DARE

To Change Your Job and Your Life

Carole Kanchier, PhD

Dare to Change Your Job and Your Life
Fifth Edition

Copyright © 2008 by Carole Kanchier
Published by Questers

First printing, Key Porter, Toronto, 1988
Second printing, Master Media, New York, 1991
Third printing, Jist, Indianapolis, 1995
Fourth printing, Jist, Indianapolis, 2000

1.888.206.0108
E-mail: Questers@daretochange.com

To order:
E-mail: Questers@daretochange.com

Visit our web site for information on other Questers products and ser vices:
http://www.daretochange.com

Quantity discounts are available.
Email: Questers@daretochange for more information.

Cover by Blitzprint
Printed by Booksurge

Library of Congress Cataloging-in-Publication Data.

Dare to Change Your Job and Your Life /Carole Kanchier—5th ed.
     p. cm.

ISBN 978-0-9810622-0-4
1. Career changes. 2. Career development. 3. Psychology. 4. Self help

HF5384 .K35 2000
650.14—dc21

Printed in the United States of Amerca

We have been careful to provide accurate information throughout this book,
but it is possible that errors and omissions have been introduced. Please
consider this in making any important decisions. Trust your own judgment
above all else and in all things.

To my father
Whose love, support and encouragement
helped me to be myself

Contents at a Glance

Chapter 1   Questers and the Contemporary Career

This Chapter describes contemporary career/life development and introduces the Questers—people like Pablo Picasso, Coco Chanel, Lee Iacocca, George Soros and thousands of less-known folks who are redefining the way we look at careers today.

Chapter 2   Quester Qualities

What makes a person a Quester? In Chapter 2 you'll read about the qualities Questers have in common—qualities you can develop for yourself.

Chapter 3   Are You a Quester?

Think you might be a Quester? Take The Quester Questionnaire to find out how many Quester qualities you already have. Then find tips for developing more.

Chapter 4   Career Change: Up–Down–Sideways

There are several routes to career satisfaction, including staying in the same field, changing fields, and going into business for yourself. Which is right for you? Chapter 4 will help you decide.

Chapter 5   The Career Cycle Meets the Life Cycle

If you look over your career, do you see a pattern emerge? Most people see definite career cycles of entry, mastery and disengagement. Learn how your career cycle meshes with your life cycle, and how you can put the process to work for you.

Chapter 6   Job Satisfiers

What makes for a satisfying career? It turns out there are several factors that are common to career happiness across all fields and cultures. How many of them are present in your job?

Chapter 7 Rate Your Job Satisfaction

How satisfied are you with your career? Take the quizzes in Chapter 7 to determine if you're suited to your job, if you're involved in your work, or if you're headed for career burnout. You'll also find tips for managing stress and increasing your energy level.

Chapter 8 The Courage to Risk: Psychological Aspects of Decision Making

Changing jobs can be risky—in fact, for some people it's down-right paralyzing. Read the case studies in Chapter 8 to learn how others have minimized their risks by using a decision-making process that works.

Chapter 9 Prepare to Change

In this Chapter, you'll put to work the decision-making process you learned in Chapter 8. Following a step-by-step approach, you'll ready yourself for the changes ahead so you can act with confidence.

Chapter 10 Dare to Change

Now that you've decided on change, you'll need some practical job search help. Chapter 10 is loaded with information on conducting a thorough, successful job search. From setting your goals to using the Internet, from writing a dynamic resume to succeeding in the interview, this Chapter covers the basics and more.

Contents

Preface: Planning for Change

If you are wondering what to do with the rest of your life—because you are dissatisfied or bored with your job, reentering the workforce, contemplating a career change, or unemployed—this book is for you. A major shift in your career direction can create important gains in your life. It forces you to step out of the well-worn groove of your life and confront yourself in some basic ways. And it offers you the chance for an expanded sense of self, personal and professional growth, and hope. It also involves some risks. I wrote *Dare to Change Your Job and Your Life* so that I could share my research and experience on the career quest with you.

A career really is a quest. As I look back over my own life, I think my quest started when I was a teenager. As the physical and emotional tumults of adolescence raged within, I tried to make sense of who I was and what I wanted to do with my life. As options floated in and out of my consciousness, I realized that what I wanted most was the same thing we all want: to enjoy every day fully.

Since a great part of my days would be devoted to work, I wanted to find a satisfying and rewarding career. I wanted to be involved, challenged, and autonomous and to have a sense of meaning and purpose in my work. I wanted to thoroughly enjoy my work and my life.

I graduated from college and struck out into the world of work with high hopes. There, I made a discovery: When I no longer felt enthusiastic about a job, I felt lifeless and dull. My satisfaction and productivity nose-dived. I left several jobs, never lasting more than seven years before my restless spirit guided me to another. My colleagues and friends seemed content to stay in one position. Why did I keep quitting positions I had initially loved and, according to society's yardstick, I had been successful at? Was it because my life lacked balance? No matter how involved I became in hobbies and relationships, the old ache returned—and the jobs changed.

Then I began my doctoral research. Slowly the answers came. As I hunted through volume after volume of theory and research in the different branches of psychology (developmental, personality, vocational, counseling and industrial) and spirituality, I began to find myself. Journeying across the country, I sought out the life stories of male and female executives to see how and why they had made career changes. I was beginning to understand my own feelings and motivations.

Since then, I have conducted research on many other aspects of career and adult development, on voluntary and involuntary career/life transitions, on purpose, energy and intuition; and, as a teacher, counselor, columnist and psychologist, I have worked with adults from many different occupations and educational backgrounds. The conclusions I have drawn—

based on research conducted with data gathered on more than 40,000 adults representing varied ages, occupations, and educational backgrounds—illustrate main themes that run through people's lives. They are presented in this book: *Dare to Change Your Job and Your Life.*

The life stories described here will give you a clearer picture of the contemporary career from the viewpoints of different branches of psychology as well as spirituality. You will learn how your career development is intricately and inextricably connected to your personality development and the transitions in other parts of your life. You will discover the complex psychological dynamics that come into play when you are considering a job change. If you have lost your job because of a plant closure, merger, downsizing, or reorganization, you will learn how to turn this crisis into an opportunity for continuing growth and revitalization.

I have included questionnaires that will help you examine your own personality and life situation. These will also help you determine how satisfied you are with your career and life, how well you are coping with both, and whether you are a Quester—the new breed of creative risk taker.

The Questers' stories included in this book will show you how to make risky decisions when you need to. Seeing how others have overcome barriers will help you to overcome them yourself when you are ready to make important changes in your life. Equally important, *Dare to Change Your Job and Your Life* doesn't encourage you to take risks for which you aren't ready or ones you don't really need.

Many of us spend much our lives trying to stop or resist change. It's human nature to be comfortable with the way things are. However, your life, your personal growth, and your career development are fueled by the dynamics of change. The energy you spend fighting to keep the status quo is energy you could be using to understand the causes and nature of the changes occurring around you. The ability to take planned risks is just what you need to manage your career in today's dynamic world. Without risk, there is no growth, no vitality, no true joy.

The ideas you will find in this book are not new. Many popular and informative books on career and adult development line the shelves of your local library and bookstore. But none provides a holistic or complete picture of the contemporary career. Most titles explore career planning and the job search. They look at how to put together the right resume, dress for success, or survive an interview. They say very little about emotions and spiritual concepts such as consciousness, intuition and purpose. None describes career growth and development throughout the life cycle. They don't provide a thorough understanding of the contemporary career, and they don't explain what makes you like or dislike your job or show how these feelings are related to your personality development and your life's many transition periods. Nor do they describe the intricate dynamics of making risky decisions which come into play when you change jobs. In *Dare to Change Your Job and Your Life,* I strive to incorporate and share all of the different elements that help each of us find and pursue our individual quests.

As you journey through this book—and through your life—don't hold back because of concerns about "success" or the availability of jobs in your field. Whether the country is in an economic explosion or a recession, whether you want to work in a broad or a narrow field, attractive jobs are available. They are created by the mobility of the workforce—the deaths, retirements, and promotions of current job holders—and by the growth of thriving companies. Regardless of prevailing economic conditions, good positions are out there for the taking. Somewhere, a company is looking for just your talents and experience and will pay you well for them. Finding that ideal job or becoming successfully self-employed is easier than you think.

Keep your options open. Focus on the opportunities available. By following the examples of the self-reliant Questers, who thrive on challenge and growth and turn crises into opportunities, you will gain the strength to take an active stance in your own career development. *Dare to Change* will teach you to become the manager of your own life, to be in charge of your own destiny. You will find the knowledge and the courage to improve the quality of your life and your work and to make your innermost dreams come true. You will have the power to achieve a more meaningful, satisfying, and productive life—to attain the life you were meant to live—in a changing, challenging, and exciting world.

Like a good meal, this book should not be gobbled up in a hurry, but savored, one bite at a time. Schedule time to read each chapter. Relish the knowledge you gain. Relate what you've learned to your own life. Take time to plan for greater happiness and more personal and professional growth and success.

Acknowledgments

I would like to express my deep appreciation to the following individuals:

The Questers, who willingly gave their time and candidly shared their experiences. Although their names (and, in a few cases, some particulars) have been disguised to maintain their confidentiality, their stories are based in fact.

The many students, clients and individuals who participated in my research over the years, taught me a great deal about adult and career development, and offered valuable feedback on the questionnaires. More recently, clients at Douglas College/Career Builder Plus Program in Coquitlam gave feedback on the modified versions of the questionnaires.

Kathy Teillet, whose creative editorial assistance helped put the first edition of *Dare to Change* in its final form.

Emmanuel Shammatutu, who took time to read and offer valuable suggestions to the fifth edition and provided needed technical assistance.

My friends and colleagues who took the time to read certain chapters and offered constructive suggestions: Bea Harks, Kent Black, Linda Pomerantz, Lynn Feingold, Marino Giancarlo, Kent Patel, Jan Jesky, Hazel Sangster and Drs. Pat Nellor Wickwire and Gibson Scheid.

Chapter 1

Questers and the Contemporary Career

Would you know a Quester if you met one? Are you a Quester yourself? Could you become one? What are Questers, anyway?

Questers

The answers to these questions come first through jobs. Questers think of their work differently from most people. Like many of us, Questers will probably spend a third to half of their adult lives working, thinking about work or commuting there. But, unlike most people, at crucial points in their careers, they set off on quests to find the missing links in their lives. Their life stories start out a lot like everyone's until the day they begin a personal journey of discovery to find a better life and a better career. You, too, can make this journey.

People with Questers qualities have been around for ages, but their numbers are increasing today. Questers know they will prevail during uncertain times by continuing to learn, change and grow.

Quester Qualities

- Are self-reliant and resilient
- Are flexible
- Have a sense of purpose
- Are willing to take risks
- Are androgynous
- Have strong interpersonal skills
- Value internal rewards such as personal growth, autonomy, challenge and achievement over external rewards such as prestige, security and money
- Periodically assess their values and goals
- Learn from their experiences
- Turn crises into opportunities
- Listen to their feelings and other intuitive cues as well as to their intellect
- Are confident
- Have positive attitudes
- Enjoy their jobs and lifestyles
- Set high standards for themselves
- Get involved in their work
- Are energetic and committed to learning
- Are independent, value personal freedom
- Feel connected to other people, the planet and the universe

Questers tend to be complex, individualistic, flexible, autonomous and open to risk. They may have the best of both male and female strengths. They tend be self-confident and have a sense of purpose and meaning in their lives. Many hunger for tasks worthy of their talents and skills, and have the courage to do what is morally right even though their actions will be unpopular. Questers question authority and often pursue socially responsible work. They have a high need for job involvement and for other vital work rewards such as challenge, self-fulfillment, a sense of achievement and opportunities for growth.

Questers accept criticism and failures, viewing defeat as a useful experience from which to grow. Their coping devices include focus, hard work, prayer or meditation, healthy lifestyles, support from friends and spouses and a sense of humor. When they experience life crises—such as divorce, the death of a relative or close friend, job loss or dissatisfaction, marriage or birth—they undergo intense critical self-analysis. At transition periods, such as the age-30, age-40 or age-60, Questers take another look into the mirror to find if they like what they see.

Questers can be found in a wide range of occupations across the world. In most cases, it is easier to develop Quester qualities in Western cultures where adolescents are permitted to choose their careers and lifestyles. However, circumstances often force people of developing countries to adapt to changing circumstances and develop Quester qualities. For example, the millions of African grandmothers have found ways to look after their orphaned grandchildren with little money, food or help.

The varied occupational fields Questers select include the trades, self employment, law, management, education, medicine, civil service and engineering. Questers may change occupations or "status levels" throughout their careers; sometimes they sacrifice financial rewards and status for self-expression and personal growth.

For many Questers, economic security and status take second place to intrinsic satisfaction and the desire to have alternatives. Questers value flexibility and can reshape their identities through self-determined career choices. They have a playful, task-centered approach to problem solving. They measure success by internal standards and value self-respect

For many Questers, economic security and status take second place to intrinsic satisfaction and the desire to have alternatives.

more than peer respect. Questers tend to be free from conventional restraints. They are independent and innovative spirits with a rich supply of inner resources. They strive to maintain a healthy balance between work, love and leisure time. They love a challenge.

Questers tend to have a cheerful, optimistic outlook. Cheated or disappointed in life? Hardly ever! Going to work usually is a joy. Few of them ever get bored because their work provides them with a sense of purpose, challenge, growth and other desired job perks. Questers generally rise with a smile, ready to meet the challenges before them.

Surely, you're thinking, Questers must be extraordinary, glamorous people. Not really. They are ordinary individuals who face career challenges common to all of us. But they have learned to do something about their difficulties—to take control.

You probably know some Questers. They have been around in every age. Organizational behaviorist Douglas Hall called Questers "protean" persons. Searching for fulfillment through self-determined career choices, they tend to continuously reshape their identities. Motivated by freedom, growth, achievement, job involvement and job satisfaction, they measure success internally.

Questers are not like Traditionalists, who tend to be passively committed to an organizational career. Traditionalists value advancement, power, position, salary and the respect and esteem of others. Their mobility tends to be low and their adaptability is tied to organization-related flexibility and survival.

Many Traditionalists are concerned about how their careers measure up against the approved timetables for their professions. Failure to stay on track may leave them feeling panicky. Conforming rigidly to a single, narrow career track, Traditionalists feel they must travel systematically from section head to supervisor, to manager, to executive; from law clerk to junior and then senior partner. Recognition, they hope, comes to those who are faithful, attentive and loyal.

Although they may achieve temporary security, their future options are severely limited. The desire for security has its cost. Traditionalists worry too much about doing the expected thing. They choose careers that conform to what is expected of them.

Self-Seekers, on the other hand, tend to be just the opposite . Motivated by a desire for personal fulfillment, Self-Seekers refuse to work as hard as their parents and contemporaries. They want the perfectly balanced life, with time for love, leisure, family and personal expression. Their happiness formula is giving and getting love, and they shun ambition and leadership in their search for the comfortable life. They want gratification now and responsibility later. Self-Seekers assume they have the right to work less and be fulfilled while enjoying life's genteel comforts.

Self-Seekers choose a lifestyle that suits them. They willingly pass up promotions and difficult business challenges that might threaten their comfortable lives. While satisfying work is important, Self-Seekers aren't prepared to sacrifice for their careers or to have their jobs dominate their lives. Their greatest fears are not having enough money and being trapped by the constant pursuit of money. This is their dilemma. To pursue freedom at the sacrifice of a comfortable life is almost unthinkable.

You can become more purposeful, confident, loving, self-reliant and willing to risk.

Questers can be distinguished from Traditionalists and Self-Seekers by their willingness to take control of their careers. Which are you: a Traditionalist, a Self-Seeker or a Quester?

You probably are more like one than the others, but you may share traits of all three. Fortunately, you can be whichever you desire. Your personality is far from set in stone. You can create and recreate it every day. You can become more purposeful, confident, loving, self-reliant and willing to risk. It's true that researchers such as James Cattell, Hans Eysenck, Arnold Buss, and Robert Plomin have shown that certain aspects of personality (such as sociability and energy levels) are genetically based. But these, too, can be changed.

To achieve the transformations you want, look to the Questers.

> *Carl* is an achiever, a winner, the kind of guy for whom life is a warm sea breeze. He is husky and handsome, with clear blue eyes. Carl grew up in an orphanage but, through hard work, won a scholarship to an Ivy League college. He taught for a while, then went on to graduate school for a master's degree in educational psychology. Eventually, he found himself in a Washington, D.C., government department, where he rose with relative ease through several offices. But something was wrong.
>
> "On paper I had it all," he explains. "Maybe more than I thought I should have had: a prestigious, secure, and well-paying job; a pretty wife and two kids; a house in the suburbs; club memberships; and a respectable backhand. But I had a persistent and nagging feeling that life wasn't working. It wasn't adding up. Something was missing. I should have talked to someone about it, but the last thing I wanted to show was my vulnerability. Search as I might, I seemed able to deal only with the symptoms. I got myself a raise, cut down on my drinking. I never looked at the big tapestry—what I really wanted—because that was too scary. And, besides, didn't I already have the American dream?"

Then Carl began thinking about changing jobs. No single event started the process (that's rarely the case). Instead, a series of small jolts forced him out of his velvet-lined rut. First, he learned that his wife was having an affair. What shocked him most was that he wasn't angry. He just didn't care. Soon the couple was on the road to divorce, and Carl was looking at life from a new angle. If his marriage had been a mistake, maybe his career was, too. In fact, his marriage and career had something in common. He had gone into both because people expected him to. But now he began questioning whether he should devote his energy to living up to other people's expectations. He had traded self-fulfillment and meaning for security. Not long after that, Carl quit his job. He stepped into the void. He had no idea what he was going to do next.

Carl was a little frightened when he took that first step. He needed someone to talk to. He found that person in the wife of a friend. "The first woman other than my wife I'd ever really confided in." His "overdone macho" had prevented him from revealing his vulnerability to any woman, Carl says now.

Carl began his search for a new job with a painful but necessary transition. He moved from his comfortable home to a bare room in an apartment borrowed from a friend. He had a bed, a light bulb, and a stereo system. He missed his house and his children; he felt especially guilty because, as an orphan himself, he'd vowed never to leave his own children. For the first time in his adult life, he allowed himself to cry. Yet, despite his loneliness and guilt, Carl also felt what he calls "the exhilaration of trusting myself for the first time."

Carl now says he was unhappier before he made the break than during the transition itself. "Earlier, I was using up more energy just justifying a life that wasn't working," he says. "But after the break, I was confronting myself for the first time. The fear and loneliness didn't begin to offset the feeling of integrity I had. The best way to describe it is to say that it was wonderfully terrifying."

Carl survived because he made the right decision. After leaving Washington, he started a management consulting firm in an Eastern city. Carl and his ex-wife became friends again. These days, his young son lives with him; his daughter lives with her mother. He thinks that switching jobs made his divorce less bitter than it might have been. "I would have been unhappy with myself and taken it out on others," he admits.

Evelynne understands what Carl went through. An attractive, petite woman with large, expressive brown eyes and dark brown hair, she looks much younger than her 45 years. But Evelynne's early life in a large Eastern city was far from happy. She was the second daughter in a family whose social standing never quite matched their neighbors'. Her school years were tough. Treated shabbily by many of the "snobs," she determined to excel at everything she did.

After high school, Evelynne joined a large clothing manufacturer as a secretary and model. At 21, she married an athlete and continued working for several years until the birth of their first child. She had a second child and, with two babies at home, found time to take a part-time job writing fashion and food articles for a local newspaper. But as time went on, boredom set in.

Evelynne turned 30 as her youngest child entered kindergarten. Joining the newspaper staff full-time, she soon graduated to a daily column. She had been on the job just over three years when a large department store asked her to manage an exclusive women's clothing department. The timing was perfect. Feeling stale and bored with her column, she eagerly accepted the new position. It proved to be challenging and full of variety. She was given the freedom to develop a department, of which she was justifiably proud.

Just after Evelynne's 38th birthday, however, things changed. Her marriage began to crumble and her freedom at work was drastically reduced by new management policies. With much of her decision-making ability taken away, the quality of her department's merchandise declined. After three years of soul searching, Evelynne decided to separate from her husband, leave the department store and open her own boutique. Her parental responsibilities were decreasing as both her children entered their late teens and became increasingly independent.

Evelynne's first step was to thoroughly investigate the banks in her city. Then, preparing a well-researched proposal, she presented it to one of the city's more liberal bank managers. Her boutique took off. And Evelynne, then 45, began divorce proceedings as she contemplated marriage to a man she had known for five years.

Evelynne thinks her 50th birthday will bring new business projects. She looks to the future with excitement.

Kathy is looking forward to the future now, too. Although she had a B.A., she didn't have a clear career goal. She was pretty, a good athlete, and had many interests and abilities. Kathy worked at a series of jobs until, at 22, she went to a state employment agency for career counseling. That led to a one-year managerial training program with a large insurance firm. Kathy enjoyed her training. The job seemed challenging enough. But within four years, her feelings had changed. Bored and suffering from extreme mood swings, she realized she needed, even craved, challenge.

Her father's death forced Kathy to take another look at her life. Again, she went for career counseling. This time she decided to leave her job, return to school, and retrain for another occupation—the law. Three years passed from the onset of her dissatisfaction until Kathy decided on a new course of action. Today, she is excited about her work in the legal field.

Like Kathy, *Luke* is also making a new start. For 30 years, Luke worked his way up from mechanic to middle manager for a trucking firm. Then, at 52, he bought a hardware store in a town 70 miles from the Western city where he had lived his whole life. Was the decision made on the spur-of-the-moment? No. "I planned my getaway. I saved my money and explored the communities within 100 miles of my hometown. I liked fixing things, and the hardware business will let me expand the store into a repair shop later, if I feel like it."

Luke is talking like a Quester. He feels like one, too. This is how he describes his job now: "It provides me with a sense of accomplishment, the opportunity to use my skills, and the feeling that I have some control over my life. I now have more energy left over at the end of the day to do other things. I feel rather peaceful and content."

Verlynne has a different story to tell. As a 38-year-old homemaker who enjoyed writing poetry and developing games, Verlynne felt pressured by her peers to return to school and prepare for a job outside the home. It seemed to be the thing to do. So she enrolled in a journalism program at a local junior college with the idea of pursuing a journalism career.

She hated it and cried herself to sleep many nights. But she stayed with it for a year because she wanted to show others that she could make and keep a commitment. Verlynne's husband, who supported her in all her ventures, suggested she seek professional counseling. By the third session, Verlynne realized that her real passion was continuing her creative pursuits at home.

Today, one of Verlynne's most recent innovations, a doll children can tell their problems to, is selling well at local stores. Verlynne said, "I'm so happy, I sing all the time!"

Like these Questers, you can take charge of your life and your career. Career, family, relationships, and leisure will cross and intersect, clash and complement. The paths you choose will depend on your own personality, goals and life situation. To understand how you can control the direction of your life and make well-informed choices, you need to understand your place in the modern work world.

Contemporary Life

Career as Movement

Your career is the path you carve out for yourself. It involves a continuing quest for a better fit between who you are and what you do. Your occupation is based on skills you've earned through education or training. But while you may have several occupations or several positions within an occupation during the course of your life, you will have only one career, because you have only one life. Your career is made up of a series of occupations or positions—yet, it is more than that. Your career is a lifelong process.

Like an obstacle course in which you climb, stretch, and swing to develop your muscles, your career spiral continues on—widening, ever-changing, mutable, dynamic, ascending, and expansive—throughout your life. It may be that one occupation satisfies just one facet of your personality. Each stop suggests more challenges ahead. Moving on restlessly, using each job as an opportunity to grow, you plot your next move. What matters is not promotion on your job but advancement of your whole person. To be fulfilled, you need work that is compatible with many aspects of your personality.

To be fulfilled, you need work that is compatible with many aspects of your personality.

Howard discovered the need for fulfillment when he reached 32.

Throughout high school, he had dreamed of becoming an executive with a large manufacturing company. He had worked part-time for the firm during high school and was excited about becoming a manager. It seemed prestigious. At 23, Howard was well on his way to middle management.

During his first six years at the company, Howard enjoyed his work. His first two supervisors were "fine people, supportive and helpful." But the next six years brought different supervisors and changing company policies. Howard's position became meaningless. The work was "monotonous" and the atmosphere "oppressive." The money and the prestige no longer seemed to matter.

Whatever his difficulties at work, Howard's marriage was in good shape, and he enjoyed playing in a local band. As he became friendly with two of the band members, both policemen, they told him the pros and cons of police work. He learned more by participating in several volunteer police programs. Then, just after his 31st birthday, his mother suddenly became ill and died. For Howard, it was a turning point. He realized that life is short. If he was going to change, it would have to be now.

So, at 32, Howard decided to enter the police training program. He had discussed his disillusionment with his wife, and she said she was willing to take a part-time job to help pay the bills. Today, Howard is a police captain. He has found a career that will let him grow, one that provides meaning, variety and an outlet for his desire to help others.

What happened to Howard? Like many, he simply outgrew his career. His needs, values, and priorities shifted. He was no longer so interested in status. Money meant less to him. The decision to change jobs did not come easily; it was agonizing and took time. Moreover, Howard and his family had to give up many comforts. But today, Howard is confident his decision was the right one. So is his family. His career grew, and so did he.

Career as Job-Person Fit

Imagine the growth and development of your career as a spiral. If you could draw it, it would look like a track moving around a continuous curve toward a central point. That central point is you. You are the center of gravity and balance for your career spiral. If you look closely at the central point in your spiral, you will see a subtle, wonderful portrait of yourself. This portrait captures everything about you. It is a portrait of you as a whole person.

From this whole person, your energy radiates—your soul, temperament, needs, values, interests, skills, aptitudes, and goals. Like a dynamo that fuels your spiral, your energy feeds into your career track. Building a successful career relies on evaluating the harmony among your portrait, your job and your goals.

Like your career, your personal characteristics and goals change as you grow. As your portrait changes, so will the results of your evaluation.

Let's take a look at Al's career to see how it developed and changed over the years.

> *Al* was born and raised in a Midwestern town. After high school, he entered a computer science program at a nearby university because, in his words, "computers was the field to be in … the opportunities for employment and making good money were excellent."

> At 23, Al graduated with a master's degree in computer science, got married, and accepted a position as a systems analyst with a large firm 1,300 miles from his boyhood home. At first, Al enjoyed his work. It gave him enough challenge and autonomy. As his star continued to rise, he and his wife had their first child.

But seven years later, as he neared his 30th bir thday, Al began to feel as if something, some sense of pur pose or meaning, was missing. For three years, he searched his soul. Then Al left his job and retur ned with his family to the Midwestern town where he was raised. Using some of his savings to realize a lifelong dream, he bought a farm. Now Al and his wife are devoted farmers. They enjoy their lifestyle and their work.

Al changed because his needs and v alues changed. But why and how did that happen? As in Ho ward's case, the changes Al made were caused by many different events. Al's job had lost its challenge. He felt stifled. The birth of his child and the joy of becoming a parent helped him realiz e that his family was more impor tant than his career. Al was also beginning to realize that time was passing. He was anxious to tr y something new—his longtime dream of becoming a f armer. The feelings and thoughts Al e xperienced were part of his Age-30 Transition, a time of questioning and e valuating earlier decisions. He had to choose betw een either deepening or abandoning his earlier commitments.

Al abandoned them. But what if, at the v ery moment that he was looking into his life, Al had suddenly received a fabulous offer—a promotion to senior analyst and a big r aise? If Al had accepted, what would have happened to his career spir al? Would it have shot forward and upward? Unfortunately, no. It would have remained precisely where it w as, in a state of suspended animation. Why? Because Al's development as a human being, as a whole person, w ould have come to a grinding halt.

Al's glance into the mirror of his dreams at 30 helped him to change. By moving back to a small to wn and buying a farm, Al created har mony between his por trait and the energy it was radiating for his career track. When he changed occupations, his career track leapt forward because Al, as a whole person, had adv anced.

14

Marion's career also developed and changed over the years. Marion worked as a microbiology researcher for eight years while her husband went to medical school. Finally, she took time off to raise their two children. She filled her spare hours with volunteer work. Then, at 39, Marion made a decision that would radically change her life.

She says, "I wanted something to do—not just a job to earn grocery money—something that would excite me. But like most women, I had the feeling that I didn't have the right to please myself. After a great deal of thought, I decided what I really wanted to do was go back to college and get a master's degree in counseling psychology. So I did.

"At first, I was terrified. What if I failed? How could I compete with young people? Who would organize my family?"

Today, Marion is a counselor at a women's resource center on the West Coast. She spends her time counseling women who are asking the same questions she once did. "I under–stand exactly where these women are, because I was there myself. Like most women, they're asking a very important question: 'What should I do with the rest of my life?'"

Like Al, Marion decided what to do with her life by checking her image in the mirror. In her early 20s, she saw a young woman in a white lab coat. In real life, she worked hard for eight years to fit that image. When Marion looked at her portrait again in her late 20s, she saw a young mother. She had changed, and so had her life situation. After eight years as a lab researcher, she was bored. Her husband was practicing medicine and could support them both. The biological clock was ticking. If Marion wanted children, the time was now. So Marion fused her portrait and her career by taking time off to have and raise two children.

The children kept her busy for many years. But nine years later, when she looked into her portrait again, the image was blurred. Marion was confused. The children were in school and her husband was busily engaged in his career. Marion knew she wanted to go back to work, but could she and should she? All of her upbringing told her that a good wife and mother should stay home to cater to her family's needs. Marion didn't want to go back to research. That job no longer suited her. Nor did being a full-time homemaker. Marion's interests, needs, and values had changed. She wanted a job that suited her new personality. But what? Marion was perplexed. It took long deliberation, talks with her family, and career counseling before Marion concluded that what she really wanted to do was become a counselor.

Now when Marion looks into her portrait, she sees a career woman. The picture is clear. Marion created harmony between her portrait and herself by moving forward when she became dissatisfied with her life. Making changes wasn't easy. But she did it.

Career as Purpose

Candice's purpose is helping others. She discovered this by accident when, at 18, she worked as a salesclerk in a Midwestern city bakery. Candice said she really enjoyed helping the customers decide which products they needed.

After taking time out to raise two children, Candice, who completed the sixth grade in Belgium, returned to work part-time as a salesclerk in a cosmetics shop, because she liked helping customers enhance their appearance. Candice gained valuable experience and knowledge in this trade by attending seminars, workshops, and conferences, and by reading. She saved her money and opened one, then a second and then a third cosmetics shop. Candice says, "I've always wanted to help people ... And despite all the frustration and debt I've experienced, I love my work. It makes me feel excited and gives meaning to what I do."

The women who work for Candice admire her as a boss, because she cares about each of them as individuals and she listens to their private as well as work-related concerns. Candice's customers always return to her shop and bring new customers because her staff is extremely knowledgeable and helpful. In her spare time, Candice leads a young entrepreneurs' group at the local YWCA. Her children, now young adults, know that their mother is always available to listen and help when they need her. Although their mother leads a busy life, she manages her time well.

Candice's life reflects a unity of purpose. Not only does her occupation reflect who she is and what is important to her, all of her activities are in harmony with her entrepreneurial position. Now 55 years young, Candice looks a radiant 40. She has never been ill and rarely feels tired, despite the fact that she works 12 hours most days.

Career as purpose helps you express your inner self. It enables you to answer the questions: Who am I? Who do I want to become? It helps you to choose an occupation and lifestyle that give your life meaning and direction.

With a mission, you have a step-by-step design; without a mission you live by default. Your mission is your compass. It helps keep you on the right path and aligns your activities when you get off track. It's the driving force in your life -- the reason you wake up in the morning.

However, Questers do not fixate on their missions. Open and patient, they are sensitive to intuitive and environmental cues to take advantage of new opportunities that arise.

Purpose is the core around which many Questers' lives are organized and directed. Questers see all their activities (leisure, work and relationships) as reflecting a unity of purpose. But different themes run through the lives of each Quester. The theme that runs through Candice's life is service to others. Other Quester themes include healing, fixing things, building, creating beauty, leading, being a change agent, learning, teaching and creating family harmony.

The occupations Questers choose help them express their life purpose and give their lives meaning. They are honest with themselves because they are living out who they believe they are. You may, for example, have a job as a teacher; but if your position does not allow you to express yourself and give your life meaning and satisfaction, then you don't have a teaching career. Teaching is just the work you do for pay.

Research shows that adults' most meaningful pursuits are related to work they enjoy and meaningful relationships; their least meaningful pursuits relate to material possessions. You must be committed to someone or something to experience a sense of purpose. Having a sense of meaning and purpose promotes health, happiness, a zest for life, successful aging and maintenance of morale in difficult times.

Having a sense of meaning and purpose promotes health, happiness, a zest for life, successful aging and maintenance of morale in difficult times.

Just as the course of your life is in constant motion, so, too, is your career. For both your career and your life to be truly satisfying, you must keep exploring the state of all your life components—occupation, family, spirituality, relationships and leisure—and make the necessary changes to bring your inner and outer worlds into harmony.

Al, Howard, Kathy, Evelynne, Luke, Marion, Carl, Verlynne and Candice are all Questers, people who dared to change so that they could be themselves. Their work gives them a livelihood, pleasure and a sense of purpose.

Today, career development has become a continuing quest to create greater and greater harmony between who you are and what you do. Surprisingly, studies show that many people would continue to work even if they inherited a vast fortune or won a lottery. But why is work so important?

Work Through the Ages

Most people spend half to a third of their waking hours at work, commuting to work, or thinking about work. How ironic it is that work, considered by the early Greeks and Romans to be punishment and drudgery, is now so important. Earlier societies considered manual labor tiring, vulgar and degrading. Leisure, on the other hand, was exalted. Once, humankind's loftiest occupation was the exercise of the mind and spirit.

Early Christianity slowly changed the meaning of work. As the centuries passed, the powerful church came to recognize agriculture, handicrafts and commerce as valuable professions. Work acquired "spiritual dignity." But not until the Renaissance was work recognized as a source of joy and creative fulfillment. The Reformation followed on its heels, shaping modern ideas about work and stimulating the development of capitalism.

The Protestant Reformation elevated work to a new status. The search for excellence had begun. Calvinism added yet another twist: Work and wealth were okay, as long as they weren't enjoyed. Calvinists considered it a religious duty to choose a calling and follow it industriously.

Hard work, worldly achievements, high profits, and individualism were already entrenched in the work ethic when developments in scientific technology gave birth to the Industrial Revolution. The world was transformed. Entrepreneurs employing specialized labor and costly equipment were needed for efficient production lines. Since

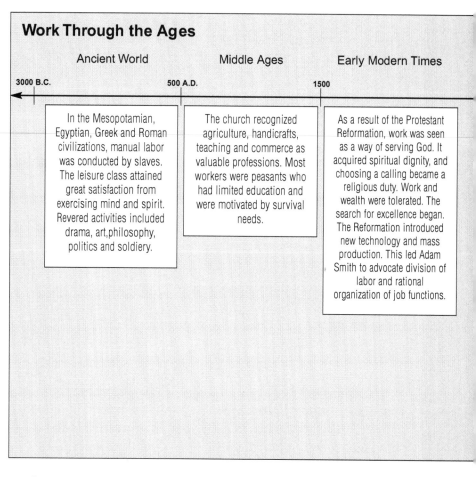

Work Through the Ages

Ancient World	Middle Ages	Early Modern Times
3000 B.C.	500 A.D.	1500
In the Mesopotamian, Egyptian, Greek and Roman civilizations, manual labor was conducted by slaves. The leisure class attained great satisfaction from exercising mind and spirit. Revered activities included drama, art, philosophy, politics and soldiery.	The church recognized agriculture, handicrafts, teaching and commerce as valuable professions. Most workers were peasants who had limited education and were motivated by survival needs.	As a result of the Protestant Reformation, work was seen as a way of serving God. It acquired spiritual dignity, and choosing a calling became a religious duty. Work and wealth were tolerated. The search for excellence began. The Reformation introduced new technology and mass production. This led Adam Smith to advocate division of labor and rational organization of job functions.

work was considered mindless and repetitive, workers could be subordinated to machines. Independent thinking, creativity and personal ability were thrown to the wind.

Adam Smith believed money was the driving force behind capitalism, and that specialization and the division of labor were vital if capitalism was to succeed. Few people really enjoyed work, Smith pronounced. Most were lazy and motivated only by selfishness and a lust for money.

The late 19th Century brought a radical change to work theory, when Taylorism was grafted onto Smith's philosophy. This theory of "scientific management" was based on Taylor's belief that most workers were stupid. Inventing time-and-

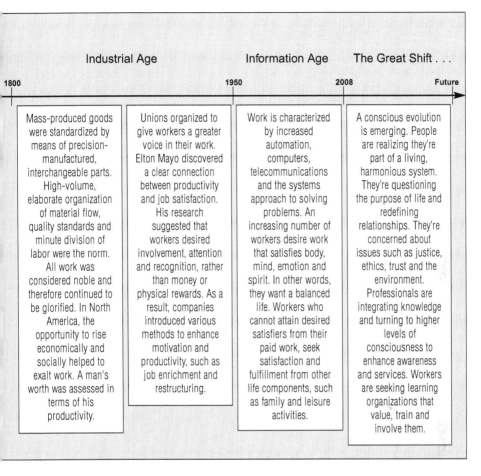

Industrial Age		Information Age	The Great Shift . . .
1800	**1950**	**2008**	**Future**
Mass-produced goods were standardized by means of precision-manufactured, interchangeable parts. High-volume, elaborate organization of material flow, quality standards and minute division of labor were the norm. All work was considered noble and therefore continued to be glorified. In North America, the opportunity to rise economically and socially helped to exalt work. A man's worth was assessed in terms of his productivity.	Unions organized to give workers a greater voice in their work. Elton Mayo discovered a clear connection between productivity and job satisfaction. His research suggested that workers desired involvement, attention and recognition, rather than money or physical rewards. As a result, companies introduced various methods to enhance motivation and productivity, such as job enrichment and restructuring.	Work is characterized by increased automation, computers, telecommunications and the systems approach to solving problems. An increasing number of workers desire work that satisfies body, mind, emotion and spirit. In other words, they want a balanced life. Workers who cannot attain desired satisfiers from their paid work, seek satisfaction and fulfillment from other life components, such as family and leisure activities.	A conscious evolution is emerging. People are realizing they're part of a living, harmonious system. They're questioning the purpose of life and redefining relationships. They're concerned about issues such as justice, ethics, trust and the environment. Professionals are integrating knowledge and turning to higher levels of consciousness to enhance awareness and services. Workers are seeking learning organizations that value, train and involve them.

motion studies and a wide range of authoritarian procedures to increase productivity, Taylor effectively chained employees into systems that controlled their every movement. Money was the reward for getting the job done on time.

Some employers still believe that employees need to be told what to do and how, and that the only (or primary) motivation for work is money. Industrial capitalism brought even more restrictions, birthing the modern corporate bureaucracy. The evolution of the bureaucratic pyramid strengthened the idea that only those at the top had the intelligence to make decisions. Once again, employees were considered mindless accessories.

In the 1920s, management began to question some of its o wn beliefs. How valuable was authoritarianism? Were people only interested in making money? Should all decisions rest with the managerial talent at the top of the p yramid? In the late 1940s, the answers emerged. Elton Mayo discovered a clear connection between productivity and work satisfaction. In fact, work satisfaction had little to do with mone y or even physical conditions. What people really wanted was a satisfying social milieu that offered involvement, attention and recognition. The human relations school of management had been bor n. Job satisfaction and career development had become impor tant issues.

The Information Age

World War II was the fountainhead of many technological, social and economic changes, which began to acceler ate in the 1950s. Knowledge became power. The information technology explosion continues today.

Forecasting the future is a challenge , of course. Some predications are accurate; others are not. Nevertheless, it's

Fastest-Growing Occupations

Jobs that are predicted to g row in the next decade include all types of health and medical ser vices; personal, professional, business, and social ser vices; hospitality services; electrical equipment and components; telecommunications; and various computer-related occupations. Jobs with the most rapid employment growth, according to projections from the U .S. Department of Labor and other e xperts, are listed below. Those in the left-hand column require a bachelor's degree or higher. Those in the right-hand column require an associate deg ree, vocational training, certificate or on-the-job-training.

The occupations listed below are based on the projections of experts. They do not include the e xciting new jobs that are emerging as a result of v arious world changes. Have you heard of steganography? How about forensic nursing or cybersecurity technician? Other emerging jobs include intelligence analyst, public safety professional and ergonomist.

These and other occupations are developing as a result of new technology, a need to prepare for the unexpected, changes in societal values and accompanying legislation changes. True Questers tend to be ahead of the 'expert' predictions—they anticipate change.

- Computer engineers
- Computer systems analysts
- Webmasters
- Computer programmers, software developers
- Telecommunications analysts
- Computer operations researchers
- Networking systems and data communication analysts
- Accountants, auditors
- Physical and occupational therapists
- Senior executives
- Management analysts
- Counselors and psychologists
- Securities and financial services personnel
- Post secondary teachers
- Elementary and secondary school teachers
- Speech-language pathologists and audiologists
- Electronic and electrical engineers
- Social workers
- Physicians and surgeons
- Medical scientists

- Maintenance and data processing equipment repairers
- General maintenance and repair workers
- Computer support specialists
- Executive secretaries and administrative assistants
- Customer service representatives
- Medical and dental assistants
- Registered and licensed practical nurses and aides
- Paralegal and legal assistants
- Personal and home health care aides
- Construction trades personnel
- Sales representatives, retail salespersons
- Physical and occupational therapy assistants
- Instructors and coaches, sports/physical training
- Paralegal personnel
- Waiters, food counter and related workers
- Supervisors of food preparation and serving workers
- Child-care workers, educational assistants
- Bookkeeping, accounting and auditing clerks
- Technicians
- Manicurists
- Guards, corrections officers
- Truck drivers

helpful to look at some labor force predictions made by authorities:

- Automation will continue to alter jobs.

- Computer-related and service jobs will increase.

- Manufacturing jobs will decrease.

- Growth will occur at two poles of the labor force—technical and professional jobs at one pole, and low-wage jobs at the other.

- Over 50 percent of new positions created will be in the high-tech areas.

- A large increase will also occur in service jobs such as sales representatives, maintenance and repair workers and home health care aides.

If you don't or won't learn about computers, word processing, and telecommunications, you'll find many doors closed to you. Machines are beginning to relieve humans of almost all dirty, dangerous, strenuous, menial and repetitive tasks.

Experts expect that more future work will be done by automatic controls and computerized equipment, and less by their human masters. Already, companies don't need as many employees to get the job done.

These days, businesses expect increased productivity, lower production costs, electronic intelligence and computerized business solutions to push the bottom line. As electronic systems become smarter and more efficient, every profession and industry feels the impact.

People can't compete with electronic solutions in achieving productivity objectives. Inexpensive offshore labor can't work as cheaply as computer chips. And as experts point out, offshoring and downsizing are just symptoms of electronic intelligence—temporary steps toward massive global change. Nowadays, electronic intelligence is displacing many manufacturing and professional jobs. There is a diminishing need for such jobs as cashiers and bank tellers. Shoppers are bagging their own groceries and automated bank machines are replacing some tellers. No need to fear, though. New occupations such as emergency medical technician, business recovery planner and information technology specialist are developing as the need for old ones diminish.

Futurists predict that in factories of the future, the only human workers will be those who install, program, monitor and repair the robots that do the actual work. In offices of the future, computers, intelligent copiers and automated information systems will eliminate such drudgery jobs as filing and stenography.

Computer-aided customization will become routine for many manufacturers. Computers will help you custom-tailor your car, your appliances and your wardrobe. Schools will be transformed by interactive multimedia and intelligent tutoring systems. These new technologies will adjust instruction to the needs and interests of each student, to make learning more effective and fun.

There are many things that computers can do much better than human brains, and vice versa. Computers are very efficient at carrying out tasks in a mechanical, "non-thinking" manner and can do these tasks without errors. On the other hand, human brains are very good at doing the thinking and acting processes required in many different, complex tasks, such as carrying on a conversation, reading for understanding, and posing and solving complex problems. That's because humans have minds and consciousness.

To thrive in the automated world, you need to strengthen your mind power. To prepare for these changes, acquire skills that can't be easily automated. Skills for tomorrow are often referred to as "meta skills." Meta skills include critical thinking, problem solving, decision making, learning, research, judgment, intuition and creativity. Trust, inspiration, caring, relationship building and ethical leadership are other abilities.

To survive in this changing world, you will need generalist skills.

In addition to computer skills, you will need to continuously upgrade your special professional skills and knowledge. You should also think of yourself as a product to be marketed. Those who succeed will be resilient and know how to take responsibility for their own careers.

The implications of all these changes are enormous:

1. *We are changing the way we define success.* A growing number of people now use their own definitions of success to derive more meaning from work and leisure activities.

2. *Dissatisfaction with authoritarian and impersonal work environments lead to decreased loyalty.* Corporate control is breaking down as employees strive for freedom and decision-making power. Organizations will have to earn the trust of the people who work for them, whether these people are their own employees or not.

3. *Organizations that value employees make employee learning and involvement key business strategies.* Progressive, learning companies understand that employee involvement and knowledge equal profit. Learning organizations train and coach leaders in meta skills such as interpersonal effectiveness, performance management and mental training. Effective leaders create work settings that respect employees. They nurture inquisitiveness and playfulness, allow privacy and avoid criticism and stress. Good leaders encourage risk-taking and innovative ways of accomplishing objectives.

4. *The lifelong occupation is disappearing.* We are seeing new social attitudes toward personal liberation and occupational change. Today changing jobs is seen as a

desire for and a reflection of personal and professional growth rather than as a sign of personal instability. Adults are learning that it's okay to periodically explore and change their values and goals. As middle-aged people realize they continue to grow and develop throughout life, many are developing new attitudes about themselves. Some people are "retiring" early, then embarking on new occupations.

5. *Self-employment and part-time temporary work continue to grow.* Increasingly, a majority of educated people who work for organizations are not employees of those organizations. They are contractors, part-timers, temps and consultants. They work for themselves and manage their own careers. Some refer to these workers as "knowledge entrepreneurs." They market their own skills to organizations internationally through computers and telecommuting.

6. *The basic unit of work is shifting from the job to a role.* Instead of being a business strategist, for example, a person assumes a blended task position such as "team member." Performance and contributions determine salary more than being at a certain corporate "level" (e.g., clerical, professional, or executive). Instead of the traditional corporate ladder, career growth is accomplished by expanding the abilities of a position. Assessments increasingly are made by "work partners"— such as coworkers, customers, and members of strategic alliances—as all workers become more accountable for their own performance as well as that of others.

7. *The microchip is reducing the need for office towers in urban areas.* These buildings were created to house documents and the many clerks who sorted, processed and filed them. Workers can now process infinitely more documents in a box smaller than a child's desk. Instead of secretaries, electrons are doing more work, at a fraction of the cost. Increasingly, because of this technology and

more flexible organizational policies, thousands of workers are choosing to work from home, and many are relocating to desired locales.

8. *Large corporations are defining and focusing on their own core capabilities, outsourcing jobs at which they are less proficient to smaller, specialized firms.* Inflexible corporate units, such as branches and divisions, are being replaced by integrated project teams and clusters that draw on skill pools to accomplish a task, then dissolve as the members move on to other projects.

9. *Companies are increasingly turning toward contract workers on whom they can call for specific projects on an as-needed basis.* Many professionals are choosing to work for one or more companies on one or more projects, selecting when and where they will work according to their skills and desires. These contract workers manage their own careers.

10. *Adaptable professionals with crossover skills such as business and technology are in demand.* Engineers and computer scientists with business or law degrees have a distinct employment edge. So do photographers who can transform images into digital formats for rapid retrieval and storage, and accountants who can program the databases of worldwide corporations. Senior executives and CEOs will be "gold-collar workers" with advanced degrees in physics, chemistry, mathematics, or computer science and a business background. As more companies shift to a transnational focus, technically trained specialists who can master a foreign language will have an added advantage.

Other factors are contributing to change, as well:

11. *Workers who keep their options open will survive and thrive in this era of rapid and sweeping change.*

12. *Well-educated adults with high expectations today insist*

on opportunities to express themselves and to make meaningful contributions to society. Volunteerism and altruistic pursuits are a growing part of our culture.

13. *The changing face of family life—which increasingly includes divorce, death, and the empty nest—is forcing people to reexamine their relationships*, to discover shifts in their goals and values, and to switch occupations more frequently.

14. *Spouses today help each other through the change cycle* by shouldering financial and family obligations while their partners study or search for more rewarding jobs. Couples often reverse roles and obligations.

15. *People are living longer*. Many different personal and environmental forces are influencing how adults feel about themselves as well as their occupational choices. Many older workers today choose to be productive by remaining in the labor force or returning to school.

16. *The expansion of the global economy continues to force many changes*. Although some workers are losing their jobs to foreign workers, others are getting better jobs created by foreign demands. Distant events bring changes to the work of many. Fluctuations in the economies of Japan or China affect the work of people around the world. "Electronic immigrants" (cross-border telecommuters) compete against workers in affluent countries in a wide variety of occupations.

The Great Shift

A consciousness evolution, a spiritual reawakening is emerging. As human beings, we have serious questions about who we are and why we are here. We are redefining our relationship with the Universe, the Earth and each other. We want to understand and talk about our responsibility in allowing a future that will be creative, loving and beneficial for all.

Numerous signals suggest humans' spiritual awareness is increasing. Disasters and crises—at the micro and macro levels—are causing people to reassess values and goals. At the micro-level crises such as job loss, illness or divorce precipitate self-appraisal. Macro disasters such as the Tsunami in South East Asia, the September 11, 2001, coordinated suicide attacks by al-Qaeda upon the World Trade Center in New York City, and global climate change have caused large groups of people to revaluate goals and work together.

Experts representing many disciplines are turning to higher levels of consciousness to expand their understanding and improve products or services. Professionals in fields such as physics, biology, medicine, psychology, philosophy and religion are integrating knowledge. Edgar Mitchell, co-founder of the Institute of Noetic Sciences, and an Apollo astronaut, knew that the world to which he was returning, after walking on the moon, is part of a living harmonious, whole system. He believes we participate "in a universe of consciousness." Mitchell and renowned scientists and philosophers conduct research to integrate scientific and spiritual thoughts to extended human capabilities.

Dr. Willis Harman, social scientist, academic, futurist, writer and visionary, who is remembered as a social scientist with SRI International, and for his work in raising consciousness within the international business community wrote:

> "We are living through one of the most fundamental shifts in history—a change in the actual belief structure of Western society. No economics, political, or military power can compare with the po wer of a change of mind. By deliberately chaning their images of reality , people are changing the world."

The New Attitude Unfolds

As these changes take place, traditional career paths are altered. Most people face tremendous pressures to readjust to the new demands of career development. To adapt, you will have to learn new attitudes and patterns of coping, new values and new skills.

To be successful in the new type of work organization, you must proactively leverage your skills by pursuing your specialty as you move from job to job. You'll need flexibility and creativity, and you must be able to work on a team. If you want to work for a progressive company, you must be innovative, flexible and willing to embrace evolving new technologies. You must develop your curiosity and be a highly motivated self-starter, a leader rather than a follower. Other qualities you will need to exhibit include risk taking, energy, enthusiasm, a positive attitude and environmental awareness. Finally, if you offer a package of capabilities—such as multiple academic degrees or fields of specialization as well as a foreign language—combined with the right personal attributes, you will have an advantage over individuals with a single focus.

To thrive in the new world of work, you will also need to find new ways of achieving a sense of belonging, personal identity, and self-fulfillment. You must know yourself—your purpose, values, dreams and beliefs, and follow these with confidence and courage. In other words, there is a whole new set of attitudes toward career development that you will have to stay in tune with to get ahead.

You have the option of creating the kind of paid or unpaid work and lifestyle you want. You can design meaningful work by modifying your current position, convincing others to hire you, taking time out to study or travel, becoming a full-time homemaker, or establishing your own business. "Success" in the changing and evolving workplace means adapting to new rules, confronting both the risks and opportunities it provides.

"Success" in the changing and evolving workplace means adapting to new rules, confronting both the risks and opportunities it provides.

These new attitudes are changing old theories about career development. To your parents and grandparents, the idea of career was a simple concept. The rewards of work usually centered on moving up the corporate ladder, achievement, individualism, and delayed gratification. Success meant social standing and respectability, being a good parent and sacrificing for the children, having money to buy the good things in life, and security and independence. No one agonized over self-fulfillment or even discussed it. No one thought of quitting a job. That was a sure sign of personal instability or irresponsibility. The future was as certain as the day was long.

Today, nothing is certain. For a growing number of workers, the career ladder is a dead issue. They speak instead about the altruistic and intrinsic—how to satisfy the body, mind, emotion, and spirit. The value of work is judged more by personal and job satisfaction and less by money and position. Status means coming up with the best ideas. Success has no one definition; it has many. A growing number of people are realizing they have the capacity to change themselves and their environments. Authenticity is making a comeback.

Tapping into Career Rewards

There are a number of rewards you can derive from your career, including a sense of identity, self-confidence, status, stability and material comforts. But if who you are is what you do, what happens when you don't find your work meaningful or satisfying? Like a steam cooker, life's pressures can build up until they explode. To relieve this pressure positively, you must discover who you are and what you want, then find a job setting that is compatible with your real self. By neglecting your needs and values, by "biting the bullet" and hanging in there (however great your excuses), you permit the malaise and lack of purpose to grow until they gnaw at every thread of your fiber.

Family life is tied into your work identity. No matter how hard you try, your family life and work life simply cannot be separated. You are a whole person. Your actions, feelings, and thoughts, your physical, psychological and spiritual well-being are one. Expressing yourself fully requires a careful meshing of all ingredients that go into making you who you are. Every experience in your life, not just those you want to, has an impact. As an adult, you must live with the experiences of your childhood. As an employee, you must live with your role as husband or wife, as parent or child. How you feel about one is interwoven with how you feel about all the others.

Family life is tied to your work identity.

Related to this is a growing reluctance to sacrifice personal and family gratifications for the sake of a job. Many people today are less willing to accept frequent transfers, even when promotions and raises accompany them. Workers today weigh desirable lifestyle and personal fulfillment before choosing or accepting a job. They are judging expectations about work hours, advancement opportunities, status, salaries, and involvement as rewarding, demanding or unreasonable. Always, there is the bottom line assumption that your occupation, or your series of occupations, and your lifestyle should fit your developing personality.

Your career may function as a way to gain varied experiences. Frequent job changes no longer signal instability or indecision. A variety of work roles can be a hedge against obsolescence and indicate personal drive, flexibility and good generalist skills. Acquiring many different skills can also be good protection against unemployment. Mergers, new technologies, unemployment, even the move to overseas locations have thrust the threat of job loss into our reluctant consciousness. Now, changing jobs is often a necessity. People who carefully attend to their careers allow their career paths to unfold in many new directions. Along the way, they increase their skills and sharpen their intellects, becoming better prepared for the future. Some monitor their careers and direct their energies to new opportunities to prepare for unemployment. They are careful not to stay too long in repetitive jobs that may rob them of their flexibility and their opportunities to grow. They know they can be easily replaced by younger and cheaper talent.

> *Abe* understands that. From attorney to retail executive to administrator in a state college system, Abe has changed occupations several times. Currently, he is director of the human development department at a state university that offers career counseling and development programs. Abe knows the key to an ever-evolving career is to monitor his own development and remain open to new opportunities. He says, "You have to attend to what is happening to you personally, as well as to your economic value. Are you growing or are you just hanging on? Ask yourself: If you had to move, could you move? And where to?"

Today, career issues are being debated in the public forum. Career is viewed as an arena for achieving social equality and humane working conditions. The movement toward civil rights in the workplace promises fair hiring and promotion practices. Organizations face increased pressure to eliminate unsafe working conditions that threaten the physical or emotional well-being of their employees. As people become increasingly aware of their rights and responsibilities in the contemporary work world, job quality and employment practices become issues for political drum beating. Studies in vocational, industrial, and social psychology show how career satisfaction and adjustment—including job involvement, organizational commitment and burnout—affect people's lives.

All of these reasons, causes, and effects influence many Questers to change the direction of their careers. They are the people who view their jobs as vehicles for self-expression and growth. They value movement—the right to grow and to maintain their usefulness. Their career goals often are open-ended. Questers find challenge in a wide variety of occupations and environments. Taking the initiative in their own career development, when they no longer derive desired rewards, they look for new ventures. So they proceed through several occupational cycles of entry, mastery and disengagement throughout their careers.

At the same time, Questers are not simply job hoppers. They tend to make appropriate choices. They usually initially like their work and are committed to and involved in it. But after three or more years, if they can no longer grow in a job, they leave. They are willing to take prepared risks. They are not irresponsible. They don't forget their families and say "to hell with obligations," or decide they couldn't care less about money, status or respectability. They usually do want some degree of financial, marital, family and material well-being. But they also struggle to make room for greater personal choice against what they consider to be institutional encroachments.

Not all Questers live to work. Some work to live? Others have difficulty separating the two. If you work for a paycheck, you probably work to live. If you're engrossed in work activities, you may live to work. Compartmentalizing work and non-work activities suggests you strive for balance. There are many lifestyle patterns from which to choose. Which is right for you? *John*, a professor, says: "I could retire, but choose not to because work is too much fun. . . "If I wasn't paid, I would continue to work. If I retire, there is only one thing left to do!"

Anil doesn't differentiate between work and play. "I like being challenged, making a difference. Work is an extension of who I am, my purpose." The entrepreneur is involved in numerous projects that enhance the quality of his own life and that of others.

Lorrie has a different perspective. "My calling is to enjoy life," she says. "I work to live. . . I work for money to supply my lifestyle. Although I do get satisfaction from doing a good job, I devote my life to hobbies and volunteer activities."

A developmental perspective to the "work/life issue" is offered by *Roxanne.* "At an earlier career stage, I tended to make work a priority. . . I took opportunities to get ahead. My family suffered. . . Now, I never work weekends, and when I leave at five, I leave work." Roxanne enjoys her work, but strives for balance.

A different life/work balance is practiced by some *Silicon Valley professionals* who work for high tech start-ups. They work long hard days for three to four years and then take time out for a few years. Thus, instead of working at a low intensity for 30 plus years, they work very hard for three to four, then take a long vacation. Some need this break from work to regenerate.

There is no best lifestyle. Each person should select a way of life that is congruent with his or her personal qualities. In essence, all life components are tied to your identity. How you feel about one area is interwoven with how you feel about others. Your physical, emotional, mental and spiritual being are one. Expressing yourself fully requires a careful meshing of all ingredients that make you special.

Some Famous Questers

You may suspect by now that many Questers are either highly successful in their careers or complete failures. The truth is that success is measured differently by Questers than by most Traditionalists, as we have already seen. Yet the Questers have included many famous successes among their ranks. Most of them also found purpose in their work.

Pablo Picasso had this to say about his work: "What is always there is your work. It is the extension of you—not

You are your work.
— *Pablo Picasso*

36

your child, but you. You are your work. The passions that motivate you may change, but it is your work in life that is the ultimate seduction."

Picasso was one of many creative people who learned to express hidden emotions through work. "Painting and making love were very much the same for me. At the greatest moment for each, painting and sex were the same. But painting you can do alone."

Eminent French designer *Coco Chanel* was indomitable at work. But in private she was totally vulnerable. Everything worried her. "I believe that every little girl should be taught as early as possible something she can do to take her through her whole life. I shall always be grateful to my work because it taught me independence. Even more important, it saved me from boredom. Boredom is a terrible thing."

Lee Iacocca suffered a devastating emotional blow before masterminding Chrysler's remarkable financial turnaround. Iacocca had spent 34 years working his way up to president of Ford Motor Company when he was fired in 1978. A generous separation agreement guaranteed him $1 million a year until 1980—if he remained unemployed. By joining Chrysler, he would trade $2 million for the helm of a faltering auto giant teetering on the brink of bankruptcy. To fail would add hundreds of thousands of Chrysler employees to Detroit's unemployment rolls. The future of Detroit was on the line. To take the job was to jeopardize his reputation. But he did. By December 1984, Iacocca's marketing genius had turned a dying company into a $2.3 billion financial giant—all for the love of a challenge and a concern for humankind.

People always thought *Barbara McClintock* was an oddball. She didn't let anyone stop her from doing what she wanted to do. She played sports when other girls didn't. She skipped school to go ice skating. When she grew up, she studied genetics when women weren't allowed to. She used an old-fashioned microscope even after high-tech ones were invented. She investigated chromosomes while everybody else was looking at DNA. And when she made the remarkable discovery of jumping genes, other scientists thought she was crazy.

Dr. McClintock knew she was right. She had a great vision in her work. Barbara McClintock won the Nobel Prize in Physiology in 1983, when she was 81 years old—three decades after she made her discovery. The other scientists had finally caught up with her. This remarkable researcher was the first woman to win an unshared Nobel Prize in any science category.

George Soros has demonstrated that he has more than one passion. This exceptional man, born in Budapest, Hungary, is an American financier, philanthropist and political activist. Soros has made his mark as an enormously successful speculator. The bulk of his earnings is devoted to encourage transitional and emerging nations to become open societies -- open in the sense of freedom of commerce as well as tolerance of new ides and different modes of thinking and behaving.

Soros' network of philanthropic organizations has expanded to include over 60 countries in the Middle East, Central Asia, Africa, and Latin America. Soros has also provided palliative care to the dying and donated to halt the spread of tuberculosis and HIV/AIDS. Despite the breadth of his endeavors, Soros is personally involved in planning and implementing many projects.

The Questers you have met in this Chapter found both the courage and the means to take command of their lives. Why did they do it? What personality trait or traits gave them the courage to risk and to persevere? Could you do the same? Are there characteristics you already possess or could develop that would turn you into a Quester?

Chapter 2
Quester Qualities

Some Traditionalists and Self-Seekers possess Quester qualities such as self-confidence, the desire for challenge, and a sense of achievement. However, most Questers have strengthened these and developed other qualities necessary to prevail in a changing world. They have learned to risk, to learn from experience, to turn crises into opportunities and to maintain career flexibility and positive attitudes.

You could say no two Questers are alike. Yet they share many of the same personality traits. A very few have them all. The willingness to take control of their careers, to periodically assess their values and goals and to listen to their inner voices is what distinguishes Questers from Traditionalists and Self-Seekers.

By reading about the courage and imagination Questers rely on to find career happiness and growth, you may discover ways to take better control of your career—and your life. Some started taking charge of their careers early in life. Others were near retirement. Maybe you share some of the personality characteristics Questers tend to have: a sense of purpose, a desire for autonomy, strong interpersonal skills, self-confidence, the ability to combine the best of male and female strengths, the desire to achieve, the need to grow and create, the courage to risk, resilience and an optimistic outlook. Where do you fit in?

Finding a Purpose

Questers give their lives purpose by pursuing activities they enjoy and that give their lives meaning and direction. They get a sense of purpose from many things—work, ideas, other people, social goals. For many, much of that purpose comes from their careers. Their careers satisfy their needs to believe in something or someone. Making commitments to projects (or other people) help them move outside themselves. They feel good because they are achieving something or helping someone. By choosing occupations that help them fulfill their life goals, Questers are being honest with themselves. The congruence of inner and outer worlds gives Questers a sense of inner peace and joy.

> *Questers give their lives purpose by pursuing activities they enjoy and that give their lives meaning. They get a sense of meaning, direction and purpose from many things— work, an idea, other people, a social goal.*

Candice, whom you met in Chapter 1, fulfills her purpose of helping others by owning and managing cosmetic shops. Her leisure and family activities also reflect this purpose. Some Questers, such as Pablo Picasso, Barbara McClintock and Coco Chanel, have become famous pursuing their passions. Other Questers accomplish their goals through homemaking or volunteer activities. They know they are accomplishing something worthwhile.

Brenda finds meaning in writing and raising her five children. She has yet to create the great American novel, but she loves to write short stories and poetry. As a young mother, Brenda knew she could pursue both her love of writing and her desire to be at home with her children. A few night courses led to short stories in magazines. Brenda squeezed in a bachelor's and then a master's degree in English while the children were growing up, graduating from college with her eldest son. Now in her 60s, Brenda does public relations work and writes in her spare time. She also finds time for her growing family. Brenda has even won some writing competitions. She is truly content with her life.

Fred is pursuing his passion in a different way. As a young boy, Fred liked fixing things—toys, bicycles, and household gadgets. At the urging of his parents, he earned a mechanical engineering degree and subsequently worked his way up to a senior management position with a large manufacturing organization. His career and life seemed relatively happy, until he was laid off at 52.

After Fred addressed his initial shock and anger, he turned the crisis into an opportunity. He pursued his boyhood passion of fixing things by becoming a maintenance man in a large apartment complex. "If you're doing something you like, then it's not really work, and you're making money ... Your best work goes into it because you like it." Fred is happily engaged in pursuing his purpose. Not only is he cheerful, he also makes everyone who comes in contact with him happy. He radiates joy.

Byron's passion is to be an "agent of change ... to influence public policy." Byron's dissatisfaction with the education his children were receiving influenced his decision, at 33, to run for the local school board. As

41

chairman of the school board, he was responsible for implementing many progressive educational policies.

Byron subsequently held a number of public service positions in which he influenced change. Now in his 50s, Byron continues his mission to be an agent of change in his position as director of programming for a national television company.

Some jobs, such as those in education, health and social services, naturally have social benefits. A dedicated principal who saves a dying school, a nurse or physician who helps the sick, a therapist who aids a troubled family—all of these professionals derive a sense of purpose from their work. But Questers go beyond the ordinary. Debra and Gerald are Questers.

Debra is petite, attractive and fragile-looking. Who would guess she is 50? When she began her career as a physical education teacher, she wanted to make gym class fun for all of her students, not just the few truly gifted. So Debra did what she could to change the system. She made sure more time, space, and effort were devoted to programs just for students. She started a keep-trim club to teach her students how to eat a balanced diet and keep their bodies healthy. She offered classes in dance and golf, activities her girls could use in later life. Debra's students went on to become top contenders in city and state competitions. But, more than that, Debra made her ideas known to her peers, superiors and parents. She pioneered a program girls of every level of ability could enjoy.

Then the challenge was over. Debra needed a new cause. She accepted a job as vice-principal, and she was quickly promoted to principal. Debra believed she could have more influence as an administrator. Her first administrative task was to help deprived children and underprivileged minorities. And, as the years passed, Debra accomplished her goals—building teacher morale, reducing dropouts and improving the behavior of her often-difficult students.

Debra's next few projects included setting up a school for unwed mothers, and training prisoners in a nearby penitentiary. In her late 40s, Debra went back to school to study in geriatrics. Helping seniors has become her new goal.

Debra's mission was, and still is, to provide educational services for the deprived. Like most Questers, Debra had to keep changing to keep the challenge alive. The sense of purpose she gets from her work gives her life more meaning and fulfillment than "a job" ever could.

Gerald feels the same way. An eye specialist in his late 40s, he started off as a general practitioner but soon became interested in the eye problems of his patients. So, in his early 30s, he returned to school to specialize.

At first impression, Gerald seems nondescript, a colorless man. But when he talks about his work, he shines. His eyes sparkle and the sympathetic, warm caring doctor emerges.

Gerald likes finding new and better ways to help his patients. Research is a big part of his life. Gerald has pioneered many projects, such as the use of laser eye surgery and radial keratotomy, which help the severely shortsighted to see better (sometimes without glasses). Many of the operations are performed right in his office, because Gerald believes the trauma of a hospital stay prolongs recovery. Those who can't pay, don't. His holidays are spent in Third World communities performing eye surgery for free. Gerald's life really is his work, though he also enjoys his family, friends and peers, plus regular workouts in the pool and on the racquetball court.

Research indicates that, in addition to giving meaning and direction to life, having a sense of purpose is related to good physical and psychological health; high levels of energy and confidence; a sense of security, involvement and enthusiasm for life; and a better than average ability to manage stress and cope with tragedy. The more clear, focused and concrete a sense of pur pose you have, the greater your attainment of these qualities will be.

Meaning in life enables a person to maintain integrity.

A number of prominent scholars in psychology, religion, and medicine explain the importance of purpose in different ways. Victor Frankl, a renowned psychotherapist who overcame extreme hardship as a pr isoner of the Nazis dur ing World War II, contends that a major illness of contempor ary society is the failure of people to find meaning in their liv es. He refers to this phenomenon as existential vacuum. Frankl stresses that meaning in life—derived from commitment, optimism and transcendence of self-interest—enables a person to maintain sanity and integrity under the most adverse conditions.

Abraham Maslow, the father of humanistic psychology, emphasizes that one must follow one's calling to be ultimately at peace with one's self. Bernie Siegal, physician and author of *Love, Medicine, and Miracles,* also advocates the importance of purpose. He advises readers to follow their bliss and warns them "not to climb the ladder of success only to find it leaning against the wrong w all." He suggests that pursuing one's purpose may even help one regain health.

Louise shows that this is possible. A nun for 31 years, she initially enjoyed teaching in the convent; but as she approached 50, she began to feel empty, helpless and alone because she was trapped in a setting she had outgrown. She became a compulsive eater and drinker, had difficulty sleeping and was diagnosed with cancer.

Part of Louise's treatment for the disease included counseling, which enabled her to develop the courage to take charge of her life. She left the convent and moved into a tiny apartment. Continued counseling helped Louise understand that her purpose was still to learn and teach, but at this period in her life it was more appropriate to continue with her teaching in another setting and to develop other aspects of her personality and life.

Louise soon began to feel alive, she smiled, she stopped eating and drinking compulsively. Now 56, Louise is teaching at a junior college and feels great. Her cancer is in remission.

Becoming Autonomous

Questers tend to motivate themselves. They make their own decisions and do and say what they want. They're not afraid to swim against the tide. Questers tend to avoid situations in which they must blindly conform. The binding ties of custom and habit do not hold them back. They move forward at their own speed, doing what they know is right for them.

Questers enjoy freedom. But their freedom is not bought by rebellion or by using someone. Nor are they unconventional in everything they do. They usually behave in socially acceptable ways and within legal and ethical structures. Questers know how to transcend their environment.

Being inner-directed is part of being autonomous. Questers know they can control their own lives. They take responsibility for their successes *and* for their failures. They say, "I was successful because I worked hard." Or, "I succeeded because I'm bright." Or, "I failed because I didn't try." Because Questers know they can control their lives, they don't depend on others to reach their goals. We know that those who take charge of their own

Questers don't dwell on failure because they know that, if they learn from their setbacks, next time they will succeed.

45

lives have higher expectations of getting what they want. Moreover, they have the marvelous, exuberant feeling of personal power that comes with believing anything is possible and what happens depends on you. Questers don't dwell on failure because they know that, if they learn from their setbacks, next time they will succeed.

Jay understands the importance of taking charge of his own career. A stocky man with an honest face, Jay quit school during the Great Depression to support his family. He was lucky to find a job as a construction worker. A go-getter, Jay worked hard to learn his trade. By 30, he was a successful contractor.

At 36, Jay decided to satisfy a longtime dream. He entered municipal politics. For the next seven years, he ran unsuccessfully for the city council. Some people laughed at this simple working man. Friends and advisers told him to change his home and his lifestyle. Jay and his wife lived in a modest two-bedroom bungalow in a lower-middle-class part of the city, dressed plainly and refused to show off their new-found wealth. Although he was now a prosperous businessman, Jay didn't forget the people who were kind to him in his hungry days. He remained loyal to his basic principles and values.

Jay is an optimist. He persevered, he knew he would win—and he did. At 43, Jay became mayor; he has been reelected for 20 years. He is a kind, honest, and caring administrator, who has increased tourist trade, renovated the city core, restored historical buildings and expanded the city's park land. Social climbers who earlier had laughed at him begged Jay to join their circles when he was elected. A perceptive and forgiving man, Jay did. But he also remained loyal to his friends and supporters.

Jay isn't afraid of social disapproval or societal pressure. He has the courage to be himself and the conviction to follow his goals. He also learns from his mistakes. Jay is individualistic, self-directed, self-reliant and independent.

This persistent man doesn't complain about being "unlucky." He listens carefully to what others say, but he makes his own decisions. He isn't afraid to admit to his errors because he knows he can correct them. Therefore, he continues to learn and grow.

Many other Quester qualities tend to fortify and are fortified by a sense of autonomy. Positive thinking goes a long way toward improving your sense of control. Getting new and better coping skills is the first step. In fact, you can become more autonomous just by learning how to set and achieve goals.

Setting goals puts you in control. You feel better when you are in charge, so you do better. Adults who are in control are better able to cope with the problems they have. Biological researchers have discovered that people who are taught coping strategies have lower levels of cortisol. Cortisol is a stress hormone produced by the adrenal glands to help the body cope with stress. Too much cortisol, caused by chronic stress, can deplete vitamins we take into our bodies, particularly C and the B complexes.

Your mind and body interact. Stress-related illnesses and behavioral disorders are really created by your body's chemistry interacting with psychological and sociocultural stressors. Because most Questers have learned to be in control of their environment, they are happier, healthier and more productive. You can be, too.

Winners See Themselves as Winners

Many Questers know they can make things happen—so they do. Questers also accept defeat. They understand that some rotten breaks are an unavoidable part of the game. But they don't let those breaks rule their lives.

Erika didn't let bad experiences hamper her career. Her first venture into the working world was a disaster. Fired from her first job for chronic lateness and laziness, Erika didn't realize that a rare but easily treatable blood disease was causing her lassitude.

"I wasn't able to get a second job because of the unfavorable reference from my first employer," Erika remembers. "It was a whole year before I was diagnosed. After I found out what was wrong, I went back to my former boss and explained. I got my old position back, and within six months I was promoted. I don't deny that I had an awful piece of bad luck, but I think you have to expect some undeserved blows sooner or later. You just have to cope with them as best as you can."

Vanessa is a beautiful, vibrant woman who lived through a disastrous marriage to a man who beat her. Hounded by this obsessive, frightening man, she came through both a divorce and the failure of her career as a professional dancer. Her unfailing aura of hope and good cheer managed to attract and keep a faithful circle of friends. "I've got nowhere to go but up," she would say, undaunted by yet another unsuccessful audition or a midnight phone call from her unbalanced ex-husband.

Vanessa critically evaluated each audition and set herself a time frame to make it on Broadway. When that time frame ended, she gave up on elusive stardom and opened a dance school. "I just admitted I didn't have what it takes to be a star. But I did have the makings of a good teacher. I faced the realities of my own talents and limitations." At about the same time, Vanessa's ex-husband remarried and dropped out of her life.

Knowing your own limitations is important. You don't have to settle for second best. You just have to find out what your best really is. Vanessa could have ended up a loser if she had single-mindedly pursued her goal without reassessing her true talents. Instead, Vanessa is now a real winner. She makes a good living from the art she loves because she shook off the chains of an unattainable dream.

Questers tend to win because they periodically reassess their strengths, limitations, and goals. If things aren't working, they take action to capitalize on their strengths, improve on their limitations, or modify their goals. But most Questers also know when to quit. They have no hesitation about abandoning unrealistic goals or ill-conceived projects. They don't beat their heads against a brick wall or blame others for their failures.

Developing Interpersonal Skills

Real Questers understand the importance of strong interpersonal skills. They can tell their deepest dreams and fears to good friends. They can also accept their friends' needs for closeness. This is often referred to as intimacy.

Developing the capacity for intimacy is the first step to developing supportive relationships. Neither marriage nor sexual relationships can buy intimacy. Even the most active sexual partners can feel isolated if they lack mature, caring attitudes and emotional intimacy with their partners.

Studies show that people who are empathetic and know how to build relationships are more successful in their careers than people who only possess intellectual smarts. Effective leaders know how to build relationships. They have interpersonal skills such as empathy, awareness and appreciation of other's feelings. Good leaders are friendly, and know how to communicate with others.

To be fulfilled, you need work that is compatible with many aspects of your personality.

Intimacy requires commitment to a relationship that may involve compromise and even sacrifice. Intimacy is the ability to share empathy, to give and receive pleasure without exploitation, to adjust your own needs to another's. It's the ability to say, "I don't want to use you. I want to love you. I want to experience you. I want to know you. I want to grow with you." Those who share real intimacy know it takes energy, risk, and adjustment. To grow and develop to your full potential, requires real intimacy.

The Intimate Relationship

Tom and Elva share real intimacy. They married when both were 26. Tom is tall, blond and athletic. Elva is a bookkeeper, tall, willowy and blond. "We are good friends as well as lovers," they say at the same time. They have an open, supportive tender relationship. As they grow closer, neither fears losing his or her own identity. They can make independent judgments, but they can also achieve intimacy because both saw themselves as valuable, competent and meaningful individuals with needs of their own before they married.

As Tom approached 30, his management position became restrictive and frustrating. Elva knew he was disturbed and encouraged him to talk. Tom didn't really know what he wanted to do, besides step off the bureaucratic treadmill. He needed time out—an extended trip, somewhere, anywhere—to rethink his goals. And he wanted Elva to go with him.

Elva was hesitant. She liked her job. Leaving it for the unknown was scary and risky. But she also saw Tom's apathy and depression. Tom, on the other hand, saw what his request was doing to Elva. So he didn't push. After a year of talking over their feelings and hopes for the future, they decided on a moratorium—a time-out from responsibilities and future commitments. They sold most of their belongings and bought a van. "But you're giving up everything—good positions, losing money on your belongings. What will you do when you come back?" their baffled, concerned friends and relatives cried.

For a year and a half, Tom and Elva drove up and down North America, from Alaska to Central America, up the East Coast and into Labrador, through northern Quebec and Ontario, and down into the Central states. They had no plans, no schedules to meet, no phones to answer. They had no one to answer to except each other. They stopped in little towns, big cities, fishing villages, mountain hamlets and mobile home parks. Finally, they settled in a scenic Oregon town. Tom wanted to work with his hands, to do carpentry, an old hobby, and odd jobs. He set himself up as a jack-of-all-trades. Elva took a bookkeeping job in a local motel.

Two years later, both are healthy and happy. They have made new friends and found activities they enjoy alone. They also have plenty of time for one another. Tom and Elva are thinking of starting a family. Their combination of autonomy and shared interests not only strengthens their marriage but also reinforces their independent strengths. Still young, they have achieved the empathy and commitment that makes a good marriage a sanctuary. As Tom says, "Your relationship becomes much more precious and intimate when you commit yourself to doing something like this together."

Not all Questers have been happily married all their adult lives. About 40 percent have been divorced—about the same percentage as the general population. But by the time most reach their 40s, 50s, 60s or 70s, they are happily involved with another mate.

Strengthening Interpersonal Skills

Intimacy is the ability to commit yourself to genuine love. But it's more than that. It is the ability to communicate at a sharing level with friends and colleagues of both genders. It means having close friends to share your dreams, sorrows and experiences. Close friends can be just as intimate as married lovers. Many Questers are more intimate with their friends than a great many married couples are with each other.

We need intimacy to grow and be healthy.

In the workplace, Questers cultivate friendly relationships with co-workers. They know peoples' names and special strengths, and celebrate their accomplishments. They listen to colleagues' needs, priorities, perspectives and problems. Questers are genuine, approachable and open to suggestions.

To Questers, intimacy also means nurturing humankind. It means helping people in trouble, assisting the less fortunate, treating others with kindness and sympathy, doing small favors, being generous and listening to confidences with empathy and understanding.

We need intimacy to grow and be healthy. When you are cared for, that person (your caregiver) helps you grow and develop by giving you positive feedback and constructive criticism about your strengths and weaknesses. This honest and caring feedback helps you see yourself more objectively. It helps you understand yourself better so you can learn to capitalize on your strengths and minimize your weaknesses.

Having successful relationships requires several qualities *you can develop*. As you develop your confidence and independence, your capacity for loving will also expand. Rather than fearing that an independent spouse might leave, Questers understand it is their individuality and belief in themselves that allow men and women to accept the emotional risks of intimacy. A popular quotation from 17th-Century poet John Donne sums up how many Questers feel about those they love: "If you love something, set it free. If it comes back, it is yours. If not, it never was." So it is with Questers. They can accept the need for intimacy without losing their individuality.

Questers know the secret of maintaining a balance between love and work. Even though many are achievers and work hard, they don't let work take precedence over the people they care about. Many try to spend some time each day with their partners. They have freed themselves from the tyranny of trying to please. Rather than looking to one man to confir m their worth, most female Questers develop multiple sources of identity. Questers tend to be comfortable revealing their innermost thoughts and feelings to their mates as w ell as their closest friends.

Questers remember they have needs, too. They can be loving and, at the same time, love themselves. Many of us forget to look after our own needs. We take care of our physical needs, such as food, shelter and health. But we forget to look after our psychological needs to achieve; to be accepted, recognized, creative and autonomous; to enjoy the world; and to grow. Unless we love and respect ourselves, we cannot love and respect others. Questers have learned this. Liking ourselves and doing things to please ourselv es is not being selfish and does not stop us from achie ving successful intimacy.

Acquiring Self-Confidence

How Questers feel about themselves colors their dealings with the world. Self-confidence gives them the courage to set higher and higher expectations, to change jobs, to risk, to dare to grow. Self-confidence is a vital component of Questers' personalities. Earl and June possess self-confidence.

> *Earl* is self-confident and self-accepting. In his mid-60s, Earl is rather short and average-looking. He is kind, caring, warm, friendly and has a sense of inner calm. Currently, he heads a research and development department at a university on the West Coast and teaches a few courses to undergraduates.

> Earl began his career at an Ivy League college on the East Coast where he was a full professor at 34. He then spent six years on the West Coast doing research for industry. Following this, Earl moved back East to teach

and set up a computer services program at a large university. Then he moved to the Midwest to head a university research department.

Earl is a brilliant man, very much in demand. He has many books and articles to his credit. But he doesn't flaunt his intelligence. He works hard to accomplish things. This gives him a humility that is neither self-depreciation nor diffidence, but one that promotes self-acceptance and self-respect.

Earl isn't embarrassed to say he doesn't know the answer to a student's question. He has learned how to be wrong. In fact, he rather enjoys having students challenge his views. Earl says this about criticism: "You need constructive criticism and feedback from other people. That's how you learn. I know I'm not infallible. I often get good advice from the criticism of others. I decided early on that I would learn how to take criticism in a positive way. I had to, to grow as a professional and a person."

Unlike Earl, many people fear criticism. They avoid experiences in which they might be criticized. They take jobs that are too easy or lovers who won't ask for too much. What they don't realize is that they are losing out on opportunities for growth.

Earl wasn't always self-confident. As a young boy, he was shorter than most and average looking. He acquired his self-confidence through friendships with other people. Success in his work also enhanced his confidence. Earl said, "As a child, I lacked for nothing but confidence. I was a small, skinny boy and I had few friends. I spent most of my time in the library. Most of the boys my age were into sports and I wasn't. But, gradually, as I became successful at work, it came. I was a success, and suddenly I had more confidence in me."

Building on Your Strengths

June has the look of self-confidence. A youthful woman of 46, with auburn hair and aqua eyes, June operates her own gift shop. She married right out of high school and had four children. Because money was tight, June went to work as a telephone operator, then as a salesclerk, and finally as a restaurant hostess.

When the children were in school, June signed up for a real estate course and sold houses. Her husband was transferred to the West Coast when she was in her late 30s. By then, June was ready for something different. She wanted to open a gift shop. Her husband didn't mind her working and by then the children were independent.

June loves her work. She feels good about her accomplishments. Because she believes she will do well, she does. Like Earl, June can take criticism and learns from her mistakes.

Looking at June, you would never guess she once lacked self-confidence. Her carriage, her well-modulated voice, and her private smile all exude confidence. Surprisingly, June says, "For a long time, I thought of myself as an ugly duckling. ... My nose was too long, my eyes were too close together, I was fat. So I played up to it ... making jokes about my looks and putting myself down.

"I know now that was a mistake. If you look at yourself in a negative way everybody will look at you that way. . . . I became involved in an exercise program, styled my hair so it emphasized my good points. But, more important, I placed more emphasis on internal qualities. I learned to be more accepting and tolerant of others, to see the good in them. I learned not to dwell on mistakes I made, but to use them as learning experiences. I learned how to stop feeling sorry for myself, how to take advantage of growing older, and how to accept myself and become more independent."

Trying too hard to make others like you makes you dependent.

Like most Questers, June has learned to accept herself for who she is, independent of other people's standards. Instead of being indecisive and afraid of criticism and change, June has learned to accept that some people will like her and some won't. She's no longer in the business of pleasing everybody. June knows you have to love yourself first.

Trying too hard to make others like you makes you dependent. Early in her life, June tried so hard to be all things to all people that she made herself feel wishy-washy and insignificant. Now she has learned to cultivate qualities she likes in herself, and others like her, too. The qualities she developed had nothing to do with good looks, status, or contacts. She learned how to enjoy her own company, to have fun with her family and friends. And they, in turn, enjoy being with her.

Liking yourself and doing things to please yourself does not mean you are selfish. June explains, "I'm not self-centered. ... I'm happiest when I'm not absorbed in my problems. When I'm nice to others, I get that back. And that makes me feel good about myself. . . . When you give money to charity, it makes you feel good. Givers get!"

Although June is content, she keeps working on herself. "I'm trying to get rid of my silly inhibitions. ... I want to be more spontaneous. Spontaneity is freeing the child in you. Not being childish, but childlike."

June and Earl have a lot of energy because self-confidence is energizing. Self-confidence and self-acceptance are qualities June and Earl developed as they grew older and more experienced. Many things contributed to their newfound self-confidence. Past experiences and triumphs; the way they handled humiliations; the way their parents, teachers, friends and other people reacted to them. And much of their confidence is the result of their successes at w ork. The positive feedback they receive from performing difficult jobs well feeds their self-confidence.

Similarly, the way Earl and June behave with their spouses and other people affects their self-confidence. Because they give and receive love, June and Earl feel good. They get positive feelings and strokes that tell them they are worthy, too.

June and Earl carry with them positive pictures of themselves, and they act on these pictures. In short, they behave like the sort of people they believe they are.

You can learn from people like Earl and June. You are never too young or too old to star t developing self-confidence and accepting yourself. Appreciating your own worth is not egotistical. Nor are you ruined or worthless because you are too short or too fat, or you have a long nose, or you made a mistake, any more than a well-crafted violin that sounds an occasional sour note is worthless. Don't hate yourself because you are not perfect. You are not alone!

Developing Androgyny

Gender roles are useful, b ut they may unfairly limit our potential. Few Questers play gender roles by the book. They possess the best of both male and f emale strengths. In other words, they are androgynous.

Androgyny is used to descr ibe people who blend traditional feminine and masculine char acteristics. Depending on the situation, Questers are both feminine and masculine, both introverted and expressive, nurturing and asser tive, confident and tender. Female Questers are loving and empathetic, but they also have ambition and cour age and are open to new experiences. Men may be asser tive, brave, and able to lead others effectively. But they are also comfortable with intimacy and nurturance. Simply speaking, Questers have incorporated

57

the characteristics of their gender opposites. For men, this means developing comfort with intimacy and cooperation. For women, it's ambition and courage.

> **Both men and women should be able to cry, to be assertive, to hug.**

Androgynous behavior is healthy. It allows you to adapt to a greater variety of situations. It also is more functional. Both men and women should be able to cry, to be assertive, to hug—whatever the situation calls for. Today, men and women are free to become manicurists, dental hygienists, housepersons, crane operators, bank presidents or breadwinners.

Rigid gender roles can cause conflict that robs y ou of vital energy. Highly masculine males tend to suffer from high anxiety, neuroticism, and low self-acceptance. The picture is not much prettier for women. Highly feminine women tend to be anxious and suffer from low self-confidence. In contrast, androgynous people have much higher levels of self-confidence, are well-adjusted and more creative and have happier marriages.

Because androgynous people have no gender-typed image to maintain, they can remain sensitive to changing situations and engage in whatever behavior seems most appropriate. For them, "masculine" and "feminine" traits simply don't exist. They are human traits. Almost all people experience some form of crossover as they age. Men and women in their 40s and 50s begin to adopt qualities typically thought e xclusively male or female. Women may become more independent and strong-minded. Men may become more emotionally responsive and interested in attachment. Older men often are more interested in giving and receiving lo ve than in conquests or power trips. Women may develop exactly the opposite traits.

Questers tend to start the process of becoming androgynous

early. Some in their 20s and 30s are already androgynous . By the time most are in their 40s and 50s , they have developed and feel comfortable with many of the emotional characteristics traditionally reserved for the opposite gender.

Enhancing Androgyny

Kathy, whom you met in Chapter 1, w as androgynous all her life. She was brought up in a mid-siz ed, Midwestern city. Her father was a lawyer, her mother a homemak er who enjoyed volunteer projects. She had one sister, two years older. Kathy's father encouraged her to be open to new experiences, regardless of whether they were typically "male" or "female." Her mother agreed. As a young child, Kathy had the oppor tunity to play with dolls and chemistry sets, to play doctor or n urse. She could take dancing lessons or pla y football, try out for the cheerleading squad or the bask etball team.

Because she had no brothers, Kathy's chores were both masculine and feminine. She took out the garbage, mowed the lawn, and shoveled the walk. She also washed the dishes, made the beds, baked cookies and sewed. To Kathy, there was no such thing as masculine or f eminine behavior. She did what was appropriate to the situation.

As a teenager, Kathy had both male and f emale friends, and she related to both as equals . She considered becoming a lawyer, policewoman, manager, geologist, physical education teacher, interior designer or dietitian. Because she was a good student with n umerous interests and abilities, Kathy had her choice of a n umber of occupations. But because she had man y options, she had a difficult time deciding. Her parents would have supported her in whatever occupation she chose. As it turned out, Kathy's first job w as as a manager with an insurance company. She will soon become a full-fledged lawyer.

Adrian's childhood and adolescence weren't as ideal as

Kathy's. Adrian also grew up in a Midwestern city. A middle child, he had an older brother and a y ounger sister. His parents divorced when he was 10. Adrian's mother worked as a nurse to support the family. But, like Kathy, Adrian came from a home where a parent modeled, encouraged, and supported androgynous behavior. Adrian recalls doing a variety of chores around the house. "We all helped at home. I learned that it was okay to do male and female activities." Parents who are warm and supportive facilitate the development of androgyny, autonomy and achievement.

A number of Questers, however, are pushed by circumstance to take on the strengths of the opposite gender when the y are in their 30s, 40s or older. Their stories show what goes into strengthening Quester traits.

Women and men forced by divorce or abandonment to fend for themselves and their children are often mar veled at for their ability to face life's challenges and overcome them. For example, Wilma started a lucrative typing business in a one-room apartment while her three children lear ned to become independent by helping out and taking par t-time jobs. Elaine completed her social work degree in the evening while she worked during the day to support her two children. Gretchen established her own drugstore while caring for an invalid husband. Yet all three were well-indoctrinated as children in gender stereotypes they never thought to question. Indeed, they set off into adulthood e xpecting to find a man who w ould take care of them. Here is Gretchen's story:

Gretchen was brought up in a small to wn on the West Coast, the only daughter of a merchant and a pampered mother. Gretchen didn't finish college after she met Matt. Together, they decided she wouldn't need her degree— she would never have to use it. Gretchen worked as a cashier in a bank until the y had their first child. Then three more children came along.

Gretchen enjoyed domestic life. When her youngest child started school, she worked as a volunteer two half-days a week at the school, watched soap operas, gossiped with the neighborhood coffee klatch, and kept a clean house. But paradise didn't last long.

Gretchen was forced to become the breadwinner when Matt was crippled in a car accident. She went back to the bank but didn't like it. So Gretchen decided to cash in the family's savings and return to school to earn a pharmacy degree. When she completed her education, she got a job as a pharmacist in a hospital. Within five years, she was promoted to director of research, a job she held for six years. The political hassles, coupled with her children's increasing independence and her own mid-life transition, led to Gretchen's decision to open her own drugstore.

It was hard at first. Gretchen was at work at 7 A.M. and didn't get home until 10 P.M. She kept her store open seven days a week. Today, Gretchen can afford to take it easier. She has two pharmacists and two salesclerks working for her.

Gretchen learned to be more ambitious, assertive, competent, and confident—the whole parcel of qualities usually associated with men. But she did not lose any of her female strengths, either. She is still loving and lovable, empathetic, warm and supportive.

As a matter of fact, Gretchen, Wilma, Elaine and other women like them have assumed male strengths at a remarkable rate. But Gretchen also had other Quester qualities to fortify her. She possessed a willingness to risk, which permitted her to change; she was open to new experiences; and she planned for her future. Her need to achieve surfaced only because she had the courage to allow it to, because she had picked up new skills to support it, and because she had the energy to follow through. As director of research at the hospital, she learned to think for herself. Among other things, Gretchen also had a strong sense of purpose in her life—her children, husband and a job that provided meaning.

> *Mike's* story is similar. Mike was a "macho man." As a young man, he nurtured the classic male fantasy. He ate, slept, played, and worked football. His little remaining time was spent in weight lifting and body building. As he now admits, he was a louse as a husband and father.
> So, at 35, with his wife gone, Mike was left to pick up the pieces of a shattered marriage with a son of 14 and two daughters, ages 13 and 11. The simple mechanics of being father and homemaker—working, shopping, and cleaning—stymied him at first. But he soon learned. It was the idea of intimacy that really threw him. "I didn't understand the language my children were speaking," he said. "I didn't know how to communicate with them. They would come home from school and spill their guts, and I didn't know what to say to them. I knew how to talk to the boys on the team, but this was different. In time, I learned. We learned together. Being a single parent is the most emotionally draining job I've ever had."

In the meantime, football and weight lifting became less important to Mike. The callous views he held as a young athlete disappeared. He needed another occupation. Sketching and painting caught his interest. Recovering from a broken hip, an athletic injury, he plunged into the paints and a how-to art book his daughter bought him. He loved it. Next came evening art courses.

Now, at 42, Mike is teaching art classes part-time at a high school and taking more courses. He wants to be a full-time art teacher and a free-lance artist. Mike's only involvement in athletics now, other than jogging, is leading a weekly weight-lifting class. He's even marrying a woman he met in art class.

Mike is a good model for younger men. He proves that a man is capable of releasing the tender side of his nature without losing his virility. Learning how to care, how to feel, and how to communicate these feelings to his children and being open to new experiences have made Mike's personality and his life more complete. The new, androgynous Mike will probably bring newfound joy and liberation into his marriage.

Being comfortable with the best of male and female strengths allows partners to achieve higher levels of intimacy and equality. Androgyny is an important part of happy relationships and marriages.

Striving to Achieve

Do you have a high achievement quotient? Many Questers do. Most are motivated by an inner drive. They strive to overcome obstacles, to achieve excellence and to do well at something difficult. This inner drive gives them feelings of accomplishment and confidence. Questers tend to seek settings in which independence of thought, creativity and growth are rewarded. Because Questers have a high need to achieve, they tend to strive for perfection, to do a good job and to attain their goals.

Jason is an achiever. Tall, lean, and well-built, with dark hair and blue eyes, Jason is an architect. He began his career when he was in his early 20s as a junior member of a large architectural firm. At 32, Jason decided to go it alone and established his own firm. Now in his early 40s, Jason has six younger associates. Because he is a perfectionist, Jason makes certain that he delivers a quality product. He'll go to great lengths to ensure that all details of a home match the personal qualities of the client. Jason particularly enjoys the challenge of doing a big and difficult job well. He feels good about an elementary school project he just completed, and so does the school board.

To survive in this changing world, you will need generalist skills.

Jason says this about success: "Success is an attitude. It makes you push hard at whatever you're doing. Success means never being satisfied that you've done well, always trying to do better. I work just as hard now as I did in my 20s. If you have passion, it will make you successful. Why else would Michelangelo have lain on his back for three years to paint a ceiling?"

Jason's positive attitude shines through his whole personality. He is driven by the desire to do his best, the need for challenge, and the will to work hard. Jason says, "I love my work. That leads to a strong identification with it and a high degree of motivation. I aim for excellence in whatever I do. Moreover, I have a 'can do' approach. I will try just about anything, no matter how difficult it appears—it's a challenge to me!"

Jason usually starts work at 7 A.M. No work appears too demeaning for him. "The more dirty work you do, the more you learn your job." He also manages to find time for fitness. He works out at the health club and plays racquetball as often as possible. Jason admits that he does become preoccupied when he's working on a project and sometimes neglects his wife and family. He can also be incredibly messy. But, he says, he's trying to improve.

How does Jason do it? He has *high levels of energy* and can stay with a task until it is completed. Having the energy to accomplish tasks and meet deadlines is vital to an achiever. Jason can go for days without sleep to complete a project. Like many Questers, his passion for work spills over into his playtime too.

Feeling energetic comes from being alive and involved. You feel wide awake and excited when you are doing things you really enjoy. A number of Questers over 30 have high energy levels because they are optimistic. They set out with high expectations, anticipate obstacles, put criticism in its place, and find meaning and direction in everything they do. They also take disappointments and setbacks in stride.

Your energy level may be determined partly by genetics. But don't let that restrain or limit you. You can raise your energy level by having a positive attitude, taking care of yourself (getting enough sleep, eating right, and exercising), becoming involved in an exciting job or project and having an intimate relationship.

Setbacks Are Good Experiences

It's always painful to experience a failure, and it's equally difficult to examine the reasons for one honestly and objectively. It's even tougher to pick yourself up, dust yourself off, and dive back into the fray. Yet failure can be one of life's greatest teachers, and many individuals who have found success have failed many times. Most manage to make those painful

> *Failure can be one of life's greatest teachers.*

experiences work in their favor by extracting valuable lessons that subsequently help them succeed.

Jason has found success. But he has also failed many times, and he has learned from his mistakes. "Setbacks are important," he says. "Maybe a rejection every few years is essential. It sort of revs up the engine. A number of bids I've made were rejected, so next time, I worked harder. I identified reasons the bids were rejected and tried to address these issues or weaknesses. People usually don't mention their rejections and mistakes, which is too bad, because you think you're the only one making mistakes. But I learned some very successful people have lived through many rejections."

Questers fail just as frequently and maybe more often than most of us. But they don't see themselves as failures. They learn not to fall victim to self-fulfilling negative prophecies.

A number of famous people failed several before attaining success. *Thomas Edison* had 10,000 trials before inventing the light bulb. This great scientist said the following about overcoming failure: "I am not discouraged, because every wrong attempt discarded is another step forward."

Michael Jordan, the retired American professional basketball player and active businessman, was proclaimed by the National Basketball Association as the "greatest player of all time." Jordan had this to say about his success: *"I have missed more than 9,000 shots in my career. I have lost almost 300 games. On 26 occasions, I have been entrusted to take the game winning shot . . . and missed. And I have failed over and over and over again in my life. And that is why . . . I succeed."*

Unfortunately, we are taught it is undesirable to fail, to make mistakes. Therefore, we walk away from opportunities and give up without even trying. We never learn what we are capable of accomplishing, and we spend considerable time and energy justifying why we can't accomplish something. Some people call this defeat—stopping the direction of life before the event has been completed. Don't let this happen to you. Learn from your setbacks. Turn these into opportunities for continuing growth.

Everyone Needs Challenge

Where does the need to achieve come from? Some psychologists believe you are born with "competence motivation," or the need for challenge and stimulation. Babies and toddlers have it. Grade school children have it. Some just have more of it than others.

Joyce is an achieving Quester. She was one of those children who strove to master difficult tasks alone. She recalls, "When I was 5, I went to the Ice Capades. I was so excited. I had to have a pair of figure skates, so I could

66

do all those fancy tricks myself. On Christmas day I went to the rink to practice 'shoot the duck' on my new skates. It was freezing. I was the only person there. I practiced until I had it mastered. I was cold and wet, and my feet and hands were frozen, but I felt good. I did it! But I didn't tell anyone. I felt good inside and that's what it's all about for me."

Today, Joyce is still "shooting the duck." She loved her first job, teaching high school history. Teaching was fun. She liked being around students and enjoyed trying to make her classes interesting and meaningful. Motivating poorly behaved students taxed her, but the rewards were worth it. Besides her classes, Joyce had plenty of other interests. She was involved in a pilot project with her school's English, history, and science departments. She also sat on a state committee that developed a values curriculum. But, by the fourth year, Joyce's enthusiasm was waning. Teaching the same old stuff year after year was losing its excitement. A failing marriage added to her lethargy. It was time for a change.

So Joyce took time off to travel and think about her life. She returned to a job offer as principal of a junior high school. Part of the challenge was working with problem students. She plunged in with gusto. Joyce was determined to help teachers deal with difficult students and to help students confront their problems. She introduced humanistic teaching to the school. Then she set up a student-staff liaison committee, so both sides could do something about their beefs. Joyce liked having the freedom to solve problems creatively. She's now in her fifth year as principal, and she's mastered her job pretty well. Now she wants to move on. To shine, she needs a challenging job she enjoys.

Oysters produce pearls to stop the irritation caused by trapped sand grains.

Success and achievement breed even more success and achievement. Joyce and Jason know from previous accomplishments that they can do well. So they set even more challenging goals for themselves next time. Every time they succeed, they are flooded with satisfaction. People who do well have the confidence to try and try again.

Wanting to Grow

Everyone needs to grow—Questers, especially. As they develop from childhood to old age, they continue to grow intellectually, emotionally, socially and spiritually. And because they are growing in all these components of their lives, physical decline that comes with old age for many is slower than for people who do not continue to develop in all life components.

Questers tend to improve with age. The accumulation of many experiences teaches them to be realistic, accepting and caring. Research shows that most individuals who possess Quester qualities look younger, feel healthier, and live longer than their peers. Questers' happy involvement in activities that give them a sense of meaning and purpose and their optimistic attitudes tend to contribute to their physical, mental, emotional and spiritual well-being.

Questers welcome new experiences, continuously try to improve themselves and the quality of their lives. Psychologists such as Abraham Maslow would say Questers are motivated by the need for self-actualization—to become all they are capable of becoming. Once Questers master a task, they tend to move on to other new and more challenging ones. The desire to grow is partly biological. Your nervous system hungers for stimulation. Looking for a job that uses all your talents allows you to grow. Most Questers place the opportunity to grow ahead of position, title or salary.

Questers, like everyone else, do not develop in isolation. They develop in a variety of contexts—environments which surround them and with which they are in constant interaction play a major role in their development. Experiences with their immediate families, along with community institutions such as the school, work, religious institutions and peer groups as well as the specific culture with which they identify, all play a role. Social institutions such as entertainment and news organizations, and historic and global influences such as the global economy and automation, all have widespread influence on the ways in which individuals develop.

Yet, Questers do not blame their environments for unhappiness or barriers to success. *Damon,* who was brought up in an abusive, alcoholic home, has this to say: "People from deprived backgrounds should not use their family experiences as excuses for their lack of success and growth. . . . They can take what they learned from these environments and use these as a springboard for growth and development." Damon, a modest, good-looking man, has been successful as a librarian and counselor.

Most Questers place the opportunity to grow ahead of position, title, or salary.

A peek at Renee's career history reveals how many Questers seek and develop growth from their jobs.

> *Renee,* now in her late 50s, is like many Questers. She needs a job in which she can grow. Renee began her career as a management trainee, then manager and head of ladies' fashion in a department store. By 36, she was a professional and financial success. But the meaning and excitement of her work were gone. So, at 38, Renee ventured into a new field—speech pathology. With a master's degree in speech pathology, she went to work as a speech therapist for a children's hospital. She loved it. Eight years later, she took a sabbatical for further training to prepare her for private practice.

Happily married to the same man for most of her adult life, Renee has balanced a career with a satisfying family life. She took a few years out to stay home when her son was young, but returned to retailing when he started school. Renee's family life hasn't always been idyllic. She admits to some pretty rocky times when she and her husband were in their early 30s. But, true to her nature, she did all she could to save their marriage. Renee sought counseling. "I guess I wanted to know in my own mind that I tried everything possible before I gave up on the marriage."

Fortunately, because Renee and her husband cared deeply for each other and wanted to make the marriage work, they re–solved their differences. Not all Questers are so fortunate. Renee and her husband now have an intimate relationship. They share many things and have a few mutual friends. But Renee also has special friends of her own.

Like many Questers, Renee feels good when she tries hard and achieves her goals. She possesses many Quester qualities. Renee is her own person.

Learning to Be Creative

Questers tend to be creative. Creativity involves imagining familiar things in a new light, finding connections among unrelated phenomena, and digging below the surface to find previously undetected patterns. The need to create is an innate human quality. Human beings all share an innate need to create.

Steve, an 80-year-old Quester who loves painting, reveals his philosophy: "You remain young only as long as you experiment. When you are content with what you have already done, happy only to repeat yourself, you've reached old age."

When Questers are creating something, they feel that they are living fully. Their work seems to originate in their souls, not from their egos. When they create—a software program, dance routine or book—they discover unknown parts of themselves. Intuitive, Questers pay attention to the signs, synchronicities and symbols around them, and they make use of that information in their work.

Questers need to express more of who they truly are than Traditionalists. They need to know the "truth." Because they are often ahead of their times, they may have to buck societal standards. Galileo Galilei, an Italian physicist, mathematician, astronomer and philosopher who played a major role in the scientific revolution, was considered a revolutionary in his time. Galileo proved the earth revolved around the sun instead of the other way around.

Creative Questers are usually driven. Many have a passion to contribute to the beauty and betterment of the world. Because of their high drive, they can produce a lot in a relative short amount of time. Famous Questers such as Pablo Picasso and George Soros are examples of this productivity. Many Questers whom you met in this book such as Jason work late into the night and persist to complete a project when less driven individuals would not.

Research has demonstrated that creative individuals tend to exhibit polar opposite traits. They are both extroverted and introverted, humble and proud. Although they usually have a great deal of physical energy enabling them to focus on their work for long hours, they also need quiet, restful times.

Questers can adapt to most situations and make do with whatever is at hand to reach their goals. While his less creative colleagues at a large department store were complaining that their productivity was hurt because the central office was doing all the ordering and purchasing, *Aaron,* a creative young manager of the jewelry department, used his creativity to do something about it. He approached his supervisor with a well-developed plan that included monthly profit and loss statements and balance sheets illustrating the kind of jewelry that was most viable for his department. As a result of his department's success, Aaron was promoted to head buyer within three years.

Questers love the process of creating. If they are unable to work, they feel a deep sense of loss and emptiness. However, when they are working in their areas of expertise, worries are replaced by a sense of bliss.

The courage to risk, to break with tradition, is an important Quester trait. Unlike Traditionalists, who lack nerve, want to play it safe, Questers play a more risky, but interesting and often successful game. Antonio, a sculptor, says this about his work: "When I am creating from my soul, I am inventive, searching, daring. . . . It does not matter whether other people accept my work or not. I am simply pursuing my calling." Fortunately, Antonio earns a good living by pursuing his passion.

Yet, some Questers have said that their need to be creative can be a "curse." Their openness and sensitivity often exposes them to suffering and pain. A badly designed machine causes pain to the inventive engineer, just as the creative writer is hurt when reading bad poetry. Being alone at the front of a discipline also leaves Questers exposed and vulnerable. The Roman Catholic Church denounced Galileo's opinions on the motion of the Earth, judging them dangerous and close to heresy.

Intuitiveness can invite criticism and vicious attacks. When an artist has invested years in a project, it is devastating if nobody cares. Deep interest and involvement in obscure subjects often goes unrewarded, or even brings ridicule. Creative thinking is often perceived as deviant by the majority, and so the creative person may feel isolated and misunderstood. Some creative people, who spend many hours alone, have not developed their interpersonal skills. As well, because they feel very deeply, they can succumb to depression and alcoholism.

Do you find yourself relating to some of these traits? If so, it's time to get started. Boost your creativity by trying some of the tips described in Chapter 3.

Developing the Courage to Risk

As we have seen, Questers with creative qualities tend to be risk takers. When we meet successful people, we may be tempted to envy them for their "luck." Of course, their success has nothing to do with luck. That's why Publius Vergilius, a classical Roman poet wrote, "Fortune sides with him who dares." And Homer wrote, "And what he greatly thought, he nobly dared." Life is all about taking risks. We willingly take chances every day. Whether we drive, walk or take public transportation to work, we risk getting into an accident.

What separates Questers from others is their willingness to take optional as well as necessary risks. For example, if you have an okay job and are suddenly offered another job with more responsibility and a significant salary increase would you take it? There are many risks to moving on. Will you like the new company, supervisors, and colleagues? What if you can't handle the responsibility? And if you lose the job, could you find another. Is this risk worth taking for you?

People who think like that don't understand what real security is. Security can never depend on outside things and circumstances. It only comes from within. Is there security in staying with your present job? Could you lose it due to corporate downsizing? Could a new regional executive come in and change policies and procedures? Would you like these changes?

If you are used to taking risks, you will have developed an inner strength, a resiliency, an ability to cope in tough circumstances. Research shows that when we learn new things we develop new neural pathways in the brain. Those who fear taking risks to protect their "security," are trapped by their fears. We can't grow without risk and change. Turtles can't move forward without sticking out their necks. We can't either. Snakes have to shed their skin before they can grow. We, too, have to shed our "comfort zone." We dislike breaking our routine, trying something new because new activities make us feel uncomfortable. But if we continue to pursue the same actives year after year, how can we grow? By following the examples of the Questers, you can learn to burst through your present comfort level. You can stretch by taking small risks first. Chapters 3 offer tips to enhance the courage to risk, and Chapter 8 helps you minimize risk when making important decisions.

Building Resilience

Questers, who have the will to risk, also tend to be resilient. They rebound from major setbacks such as relationship difficulties, health issues, or workplace and financial stressors, stronger than before. Being resilient does not mean that they do not experience difficulty or stress. Emotional pain and sadness are common in Questers who suffer trauma or adversity. But Questers learn how to cope with these stressors.

Resilience is essential in today's rapidly changing world. A person's level of resilience often determines his or her success or failure in the workplace or other areas. Resilient people also recover from traumatic experiences stronger and wiser.

Questers believe setbacks are temporary, not permanent. This enables them to move on to their next goal. They don't take setbacks personally. They don't generalize defeats into larger more ominous problems. Instead, they focus on their accomplishments and desired goals.

Ivan experienced several setbacks in his 20s including a divorce and a bout with cancer. Brilliant with and intelligent quotient several notches above average, Ivan felt stuck in his job as a laborer. Dissatisfaction with his job and no clear goals, contributed to Ivan's depression and related stress. His doctor prescribed medical leave and counseling. Counseling helped Ivan identify his purpose, needs, strengths and other attributes. He learned which part of his life he and others controlled. Ivan realized he did have many career and lifestyle options which he explored and narrowed. Now 33, Ivan is pursuing a forgotten dream—a retail business in a small city near the mountains. He is also engaging in activities that he enjoys and finds relaxing. He is making time for friends and fishing which are providing balance in Ivan's life, and acting as a hedge against possible future stressors.

Ivan's negative thoughts about his job and his inability to see options were barriers to building a better future. By expressing his negative feelings, changing his negative thought patterns to more positive beliefs, and identifying and researching options, Ivan was able to prepare for and look forward to an exciting future. He no longer dwelled on the negative or saw himself as a victim. Instead, he reviewed what he learned from these experiences turned these into opportunities for further growth and revitalization.

Developing resilience is a personal journey. No two people react the same way to traumatic and stressful life events. Ivan's approach to building resilience may not work for you. Coping strategies may reflect cultural differences such as how one communicates feelings, and whether and how one connects with significant others, including extended family members. Tips for building resilience are discussed in Chapter 3.

Being Optimistic

Optimists learn from failure, and they hope for and expect the best. A crucial component to a happy and successful life is what we say to ourselves when we experience the failures and disappointments that inevitably come our way. We learn to explain our setbacks in positive or negative styles early in childhood. For some individuals an automatic response might be, "It's going to last forever and undermine everything I do." But others are able to say and believe, "It's just circumstances I can overcome—and, besides, there is so much more to life."

A pessimist who is having difficulty with her significant other might say, "Men are tyrants." An optimist would say, "My husband was in a bad mood." A pessimist who is presented with the possibility of cancer might say, "This lump is probably cancerous. It looks like I may not have long to live." An optimist would say, "This lump may not be cancerous; but if it is, I will do everything I can to beat it."

When Questers are confronted with hard knocks, they perceive these as challenges to be met. *Walter,* an aeronautical engineer who lost his job as a result of cuts in defense spending, went through the typical transition stages experienced by most dislocated workers. (These are shock, denial and disbelief, fear and anxiety, resistance, anger, acceptance and exploration, and commitment, described in Chapter 4). But Walter didn't get stuck for long in the earlier stages. Seeing the glass as half-full, he told himself that he had a lot to offer, that there were positions out there for him, and that he would be employed within two months.

You create your own script in life by the thoughts you think.

Walter proceeded to work hard at his job search. He attended workshops on how to write resumes, research companies, network, contact employers, market himself and follow up on interviews. He job searched five days a week and didn't take rejection personally. He believed he would find a job that would enable him to use his skills and make a contribution. Within two months, he had attained his dream position with another firm.

By contrast, when *Bill* lost his position with the same company, he told himself and others that there were no longer any jobs in the defense industry. Believing the glass to be half-empty, he made a half-hearted attempt to contact employers. A year later, he still had not found a job. Fortunately, he finally enrolled in a career transitions group and sought private counseling. With the support of the group and a counselor, and a change in attitude, Bill attained a suitable position 18 months later. He learned to become more optimistic, developing a new set of skills on how to talk to himself when he suffered a defeat.

Optimists usually achieve happiness and success because they think positively about what they want to happen. Their vivid imaginations about their desired outcomes help to bring these about. Walter saw himself in his desired position, believed he would attain it within two months, and wrote down all the reasons why he would be successful. He reminded himself three times a day that he would attain his desired goal, and he developed a plan of action. He kept in contact with positive individuals who supported his endeavors, and he continued to look after his mental, physical, emotional and spiritual needs. He worked. He acted confident and successful.

Bill, on the other hand, saw nothing but a lack of suitable positions, and he constantly verbalized this to himself and others.

How you think about a problem can either relieve it or aggravate it. You create your own script in life by the thoughts you think. Fortunately, you have the freedom to change these thoughts. You have the choice of making each day terrific or terrible. Habits of thinking need not be lifelong. One of the most significant findings in psychology in the last 25 years is that individuals can choose the way they think. Pessimists like Bill can learn to be optimists by changing their attitudes and learning a new set of cognitive skills. For suggestion on building positive attitudes, read "Tips for Becoming More Optimistic" in Chapter 3, and "Developing Positive Attitudes and Behaviors," in Chapter 9.

Scientific evidence indicates that optimism is vitally important in overcoming defeat, promoting resilience and achievement, and maintaining or improving health. Studies show that optimists do much better in school, at work, and on the playing field than pessimists. They regularly exceed the predictions of aptitude tests, and when they run for office, they are more likely than pessimists to get elected. Their health is unusually good, and evidence suggests they may even live longer.

Of course, a little pessimism, like a little fear, can play a constructive role in our lives. In mild forms, pessimism serves the purpose of pulling us back from risky exaggerations of our optimism, making us think twice, keeping us from making rash, foolhardy gestures.

But it is the optimistic moments of our lives that contain the greatest plans, the dreams, and the hopes. Without these dreams we would never accomplish anything difficult and intimidating, we would not even attempt the barely possible. Space exploration would remain a pipe-dream, and the four-minute mile would be unrun. The genius of evolution lies in the dynamic tension between optimism and pessimism, continually correcting each other.

You, Too, Can Become a Quester

Questers tend to possess many other common characteristics. They come to terms with the transitions of their life cycles. They deal with developmental issues and struggle with whether to stay in destructive careers or relationships. Questers learn how to use life crises—such as accidents, financial reversals, being fired or abandoned, and even sudden death—as maturing experiences to take stock, and they emerge from these crises as fuller, better human beings. Most Questers recognize the importance of a healthy lifestyle and strive to strike a balance between work and family, relationships and leisure activities.

Questers know that surviving in uncertain times means being flexible and willing to risk.

Questers aren't dependent on others for their well-being. They take charge of their own destinies. But they keep their options open, finding satisfaction and success in a variety of occupations and organizations. Questers know that surviving in uncertain times means being flexible and willing to risk. They have the courage to be open to new experiences and to let go of familiar people, places and lifestyles. Questers have learned to move forward.

Which of the Questers' personality characteristics—purpose, autonomy, intimacy, self-confidence, androgyny, achievement, growth, resilience and risk—is most important? They all are, because they all complement one another. Mastering new skills helps Questers gain the confidence to set their sights even higher. They grow and change.

You may not think you are a Quester. But you can strengthen Quester qualities, if you want to, by small acts of courage. You can move forward, too. Complete *The Quester Questionnaire* in the next chapter. Dare to change and take the first step.

Chapter 3
Are You a Quester?

Are you a Quester? Would you like to become one? We are all born with Quester qualities. You can see these characteristics in babies and young children. They continuously strive to learn by exploring the world around them. Infants reach out to grasp their parents' ears, eyes or clothing and various objects in their cribs or playpens. As they learn to crawl and walk, they have fun exploring every cupboard and object in their homes.

Infants and toddlers learn to crawl, walk and build with blocks by persevering and risking. They are not deterred by setbacks or falls. There is no word for failure in their vocabularies. Children feel good about accomplishing challenging tasks, as you can see by their sparkling eyes, excited waving of arms and legs, and smiles and laughter.

Unfortunately, as people grow older, many lose this excitement for learning; they forget the good feelings that come from accomplishing difficult tasks. Various reprimands, don'ts, shouldn'ts, and shames result in embarrassment or fear of trying and failing. Many adults set up barriers to growth that are manifested in expressions of resistance such as fear, denial, delaying tactics, impatience, false beliefs and low self-confidence. They lose touch with their inner child and their Quester characteristics.

You have Quester qualities within that you can strengthen if you want to. Contrary to popular belief, the personality you developed through your childhood and adolescent experiences needn't be your wardrobe for life. In fact, you can do a complete makeover any time you want. Naturally, before you do that, you'll need to draft a map of who you really are and where you want to go. You should also identify your strengths and limitations, so that you can maximize your strengths and minimize your limitations. *The Quester Questionnaire* can help you see how you rate on the various Quester characteristics. By responding to the statements and reading the interpretations carefully, you can gain a greater understanding of who you are and who you could become.

The Quester Questionnaire

The *165* statements in the Questionnaire will help you identify how your personality characteristics compare with those of the Questers. Indicate how much you agree or disagree with each statement by circling a number from *5 (strongly agree)* to *1 (strongly disagree)*. You'll find scoring procedures and an interpretation of the results at the end of the Questionnaire .

Make your responses as honest as possible. Don't choose the answer you think others would expect of you. This is a quiz for you, and you alone. Because your attitudes about yourself can also be colored by how you feel at any given time, complete the Questionnaire when you are feeling refreshed. For best results, find a quiet spot where you can devote two concentrated hours to completing and scoring it.

One final point: In the field of psychological evaluation, there are no absolute rights or wrongs. This Questionnaire is not infallible, but you will find it intriguing and revealing. In fact, you may never see yourself in the same way again.

The Quester Questionnaire

Degree of Agreement

Very High   Very Low

		5	4	3	2	1
1.	Facing my daily tasks is a source of pleasure and satisfaction.	5	4	3	2	1
2.	I can usually manage strong feelings and impulses.	5	4	3	2	1
3.	When I do a job, I do it well.	5	4	3	2	1
4.	I am determined I will succeed in everything I do.	5	4	3	2	1
5.	I often wish people would be more definite.	5	4	3	2	1
6.	When I want something, I'll sometimes go out on a limb for it.	5	4	3	2	1
7.	When I want to buy something, I rarely consider others' opinions.	5	4	3	2	1
8.	It's easy for me to start conversations with strangers.	5	4	3	2	1
9.	I rarely contribute new ideas at work.	5	4	3	2	1
10.	Most of my misfortunes and successes were the result of things I did.	5	4	3	2	1
11.	It's very hard for me to tell any one about myself.	5	4	3	2	1
12.	I have been doing quite a bit of self-assessment lately.	5	4	3	2	1
13.	I have clear goals and aims in life.	5	4	3	2	1
14.	Most choices I make are based on my true feelings and beliefs.	5	4	3	2	1
15.	I have much to be proud of.	5	4	3	2	1
16.	I feel great after completing a difficult task well.	5	4	3	2	1
17.	A well-ordered way of life with regular hours suits my temperament.	5	4	3	2	1
18.	If the possible reward was very high, I would not hesitate to put my money into a business that could fail.	5	4	3	2	1
19.	I rely on my own power and resources in most situations.	5	4	3	2	1
20.	When I'm in a group, I hesitate to make suggestions.	5	4	3	2	1
21.	I like a job that demands skills and practice rather than inventiveness.	5	4	3	2	1
22.	I usually count on good things happening to me.	5	4	3	2	1
23.	I always try to consider others' feelings before I do something.	5	4	3	2	1
24.	I have experienced at least one traumatic event in the past year.	5	4	3	2	1
25.	If I should die today, I would feel my life has been worthless.	5	4	3	2	1
26.	I like to withdraw temporarily from the rest of the world.	5	4	3	2	1

27.	I feel good about myself.	5	4	3	2	1
28.	I don't have much ambition.	5	4	3	2	1
29.	I'm confident I will achieve my goals.	5	4	3	2	1
30.	If I want something, I'm willing to take a risk to attain it.	5	4	3	2	1
31.	I'd rather spend time and energy doing an interesting job than being successful at a job I dislike.	5	4	3	2	1
32.	I'm usually a good listener.	5	4	3	2	1
33.	I seldom bother to think of original ways of doing the same thing.	5	4	3	2	1
34.	My successes are the result of hard work, determination and some ability.	5	4	3	2	1
35.	I like to play with kittens, puppies or babies.	5	4	3	2	1
36.	I'm very satisfied with my job.	5	4	3	2	1
37.	I have a sense of inner peace and joy.	5	4	3	2	1
38.	I focus on my accomplishments more than losses.	5	4	3	2	1
39.	I believe that I am as successful in achieving my goals as most of my graduating class.	5	4	3	2	1
40.	I will never profit much.	5	4	3	2	1
41.	I'm usually hopeful about my future.	5	4	3	2	1
42.	I would accept a job that had exciting challenges as well as uncertainties.	5	4	3	2	1
43.	I refuse to behave like everyone else just to please people.	5	4	3	2	1
44.	I'm critical about the dress, manner, or ideas of some of my friends.	5	4	3	2	1
45.	I hope to develop a new technique in my field of work.	5	4	3	2	1
46.	When I make plans, I am almost certain I can make them work.	5	4	3	2	1
47.	I am adventurous and like to try new things.	5	4	3	2	1
48.	I feel that I'm passing through a transition.	5	4	3	2	1
49.	I have seriously thought of suicide as a way out.	5	4	3	2	1
50.	I accept and encourage constructive feedback.	5	4	3	2	1
51.	I allow relatives and colleagues to take advantage of me.	5	4	3	2	1
52.	All I want out of a career is a secure, not-too-dif ficult job that pays enough to buy a nice car and home.	5	4	3	2	1
53.	I like to work on problems that have ambiguous answers.	5	4	3	2	1
54.	I don't fear failure.	5	4	3	2	1
55.	Generally, I don't concern myself with what others think of my abilities.	5	4	3	2	1

84

56. I feel comfortable with all types of people—from the wealthiest and well-educated to the poorest and least-educated. _____ 5   4   3   2   1

57. I usually continue to do a job in exactly the same way it was taught to me. ___5   4   3   2   1

58. Many times I feel I have little influence over the things that happen to me. ___5   4   3   2   1

59. I'm not afraid to take a stand even though it may be unpopular. _____ 5   4   3   2   1

60. I believe the probability is good of finding an acceptable job elsewhere. ___5   4   3   2   1

61. I regard my ability to find meaning and purpose in my life as practically nonexistent. _____ 5   4   3   2   1

62. I will continue to grow best just by being myself. _____ 5   4   3   2   1

63. I am a person of worth at least equal to others. _____ 5   4   3   2   1

64. Being successful in my goals is very important to me. _____ 5   4   3   2   1

65. It bothers me when something unexpected interrupts my routine. _____ 5   4   3   2   1

66. I trust decisions I make spontaneously. _____ 5   4   3   2   1

67. What the general public thinks does not affect my standards or beliefs. ___5   4   3   2   1

68. I can take a joke when it's on me. _____ 5   4   3   2   1

69. I prefer activities I know I will enjoy to ones I have never tried. _____ 5   4   3   2   1

70. I believe I can get a job in a tight job market. _____ 5   4   3   2   1

71. I have both male and female qualities. _____ 5   4   3   2   1

72. There is much to be gained by staying in my current job for the rest of my career. _____ 5   4   3   2   1

73. I would not change my life drastically if I knew I had only six months to live. _____ 5   4   3   2   1

74. I would like to make a contribution to society. _____ 5   4   3   2   1

75. I am a useful person to have around. _____ 5   4   3   2   1

76. I'm nonjudgmental about people and can adapt to their diverse personality styles. _____ 5   4   3   2   1

77. I like things to be certain and predictable. _____ 5   4   3   2   1

78. In games, I usually go for broke rather than playing it safe. _____ 5   4   3   2   1

79. I would enjoy being a vagabond for a while. _____ 5   4   3   2   1

80. I do not have a small circle of very close friends. _____ 5   4   3   2   1

81. I like trying different kinds of foreign foods. _____ 5   4   3   2   1

82. I take my horoscope seriously. _____ 5   4   3   2   1

83. I'm sensitive to the needs of others. _____ 5   4   3   2   1

84. My employer inspires me to do well.	5	4	3	2	1
85. In thinking about my life, I see a reason to be here.	5	4	3	2	1
86. I am growing and developing personally and professionally.	5	4	3	2	1
87. I certainly feel useless at times.	5	4	3	2	1
88. I often do as little work as possible to get by.	5	4	3	2	1
89. I can define my life mission.	5	4	3	2	1
90. Overall, I anticipate more good things will happen to me than bad.	5	4	3	2	1
91. I find it hard to work under strict rules and regulations.	5	4	3	2	1
92. I can like people without having to approve of them.	5	4	3	2	1
93. Few topics bore me.	5	4	3	2	1
94. If something can go wrong for me, it will.	5	4	3	2	1
95. Once I master a task, I move on to other new challenges.	5	4	3	2	1
96. I never think of quitting my job.	5	4	3	2	1
97. My job gives my life meaning and direction.	5	4	3	2	1
98. I read people well and trust my intuition.	5	4	3	2	1
99. I usually learn from my mistakes.	5	4	3	2	1
100. I set high standards for myself.	5	4	3	2	1
101. I need the approval of others to feel good about myself.	5	4	3	2	1
102. I would prefer a stable position with a moderate salary to one with a higher salary but less security.	5	4	3	2	1
103. When I was a child, I didn't care to be a member of a crowd or group.	5	4	3	2	1
104. I feel secure in my relationships.	5	4	3	2	1
105. I like to participate actively in intense discussions.	5	4	3	2	1
106. I tend to have bad luck with supervisors.	5	4	3	2	1
107. I believe men and women should follow any career they want.	5	4	3	2	1
108. I am currently achieving my dreams.	5	4	3	2	1
109. I can see past, present, and future as a meaningful continuity.	5	4	3	2	1
110. I know and accept myself.	5	4	3	2	1
111. I welcome criticism as an opportunity to grow.	5	4	3	2	1
112. I always try to do at least a little better than is expected of me.	5	4	3	2	1
113. I think mothers should stay home with their children until they start school.	5	4	3	2	1

114. I try to avoid situations that have uncertain outcomes. _____ 5   4   3   2   1

115. Before making a decision, I often worry whether or not others
will approve of it. _____ 5   4   3   2   1

116. I would not dare reveal my weaknesses among friends. _____ 5   4   3   2   1

117. I always feel I must look into all sides of a problem. _____ 5   4   3   2   1

118. Even when there is nothing forcing me, I often find
myself doing things I do not really want to do. _____ 5   4   3   2   1

119. I believe there are no genetic differences between
the genders in intellectual ability. _____ 5   4   3   2   1

120. I attend to my needs, and engage in activities I enjoy and find relaxing. _____ 5   4   3   2   1

121. I have the knowledge and experience to be helpful to my family,
friends and acquaintances when they ask for advice. _____ 5   4   3   2   1

122. I enjoy doing challenging things. _____ 5   4   3   2   1

123. I like to associate with positive, supportive people. _____ 5   4   3   2   1

124. I probably would not take the chance of borrowing
money for a business deal even if it might be profitable. _____ 5   4   3   2   1

125. It's important for me to have a job in which I have the
freedom to perform the tasks my own way. _____ 5   4   3   2   1

126. If I sense a colleague has a problem, I'll volunteer to help. _____ 5   4   3   2   1

127. I think of myself as a straightforward, uncomplicated person. _____ 5   4   3   2   1

128. What happens to me is my own doing. _____ 5   4   3   2   1

129. It is possible for women to combine home and career,
and do both successfully. _____ 5   4   3   2   1

130. I find it difficult to express my feelings to others and ask for help. _____ 5   4   3   2   1

131. I'm flexible and adjust quickly to new situations. _____ 5   4   3   2   1

132. I would like a job that provides good opportunities for self-expression. _____ 5   4   3   2   1

133. I can accept my mistakes. _____ 5   4   3   2   1

134. I think I could accomplish almost anything I wanted if I tried hard enough. _____ 5   4   3   2   1

135. It takes time for me to adapt to new developments. _____ 5   4   3   2   1

136. There's nothing I can do about my dissatisfying work situation. _____ 5   4   3   2   1

137. I would enjoy a job in which I have to adapt quickly
to new situations and to emergencies. _____ 5   4   3   2   1

138. I prefer a job in which I am not closely supervised. _____ 5   4   3   2   1

139. I find it difficult to recover emotionally from losses. _____ 5   4   3   2   1

140. I feel free to express both warm feelings and constructive criticism to my friends.	5	4	3	2	1
141. It is important for me to have a job in which I can create original things or ideas.	5	4	3	2	1
142. I feel free to not do what others expect of me.	5	4	3	2	1
143. I'm playful and find humor in rough situations.	5	4	3	2	1
144. It's ridiculous for a woman to run a locomotive or for a man to darn socks.	5	4	3	2	1
145. When I'm no longer learning on the job, I need to move on to one that will better satisfy my needs.	5	4	3	2	1
146. I feel comfortable in social situations and can express my true feelings and opinions.	5	4	3	2	1
147. I want to know how things work and like trying new ways of doing these.	5	4	3	2	1
148. I spend my life doing what I should rather than what I want.	5	4	3	2	1
149. I would take a job I enjoy even if strikes and layoffs are expected.	5	4	3	2	1
150. I would like a job in which I can express my creativity.	5	4	3	2	1
151. I dislike working without a written job description.	5	4	3	2	1
152. A good education is equally important for men and women.	5	4	3	2	1
153. I feel comfortable talking about very personal things with my partner or close friends.	5	4	3	2	1
154. I tend to be cautious, anxious and apprehensive when making big decisions.	5	4	3	2	1
155. I have been made stronger and wiser by difficult experiences.	5	4	3	2	1
156. There are few suitable jobs available for me.	5	4	3	2	1
157. I tend to visualize or imagine my career and life goals.	5	4	3	2	1
158. I feel blessed.	5	4	3	2	1
159. I often blow painful events out of proportion, and predict negative outcomes.	5	4	3	2	1
160. In a chaotic situation, I calm myself and focus on taking action.	5	4	3	2	1
161. My behavior is often determined by the demands of the situation.	5	4	3	2	1
162. I think it's acceptable for the man to stay home and look after the children while his partner builds her career.	5	4	3	2	1
163. I can be both assertive and accommodating depending on the circumstances.	5	4	3	2	1
164. I measure my accomplishments by standards set by my peers.	5	4	3	2	1
165. I find it difficult to adapt to new and varied social settings.	5	4	3	2	1

Scoring

Part A

To determine your score for Part A, *give yourself 3 points for each 5 (very strongly agree), 2 points for each 4 (agree), and 1 point for each 3 (uncertain or undecided)* you recorded for the forgoing statements. Place a 3, 2, or 1 in the b lank beside each statement. Then add up your total score for each personality characteristic and place these in the b lank labeled, Subtotal.

Interpersonal	Self-Confidence	Purpose	Autonomy
8 _____	3 _____	1 _____	7 _____
23 _____	15 _____	13 _____	10 _____
32 _____	27 _____	25 _____	19 _____
56 _____	39 _____	37 _____	43 _____
68 _____	51 _____	73 _____	55 _____
83 _____	59 _____	74 _____	67 _____
92 _____	63 _____	85 _____	79 _____
104 _____	75 _____	89 _____	91 _____
126 _____	111 _____	97 _____	103 _____
140 _____	121 _____	109 _____	125 _____
146 _____	133 _____		128 _____
153 _____	134 _____		138 _____
			142 _____

Subtotal _____   *Subtotal* _____   *Subtotal* _____   *Subtotal* _____

Achievement	Creativity	Androgyny	Resilience
4 _____	21 _____	35 _____	2 _____
16 _____	45 _____	43 _____	38 _____
31 _____	47 _____	71 _____	76 _____
34 _____	59 _____	107 _____	98 _____
64 _____	81 _____	119 _____	120 _____
95 _____	93 _____	129 _____	31 _____
100 _____	117 _____	152 _____	143 _____
112 _____	137 _____	161 _____	147 _____
122 _____	141 _____	162 _____	155 _____
_____	150 _____	163 _____	160 _____
Subtotal _____	Subtotal _____	Subtotal _____	Subtotal _____

Risk	Growth	Optimism	Ways to Identify Potential Questers
6 _____	14 _____	22 _____	12 _____
18 _____	26 _____	29 _____	24 _____
30 _____	50 _____	41 _____	48 _____
42 _____	62 _____	46 _____	60 _____
53 _____	66 _____	70 _____	_____
54 _____	86 _____	90 _____	_____
78 _____	105 _____	99 _____	_____
137 _____	110 _____	123 _____	_____
149 _____	111 _____	136 _____	_____
_____	132 _____	157 _____	_____
_____	145 _____	158	_____
_____	150 _____		_____
Subtotal _____	Subtotal _____	Subtotal _____	Subtotal _____

Part B

To score part B, *give yourself 3 points for each 1 (strongly disagree), 2 points for each 2 (disagree), and 1 point for each 3 (uncertain or undecided).* Place 3, 2 or 1 beside each item under a personality characteristic. Again, add up your scores and place the results for each characteristic in the blanks labeled, Subtotal.

Interpersonal	Self-Confidence	Purpose	Autonomy
11 _____	20 _____	25 _____	58 _____
44 _____	51 _____	49 _____	82 _____
80 _____	87 _____	61 _____	115 _____
116 _____		148 _____	118 _____
Subtotal _____	*Subtotal* _____	*Subtotal* _____	*Subtotal* _____

Achievement	Creativity	Androgyny	Resilience
28 _____	9 _____	113 _____	65 _____
52 _____	21 _____	144 _____	130 _____
88 _____	33 _____	165 _____	135 _____
164 _____	57 _____		139 _____
	69 _____		151 _____
	127 _____		154 _____
			159 _____
Subtotal _____	*Subtotal* _____	*Subtotal* _____	*Subtotal* _____

Risk		Growth	Optimism	Ways to Identify Potential Questers
5 ____	17 ____	52 _____	40 _____	36 _____
65 ____	77 ____	101 _____	94 _____	72 _____
102 ____	113 ____		106 _____	84 _____
114 ____	124 ____		156 _____	96 _____
				108 _____
Subtotal _____		*Subtotal* _____	*Subtotal* _____	*Subtotal* _____

Part C

Now determine your *combined overall score by adding together your subtotals for each personality characteristic under Parts A and B.* For example, if under Resilience, you scored 20 in Part A and 12 in Part B, your combined overall score will be 32 (20 + 12 = 32). List each of these combined overall scores in the spaces pro vided below. You may want to compare your scores to the highest possib le totals (shown in the far-right column). Once you have determined your combined overall score for each personality char acteristic, add them up and place the total in the space beside Ov erall Score. Do *not* include your score on Ways to Identify Potential Questers in your overall score. Read on to discover what your scores reveal.

Personality Characteristic	Score	Highest Possible Score
Interpersonal	_____	(48)
Self-Confidence	_____	(45)
Purpose	_____	(42)
Autonomy	_____	(51)
Achievement	_____	(39)
Creativity	_____	(48)
Androgyny	_____	(39)
Risk	_____	(51)
Growth	_____	(51)
Optimism	_____	(45)
Resilience	_____	(51)
Ways to Identify Potential Questers		_____ (27)
Overall Score	_____	**(510)**

Your responses to the statements in the Questionnaire reveal how closely you resemble the Questers. A high score means you have many Quester qualities. An intermediate score means you are a potential Quester. A low score means you are quite different from the Questers. Keep in mind that your scores are not fixed. When events are going well, your scores will probably rise. Under stress, they will be inclined to drop.

Quester qualities are positive ones. However, if they become excessive, they lose their value. People with extremely high overall scores may be overly anxious, tense and unrealistic. People who seek intimacy compulsively may miss the joys of solitude. Those who have too much self-confidence may be arrogant, unrealistic and blind to their own limitations. Those whose sense of purpose is all-consuming may become narrow and boring to others. Overly autonomous people may refuse help even when they need it. Those driven by too great a need for achievement may be ruthless in their single-minded pursuit of major accomplishments. And occasionally, rampant innovators miss the value in the tried and true, wrongly believing there is value only in the new and novel.

Some people, recognizing the trendy value of androgyny, foolishly suppress some of the fine strengths of their own gender. A willingness to risk, when carried to extremes, may be hard to distinguish from irresponsible gambling. Obsessive preoccupation with growth can be found among boring people who are too absorbed in themselves.

What Does The Quester Questionnaire Say About You?

Interpersonal
34 or higher: Your feelings closely match those of the Questers. You tend to place great value on personal relationships, probably have a small circle of very close friends and get along well with work colleagues. Your

friendships are emotionally rich. If you are married or living with someone, the relationship is close and loving. You have nothing to hide from family and friends, and you readily reveal your problems, foibles, and concerns to them. You are candid and care deeply about others, and your excellent interpersonal skills allow you to empathize with and relate effectively to people from all walks of life. Your self-confident, trusting nature draws people to you.

15 to 34: You are a potential Quester. Your dealings with people may fluctuate. For instance, you may be empathetic and have a caring relationship with your partner, but find it difficult to start conversations with strangers and hesitate to make suggestions in a work setting. Go back over the statements and see what you could change about yourself to enhance your ability to strengthen interpersonal skills.

14 or lower: You are probably shy, have few close friends, feel uncomfortable being intimate with your partner, and feel ill at ease in social situations. Work on improving your interpersonal skills. Your attitudes about love, other people, and yourself may be preventing you from enjoying close relationships. Like anything else, you can change your attitudes. By learning to become more outgoing and a more effective communicator, you can not only improve your interpersonal skills, but also take better control of your own behavior.

Tips for Strengthening Interpersonal Skills
- *Get out and associate with others.* The act of mingling and making friends usually requires no more than suffering through the 10 or 15 awkward minutes it takes to get to know someone. Start a conversation. As soon as the conversation starts rolling, see if your shyness doesn't disappear. A hello, a smile, a handshake, a nod, a wink— any one of these little communication devices can help you overcome shyness. Force yourself to smile at and speak to someone you previously ignored. During an office coffee break, strike up a conversation with someone

new. Go out into the world, even when you don't feel like it. Make small talk. Become more visible. Compliment others—or, better yet, ask for their advice. Sit down next to a stranger or a new acquaintance on the plane, bus or train. Pick up the phone.

- *Enhance your social skills.* Try honing your interpersonal skills in a small task-oriented group, such as a PTA committee, or in a social group, such as a book club. A restricted, focused situation is much easier to deal with than the ambiguous, unstructured atmosphere of a party, where words can easily fail most of us. Come to the group prepared to participate. Or, volunteer to collect for the cancer fund, so you feel forced to speak to strangers.

  Before attending a party, find something fresh to discuss by reading a newspaper or magazine. Seek out the host or hostess and ask for introductions. Most of all, be aware of your own body language. Don't close out others by looking away or crossing your arms. Look people in the eye.

  Set realistic goals. Talk to just a few new people each week. And don't feel hurt if someone doesn't respond. Move on to the next person. Introduce yourself to several strangers, then set out to discover three identifying characteristics about each one. Next time you meet, you'll be able to put names, faces and facts together for a fun and fascinating conversation.

  Probably the biggest payoff from practicing these small steps is that they will help you to stop dwelling on yourself and open you up to the rest of the world.

- *Listen to what people are really saying to you.* To avoid misinterpretations, listen not only to people's voices but to the tone of their voices, as well. Are they saying, "Notice me," "Help me," or "Care about me?" A good listener shows that he or she understands and cares about the messages others are sending. A good listener hears feelings and probes for thoughts, intentions and actions, as well as for statements.

To become a good listener, learn to recognize nonverbal cues such as facial expressions, body movements and breathing rates. Acknowledge and let someone know you are really listening by paraphrasing or by reflecting your interest through nods, smiles, and comments such as "Uh huh." Encourage or invite the speaker to tell you more, and check out your interpretations so that you know what you are hearing is what is being said. (You will want to recycle the message back and forth until what is being sent and what is received are identical.)

As you practice what are called attentive or empathetic listening skills, try to imagine what your speaker's experiences may feel like. Doing so will help you better appreciate the message being spoken.

- *Say what you feel.* Learn to share your deepest feelings and to express anger without blaming or attacking. Learn how to express affection and discuss problems with friends as well as lovers. Express your emotions indirectly or symbolically, perhaps through a gift, or nonverbally through kissing, hugging, crying or even slamming doors. Such nonverbal demonstrations of emotions are certainly okay. In fact, actions often have greater impact than spoken expression.

  Remember, however, that feelings and actions that are unsupported by words can be ambiguous. Crying, for example, can express joy, sadness, disappointment, anger or relief. Direct statements of feeling are much more powerful. Next time you feel upset, say so. Next time you feel excited, tell someone. Most people will readily respond. You can express your feelings honestly and directly in many ways. Expand your emotional vocabulary by adding these powerful feeling words: pleased, calm, comfortable, satisfied, bored, fearful, confused, lonely, excited, uneasy, silly, surprised, eager, angry, weary, glad, gleeful, content, confident, awkward, anxious, hopeful, sad, proud and relieved.

- *Practice makes perfect.* Using these techniques will help you connect with others more quickly and easily than you may ever have dreamed possible. All it takes is one positive response to send your shyness into seclusion. You are not the only one who feels awkward and left out in social situations. Many others feel that way, too. As you make a conscious effort to be pleasant, others will respond in the same way. Pleasing people can be reward enough.

Self-Confidence

33 or higher: You like and respect yourself. You have learned to accept both your positive and negative qualities. Because you feel good about yourself, you are happy and content with life. Being confident is quite different from being selfish and conceited. When you like yourself, you can accept life as a gift. Like most Questers, you can give yourself permission to tread life's path with enthusiasm.

13 to 31: You are a potential Quester with respect to this trait. You probably feel quite confident in some areas of your life, while in others you may feel weak and vulnerable. Alternatively, your mood at the time you completed the Questionnaire may have a lot to do with your score. Are you being overly hard on yourself? All too often achievement-oriented people set unrealistically high standards that virtually ensure feelings of personal failure or inadequacy. Try to be realistic about what you can and can't do. Perhaps you are a perfectionist and just can't seem to give yourself the credit you deserve. Congratulate yourself on your accomplishments, your willingness to risk and your initiative.

On the other hand, you may not have learned how to translate criticism or mistakes into learning experiences. Go back to the Questionnaire and reexamine your low scores. Work on improving these aspects of your personality. Soon your level of self-confidence, and your career development, will begin to grow.

12 or lower: Your low self-opinion may be taking the fun out of life. With this sort of attitude, you can't possibly hope to feel happy or to establish healthy personal and work relationships. The gulf between having an inferiority complex and recognizing your own limitations is vast, but not insurmountable. While a few of your limitations may be genetically based, most are due to bad life experiences. Just as it is important to recognize and accept your limits, it is important to try to change those you can. Stop agonizing over those you can't change. You are never too old or too young to learn.

Tips for Building Self-Confidence

*   *Know and accept yourself.* Think of yourself as you really are, rather than as you think you should be. See yourself as others do. Be objective. Don't feel bad if your clothes are two sizes larger than when you were in high school, or if your viewpoints are occasionally biased, or if you have wrinkles and a receding hairline. Compare the picture in your mind to the reality of your presence. You may not like what you see, but not acknowledging disparities can create immense disharmony, both within yourself and with the people in your life. Know what you can and cannot do and what you want out of life. If you can change your limitations, do it. But, at the same time, maximize your strengths.

*   *Acknowledge and accept your accomplishments.* Prepare a list of your positive achievements and personality characteristics. Post the list on a bulletin board or a door where you can see it and read it every day. When negative thoughts or experiences creep into your consciousness, reread your list. By competing with

yourself, you will learn how to accept who you really are, not who you think you should be. Don't limit your potential by only half-knowing yourself. Get acquainted with your strengths and your limitations, then dedicate yourself to making daily improvements. If you love and accept yourself, others will do the same.

- *Be yourself.* Don't be influenced by those who reject your opinions. You don't have to change to please others. Your opinions are extensions of your individuality. Even though others may not like what you say, most will respect your right to say it. Being overly concerned with what others think or trying too hard to please them can result in excessive inhibitions and poor performance. Don't inhibit your creative self or compare yourself to others. Instead, try to maximize your strengths and improve your performance.

- *Reward yourself.* Start putting yourself first more often. A little self-indulgence is healthy for your ego. Begin your morning by thinking of something positive you can do for yourself. Instead of going to the symphony because you are expected to, stay at home if you feel like it. Start dressing the way you would like to, not the way others say you should.

- *Trust and follow your intuition.* Take time to listen to your inner voice. Your intuition may present itself to you in a visual, auditory, kinesthetic, sensual or mental way. To identify and develop your intuitive strength, think about the different life experiences you have had in which your intuition came into play.

For example, have you ever met someone and, without knowing anything about her, taken an immediate liking or disliking to her? Did this hunch or gut reaction turn out to be accurate? Have you ever awakened in the morning with the feeling that something was going to happen to you completely out of the blue—that you'd get an unexpected promotion or demotion, for instance—and then what you imagined became reality? What emotions, thoughts, auditory signals or body sensations were you experiencing when you felt your hunch?

Make a list detailing the circumstances. Then compare the various episodes. When you have a hunch, does a vision flash in your mind, or are you apt to hear a voice? If your reactions are, for the most part, kinesthetic (felt through your nerves and muscles), is the sensation always the same? Does it ever vary in intensity or occur in different parts of your body? Does your physical response to a hunch depend on the type of situation?

- *Keep an intuition log.* Record your intuition "awareness" and note how accurate you are in differentiating your intuition from your hopes and fears. With practice, you will become good at listening to and understanding your inner cues.

- *Enjoy your success.* Measure yourself by what you have done, what you are doing now, and what you can do. Keep a daily, weekly, or monthly record of your accomplishments and build on these. For example, develop an exercise routine. Start with five minutes of easy exercises every morning. Then get up three minutes earlier each week to work on it. Add a new routine each week. Mark this down. Be proud of yourself. Remember, change comes gradually. Strive every day to do something just a little better than the day before. The exhilaration of achievement and growth will help you feel better about yourself.

- *Be image-conscious.* Your demeanor—the way you look, act, and express yourself—is your calling card; it's what you leave behind for people to remember you by. Act self-confident, and you will be self-confident.

- *Use creative visualization.* You can create whatever you want in life. For example, set a desired goal such as losing 15 pounds or asking for a raise. Relax and see yourself 15 pounds lighter. Experience the good feelings you have from accomplishing this goal. See, hear and trust compliments and positive feedback you receive from friends. Of course, appropriate diet, exercise and positive attitudes will facilitate goal attainment. (Read "Attaining Your Goal" in Chapter 9.)

- *Be heard.* Your speech is often a profound indicator of your level of self-confidence. Take responsibility for what you say. Speak clearly, not just loudly or aggressively. You can control others' reactions by controlling the pace, pitch, inflection and tone of your voice. Strive for an energy level that matches your normal conversation. Speak briskly, but pronounce words clearly. Keep your tone attentive, interested and friendly.

- *Believe in yourself.* Affirm yourself. This will help you to replace negative thoughts with positive ones. Tell yourself, "I am confident, intelligent, caring and attractive" (or whatever you really want to be). Make this a part of your daily routine. Do it at the same time every day.

- *Be flexible.* Welcome the new and the unexpected. Listen to your hopes, dreams and desires. Often, your creativity is challenged to the fullest by the new and unexpected. Open up, take a risk, explore new possibilities in your life. Be determined enough to achieve your goals, but flexible enough to change directions if necessary.

- *Maintain your perspective.* Time and distance can make once seemingly insurmountable mountains seem like inconsequential molehills. Why let what happened yesterday affect what will happen today or tomorrow? Face each new day and each new challenge with an open mind. They may not be as difficult as you thought they'd be.

- *Persevere.* Into every life a little rain must fall. Weather it out. Power comes from persevering in the face of adversity. Remember, achieving worthwhile goals takes hard work, patience and enduring temporary setbacks.

- *Prepare.* Preparing and planning to accomplish a goal such as losing 15 pounds give you control and the strength to carry on. Keep your hands on the wheel and your road map before you. If you know where you are going, you will get around the roadblocks.

- *Maintain your focus.* Look ahead, not back. Keep your energy focused on the challenge, and sooner or later you'll find a solution.

- *Depersonalize disappointments.* Omit the word failure from your vocabulary. View setbacks as necessary learning experiences that will help you grow and move you toward your goal. Ask yourself, "What did I learn?" "What should I do differently next time?" Then do things differently, if necessary. You tried. Next time you will succeed.

- *Learn to accept compliments.* Accept well-meaning remarks about your appearance or ability with grace and a simple, "Thank you."

- *Become an expert.* Learn as much as possible about some subject. Take responsibility for your area of expertise, then enjoy the power and authority that comes from being an expert. An additional payoff will be the renewed confidence that comes from knowing a lot about your particular interest.

- *Accept responsibility.* Be responsible not only for performing your work, but also for maintaining your health, developing your personality and enhancing your lifestyle.

- *Remember, you are an intelligent person who has succeeded in the past and can succeed again.*

Acknowledging this allows you to fully enjoy and appreciate your successes without the doubt and anxiety that may have accompanied past efforts. Only you have the power to project a confident image. Exercise it, nurture it, delight in it. You can make anything happen.

Purpose

30 or higher: Like many Questers, you tend to be involved in activities that give you a sense of purpose, meaning, direction and satisfaction. You are true to your inner self and have a zest for life. You probably have both short- and long-term goals, and you seem to be achieving them. Your various activities—such as work, leisure, family time and relationships—tend to reflect a unity of purpose.

13 to 29: You are a potential Quester with respect to purpose. You may need to clarify your purpose and goals. Do your job and life roles help you live out who you really are? Are you having difficulty achieving your goals? Review your responses to the Questionnaire items to get additional insights into areas of your life you could enhance. You may benefit from the suggestions offered below.

12 or lower: You seem to have little meaning and few goals in your life. You may be bored, anxious, frustrated and lack direction. To develop more meaning in your life, you should reconsider your basic philosophy of life. Then take the necessary steps to change your family, relationships, spiritual, occupational and other life components.

Tips for Developing Purpose

- *Be patient.* Identifying your mission or purpose will take time, particularly if you are not accustomed to looking inward. A good start, however, is to identify and acknowledge your deepest dreams and hopes. Some people have one major purpose or theme running through their lives, while others may have two or three that vary slightly or change drastically over the life span. The following activities will help you begin to better understand yourself and your raison d'être.

- *Identify what's important to you.* Success may mean something different to you than it does to your spouse, parents or best friend. When you try to live up to others' expectations, it's easy to become anxious about failing. Don't try to live by others' definitions of success. Learn how to say "no" politely to those who try to pressure you into doing something you don't really want to do. Don't share your dreams with or associate with negative people.

- *Consider how you would change your life if you knew you had only six months to live.* Your answer to this question will be revealing and help you become more candid and straightforward with yourself. If you would make some drastic changes, then you are not living your life with integrity. Thinking in terms of six months is useful, because it gives you enough time to act on things that are important to you. If you would change jobs, relationships, locations, friendships, lifestyles, means of communicating with your loved ones or anything else, then get on with it! What's stopping you? Don't take your life for granted. What do you really want to do? Who do you really want to be? Concentrate on the now. Mean what you say.

- *Decide what you would do if monetary rewards did not matter.* Ask yourself what you would do if you had billions of dollars, and never had to worry about money. If you are spending your time struggling at something that has no meaning for you and justifying it by saying you do it because it pays the bills, then you have made money more important than your own sense of purpose. You can make money doing what you really enjoy. Most Questers do. For example, Melissa teaches computer classes, and Ross, a former accountant, makes and sells pottery. How could you make money doing what you enjoy?

- *Identify what kind of personality you would choose if you could begin your life today.* Would you be more assertive, less shy, more humorous, more outgoing, more confident, easier to talk to, or more caring? No one forces you to remain shy, anxious, and nonassertive. You make these life choices, and you can remake them, if you really want to.

- *Describe yourself without using any labels.* Don't tell how old you are, where you live, what you studied in school, your job history, your marital status, your economic status, your hair color and height, or even your name. Instead, describe precisely what kind of human being you are. For example, "I am warm, sensitive, caring, intelligent, creative, intuitive, energetic, enthusiastic, confident, a loving spouse and have a sense of humor.

  If you continually resort to labels and describe yourself as if you are filling out a job application, you may start to view yourself as a statistic sheet rather than as a special human being. This very image, in fact, may become the reality you choose for yourself. Many people have difficulty finding out what they really want to do because they confuse success as judged by others with success according to their own inner feelings of purpose. It is not what you choose to do that will bring you total honesty; it is knowing that the reason you are doing it corresponds with your feelings of self-worth.

- *Describe the person(s) with whom you would choose to live if you could live with anyone in the world.* Imagine that you have no legal obligation to stay with your immediate family, assuming you have one, and that you know of no reason why you could not legally live with anyone outside your immediate family. With whom would you choose to live? What's stopping you from living with that person(s)? If you are living in a relationship (family or otherwise) in which you feel obligated (rather than genuinely wanting to be there), ask yourself why you made this choice and what you can do about the situation to make it more satisfying to everyone involved.

- *Adopt a cause.* Do something worthwhile. Volunteer your time or share your expertise with others. Make helping others a goal. Sign up to work in a senior citizens' home or with the mentally challenged. Make clothes that can be given away to social agencies. Join a citizens' action group that fights for a cause in which you believe. Look around your community, and you'll discover a wealth of ways in which you can get involved.

- *Complete the Life Cycle Exercise.* First, think about the various periods of your life (birth to 10 years, 11 to 20 years, 21 to 30 years and so on) and write down those experiences that gave you a sense of joy and completeness—activities that totally absorbed you. Next, list activities you would really love to do in the future. Finally, reflect back on your life as an old man or woman, and list the qualities and achievements for which you would most like to be remembered. If you could make any changes in your life, what would they be? Can you make them now?

- *Make an Inventory of Your Dreams.* Write down the things you want to have, do, be, and share. Keep your pen moving nonstop for no less than 15 minutes. Abbreviate whenever possible. Do not allow security or financial considerations to stop you from dreaming. Create the people, feelings and places you want to be part of your life. Include a broad sampling of goals and outcomes related to work, family relationships, leisure and spiritual activities. Consider everything as possible. Throw away all your limiting beliefs. Identify two goals you really want to attain this year. Write them down, indicating why you want them and how you will achieve them. Be clear, concise and positive.

- *Complete the Guided Fantasy Exercise.* Close your eyes and imagine yourself in a typical workday of your ideal occupation and lifestyle. Describe your whole day in detail, beginning with waking up in the morning and ending with going to sleep at night. Pay particular attention to the details of your home and work environments, your work tasks and responsibilities, your leisure activities, and your feelings about the various tasks and people you encounter. Then ask yourself, what made you feel excited, happy, challenged, or bored? Your feelings will help you identify the kind of work and lifestyle you really want. Once you know what you want, you will be more willing to take the risks necessary to achieve your goals.

- *Identify major themes or patterns.* To clarify your mission, look for themes that emerge from the exercises above, as well as from the questions below. Write your answers to the following:

  - What accomplishments in any area of your life (social, work, school, civic) are you most proud of?

  - What do you want work colleagues to say about you?

  - What activities absorbed you as a young child?

  - What is your recurring dream?

  - What would you do if you knew you couldn't fail?

  - What prize would you select for yourself for being the best in the world (e.g., literary, athletic, social, other)?

  - What would you wear to a costume party?

  - What people (living or dead, famous or not) do you admire, and why?

  - What kind of person do you want to be five years from now?

  - What skills you want to use in your ideal job?

  Write a "working" mission statement that represents your mission based on these recurring themes. Discuss your theme or themes with a supportive partner or friend. Brainstorm how your purpose can be expressed in various components of your life. For example, if your purpose is to help others, you could express it in work by being a social worker, a considerate employee, or a helpful colleague. If your purpose is to promote justice, you could express it by being an attorney, a public prosecutor, a police officer, an investigative reporter, a broadcaster, a teacher or a criminologist. In family activities, you may express your purpose by being a loving spouse, parent, son, daughter or sibling. Brain storming will also help you find contacts and practical help. Do not allow age, lack of education or money, or some physical disability stop you from pursuing your mission.

- *Explore occupations that will enable you pursue your purpose.* Get your feet wet. Look for ways to get involved right now, without acquiring more skills, credentials or money. For example, volunteer, take a course, participate in a group activity, or commit yourself to a worthy cause. Write a long-range goal that will help you pursue this purpose in an occupational, leisure, or social activity. Visualize your goal. Include as many details as possible. Make specific plans for the next three months toward achieving the goal. Write your plans. Be specific. Indicate when, where, with what and with whom. Be flexible. Realize that your mission statement, goals and plans may change as you get to know yourself and your options better.

Having a sense of purpose and striving towards goals gives life meaning, direction and satisfaction. It not only contributes to health and longevity, but also makes you fell good in challenging times. Purpose is a common denominator for success and failure. Knowing your purpose will give you courage to do what you've always longed to do. You'll be empowered to achieve your goals. It will be easier to risk and to manage fear. You'll be able to change your life for the better.

Autonomy
37 or higher: You tend to think like many Questers. You are your own person. You believe in yourself and are independent,

self-sufficient and inner-directed. You honestly believe you are in charge of your own destiny and you seldom blame others for bad experiences. You try to express your genuine self, your talents, interests and unique personality. Rather than functioning as an adapted person or following someone else's script, you try to make your own decisions and, when necessary, even swim against the tide. Far from being unnecessarily unconventional or prone to illegal or socially unacceptable behavior, you seem to have the courage to transcend your environment when it infringes on your personal and professional growth.

15 to 36: You may be overly concerned with other people's opinions. Status, success or others' opinions may be controlling your life. You may believe that chance or luck play an important part in your life. Review the statements in *The Quester Questionnaire* to find a greater understanding of your score. What changes can you or do you want to make?

14 or lower: You seem to be quite dependent. Your levels of growth, creativity and self-confidence are probably quite low. You may believe that what happens to you is determined by powerful others fate or chance. You tend to be influenced greatly by pressure from authority figures and peers and you probably lack clear goals. You may have decided to settle for less than necessary. You seem to have chosen to take the path of least resistance by not facing up to the anxiety that accompanies growth. You can enhance your sense of autonomy and control. Put more faith in your own ability to make good things happen.

Tips for Enhancing Autonomy
- *Know and accept yourself.* The first step toward constructive action is letting go of old ideas about who you are or who you should be. Learn to accept yourself, flaws and all, for who you really are. Own your successes. Don't attribute them to chance. They are the result of your hard work and abilities. Stop setting up self-fulfilling negative prophecies. Think positively about yourself and

your abilities. Keep an open mind, learn to tolerate ambiguity and trust your own decisions. Besides, a wrong decision may simply be a detour on the way to discovering the right one.

- *Believe that you do have options.* You can create your desired work and lifestyle. You can get another job, study, travel, establish a business, restructure your current position or pursue volunteer activities that give you a sense of purpose, accomplishment and confidence. Testing your options may mean tradeoffs, but usually they are worth the inconvenience. Knowing that you have choices in life can eliminate a lot of the distress and uncertainty that accompany difficult experiences. Studies have shown that the more freedom you believe you have, the more able you are to meet and master life's challenges.

- *Act on your options.* Independence requires action. Don't let your fear of not being perfect prevent you from trying. If you are socially insecure, try settling for less than the perfect date. Learn to speak up, even if you think what you have to say isn't brilliant. Invite friends over to your home more often. Do what you want to do, not what others think you should do. Rather than trying so hard to please others, learn to please yourself.

- *Confront your fears.* Anxiety and fear can be major blocks to independence. Identify your fears. What's stopping you from pursuing your desired career goal? Is it fear of failing, of not knowing what to expect, or of inability to afford material comforts? What's the worst thing that could happen if you let go? How can you minimize this?

- FEAR stands for False Expectations Appear Real. Live in the present. Don't worry about what might happen. Instead, research your goal to minimize setbacks, then develop an action plan. Speak up to your boss, take that vacation alone or approach your partner or spouse with your concerns. Let go of attachments, the more attached you are, the greater the fear of losing something

- *Become more assertive.* Assertive behavior differs from aggressive behavior. Aggressive people accomplish goals at all costs. They can be manipulative, threatening. Assertive people let others know what they want while preserving their own dignity and that of others. Do you get the kind of work you want? Do others take advantage of you? Do you want this to continue? Recognize that you need to change. List three recent incidents when you wish you had been more assertive. Indicate what you really wanted to do. List three things you need to change to be more assertive. When will you take the first step?

  Establish appropriate limits for your personal and professional life. Start by expressing your feelings to people you trust. Set limits on your time and energy. Let others know these. If you don't want to do it or give it, politely say "no." If you don't want to go for lunch with co-workers, say so.

- *Identify colleagues who feel they have control over their work.* What are they doing differently from you? Are they taking more initiative? Volunteering for new assignments? More assertive at meetings? More politically astute? If so, what does this tell you? Take the initiative. Look for jobs that need to be done in your company. Identify the project manager, research ways you can enhance the project and offer assistance and suggestions.

- *Challenge your irrational beliefs.* For example, spell out your negative predictions ("people will stare at me if I dine alone"), then devise ways to test them (venture out alone to a favorite restaurant). Now develop a way to measure the outcome (look around and see how people are reacting). Finally, draw a conclusion ("I can dine by myself"). Keep a record of your limiting beliefs and devise experiments to challenge their validity.

111

- *Think for yourself.* Don't echo others' opinions. Just because others have opinions doesn't mean yours aren't appropriate. Your own ideas are just as good, and maybe better, than anyone else's. So are your tastes in art, music, food and other cultural pursuits. Express support for, and defend your opinions. Consider stating your ideas at the next meeting. You have value and your opinions count.

- *Practice makes perfect.* Learning to become more independent is like learning to ride a bike. Repetition helps. Repeat to yourself, "It's better to do as much as possible for myself," or "I can do it, no matter what. Now practice this skill in different situations, starting with the most comfortable and then progressing to the least comfortable.

Being in control takes time, effort and transformation. But, chances are, you'll find that taking charge of your own life makes you feel better about the direction of your life. Soon, you will discover that you have more choices, more independence, more strength and more control than you ever thought possible.

Achievement
27 or higher: You tend to measure success by internal standards, rather than by status symbols or material wealth. You enjoy the whole process of learning, accomplishing, and mastering. You are fortunate to find your work fulfilling and are probably getting opportunities to do things you are capable of and really enjoy. Your work may also be your leisure. You would rather spend time and money at an interesting job than be an outstanding success at one that bores you. You want the best for yourself and are uncompromising about your standards of excellence. When you finish a project, you want to move on. Do you take enough time for leisure and fun? If not, put more spice into your life. This will increase your creativity and energy.

13 to 27: You seem to be a relatively easygoing person who is quite satisfied with your work and lifestyle. However, you may avoid difficult tasks for fear of failing. If you want to change, check your low scores for clues, then decide where you can make some modifications.

12 or lower: You may lack ambition. If you fall into this category, you tend to have a rather lackadaisical approach to life. You do as little work as possible and have a tendency to give up when the going gets tough. If you are happy with your lifestyle, that's okay. If you aren't, try accomplishing something you will feel good about. Bake a torte or build a great recreation room. Learn to fix your car. Develop a respectable game of tennis. Consider looking for a new job that will give you a better sense of accomplishment.

Tips for Achieving

- *Set attainable goals in harmony with your mission.* Intend to achieve them. *Try to establish* each new goal one level beyond your present level of accomplishment. Make goals specific. For example, instead of stating, "I intend to lose weight," state "I intend to lose 15 pounds ." Goals should be measurable and *achievable*: Unfulfilled goals make you feel incompetent. Instead of trying to lose 50 pounds, try to lose 15 pounds first. Track your weight loss progress.

  Write a plan for achieving your goals in specific and doable actions. Give yourself a clearly defined end date. "I want to lose 15 pounds by July 1." Outline your goals, time lines and activities on an organizer. Allow for the unexpected. Make a contingency plan in case things don't go as you thought they would. Enjoy the process and learning involved in achieving your goal.

- *Experiment with standards of excellence.* Set your own criteria. Instead of aiming for 100 percent, try 80 or 90 percent for some projects. Realize perfectionism is an unattainable illusion. Perfectionism refers to self-defeating thoughts and behaviors which cause some people to set unrealistic goals, fear making mistakes. Some perfectionism is good, but excessive perfectionism may make you afraid to try. Accept the "ideal" as a guideline, a goal to be worked toward, not to be achieved 100 percent. Give yourself credit for good performance and effort, even though not perfect. A healthy achiever has drive. A perfectionist is driven. *Pablo Casals*, the Catalan cellist and conductor, advises: "The main thing in life is not to be afraid to be human."

Emphasize task mastery. Focus on what you can do to develop a better product or service for your employer or for yourself. Consider money a byproduct of achieving your goal, not an end in itself.

Silence your inner critic. Learn to ignore the nagging voice in your head that says you're not good enough, smart enough, or good-looking enough to succeed. Set goals, make plans and move forward in spite of that voice. Soon it will start losing its power over you.

Accept failure graciously. Recognize that mistakes are part of the achieving process. Learn from mistakes. Acknowledge your right to have setbacks. When you stop making errors, you stop learning. If you do fail, examine the reasons why and move on. The only real failure is the failure to learn from your mistakes. Accept criticism. Don't take it personally.

- *Practice mindfulness.* Mindfulness, the heart of Buddhist meditation, is about attention and awareness. It means purposely and nonjudgmentally paying attention in the moment. This kind of attention nurtures awareness, clarity and acceptance of present-moment reality.

Experiment with mindfulness in your work and personal life. Focus on each experience for the moment without drifting into thoughts of the past or concerns about the future. Concentrate on each task. Don't watch TV, read the newspaper, or listen to the radio while brushing your teeth. Attend fully to the report you're reading or writing. Give face-to-face meetings and phone conversations unwavering attention.

- *Manage time. Use linear and holistic strategies.* Identify self-defeating habits and work patterns. Review your work schedule over several weeks. Note whether you underestimated time required for tasks, and made use of waiting and commuting times. Indicate what you can do differently to save time.

Get up an hour earlier each day to think and plan. These periods of uninterrupted concentration will enable you to complete projects, meet deadlines. If possible, commute to work before or after rush hour traffic. Schedule "no phone hours." During the phone hour, return calls and make needed calls. Check emails twice a day. Reply, file or ruthlessly discard messages. Guard against unwelcome interruptions. Maintain a closed and open door policy. An open door communicates welcome and encourages colleagues to drop in. A closed door indicates no interruptions.

Establish appropriate limits for your personal and professional life. Say no to the request without rejecting the requester. *Focus on activities that use talents.* Delegate or exchange tasks you dislike, aren't good at or find draining or time-consuming. Also explore ways to minimize time-wasting domestic chores.

Use your *intuition* to help you manage time, as well. When you fine tune your intuition, you can make quick decisions that you might have agonized over previously. Four interrelated Taoist principles form the underpinnings of this way of looking at time: nonresistance, individual power, balance and harmony.

Nonresistance refers to trusting the moment and allowing events to develop naturally instead of forcing them. When you use your individual power, you trust your intuition and assert your right to control your time. Trusting intuition enables you to remove extraneous details. You enhance clarity and efficiency. To be balanced, you need to find your "center," and listen to and act upon inner cues . Harmony suggests you're synchronized with your environment. You are an intrinsic part of time and the grand scheme of the universe.

In summary, nonresistance teaches you to let go of the prepackaged approach to time management and allows events to unfold. Individual power enables you to assert your right to control your time. Listening to and trusting your intuition help you live in the moment and balance daily activities. Centered, you no longer feel guilty about past actions or fear future choices.

As you rediscover your natural rhythms, clocks and schedules won't control you. You can use them as tools rather than absolutes. Can you find a balance between the holistic and linear ways of perceiving time? How can you integrate Taoist concepts into your management of time?

- *Establish a support group.* A group of like-minded people with similar goals can provide needed motivation. Not only will they understand what's holding you back, they may have tips that can help you overcome your blocks.

- *Enjoy your successes.* Measure yourself by what you have done, are doing and can complete. Keep a weekly tally of your accomplishments. Record every achievement you've attained or hope to complete. Post a list of these over your desk, on the refrigerator door or on the bathroom mirror.

- *Reward yourself for completing a challenging project.* A

little self-indulgence is healthy. Take time for enjoyable breaks such as reading a favorite magazine or sleeping in late. Major projects could be the impetus for larger rewards, such as a ski weekend, a trip to the lake or a new outfit.

- *Continue to learn.* Take courses to enhance your knowledge and skills. Many employers pay for training that improves on-the-job performance. Find something enjoyable in every task you undertake. Stretch yourself. Experience the good feelings that come from testing yourself and excelling. You will be energized and turned on by your work. The exhilaration of achievement and growth will enhance your purpose and confidence.

Creativity

34 or higher: You tend to be an innovator. You embrace change and use your imagination to find new ways of doing many things, both work-related and personal. Shaping fresh, new perspectives about yourself, life and the world brings you great joy. You are complex, self-accepting, and have many diverse interests. You are generally independent, intuitive and capable of seeing many sides of a problem. To you, routine is boring. You would much rather tread new ground than follow in your colleagues' footsteps.

15 to 34: You may enjoy creating in your personal life but dislike change in your work routine. Or the opposite could be true: You may be innovative at work but conservative at home. To enhance your creativity, try some of the suggestions below.

14 or lower: You probably dislike change. You tend to enjoy the status quo and prefer the tried-and-true way. If you are satisfied with your life, don't change. But if you want to add more excitement, learn to free and release the creative potential within so that you can express your real self. Learn to bring out the child deep inside you.

Tips for Increasing Creativity

Creativity is a quality everyone is born with. Unfortunately, few people know how to tap into it. The suggestions below will help you develop your creativity by quieting your inner voices of reason, disbelief, certainty, time, routine and social structures. In their rush to point out the rational and logical, these voices can drown out your intuitive voice. While experimenting, don't think in terms of right or wrong. Let ideas suggest others. Devise your own ways of freeing your creativity. But remember, transformation does not happen overnight. Give the process time.

- *Learn to use "hurricane thinking."* Suppose you had to give a talk or write a paper about Cape Cod (or any place you choose). First, write Cape Cod in the center of a piece of paper and circle it. This is the eye of the hurricane. Now, write down the first thoughts that come to your mind. Place these somewhere around the eye. If this process generates related ideas, jot these down close to the parent thoughts. Draw lines to connect these related ideas. Should a completely unrelated association come to mind, record it on the opposite corner of the page. See if this new idea will produce offspring as well. Continue this process until the page is filled with major points swirling around the calm eye of Cape Cod.

  What is important in this exercise is not to evaluate your ideas, but to write down all the ideas that come to mind. Let your mind roam freely to produce as many ideas as possible. Next, organize your thoughts and ideas. Link them or circle them with different-colored pencils to see where they logically belong. What sequences seem most appropriate? Finally, research the feasibility of your ideas.

  Kirsten used this strategy to brainstorm career options. First, she wrote "Dream Job" in the center of piece of paper and circled it (the eye of the hurricane). Then she wrote down all ides that came to mind (gardener, florist, equestrian, set designer, architect, horticulturist, photographer, landscaper).

Kirsten placed these near the eye. This process generated related ideas that she recorded. Kirsten also noted unrelated ideas and their offspring on the corners. She continued the process until the page was filled with ideas swirling around. Kirsten then drew lines with different colored pencils to connect the ideas. This was when the notion of landscape architect hit her.

Extend hurricane thinking throughout your personal and career life. Be on the alert for those "crazy ideas" that could be the spark of genius.

- *Make friends with your inner child.* List all those things that parents or authority figures always warned you about. Note what you went ahead and did anyway and then succeeded at despite their predictions of failure. Examine the attitudes and beliefs you developed as a result of these early teachings. Consider how, given your age and circumstances, they may no longer be appropriate.

  Do admonitions such as "Don't question authority," "Boys don't cry," "Never eat in bed," and "Save for a rainy day" apply today? Examining long-held attitudes and beliefs, particularly those that stifle creativity and change, can open you to new ways of being. No one is encouraging you to throw socially acceptable behavior to the wind. But perhaps it is time you determined which attitudes and values are crucial to your current lifestyle, and which may be cramping your creativity.

  Jake reassessed his values and goals during his Age-50 Transition He realized that he pursued his academic career because his parents placed great importance on scholarly pursuits. This insight gave him the courage to follow his dream.

- *Draw or doodle.* Write a question that clearly states what you want to know. Underneath it, draw (with colored pencils) whatever comes to your mind or flows though your hands. Continue to draw until you feel you have nothing to add to the picture. Now, use your intuitive skills to interpret the meaning behind the drawing and the symbols within it. Note the sequence of steps and your thoughts and feelings, such as the joy or sadness you experience as you study the drawing.

Unsure of whether to establish her own consulting business, *Samantha* wrote, "Should I establish my own business?" at the top of the page. She drew a scene with lush green vegetation. She interpreted this as a sign to get started. She is doing great.

- *Identify face-to-face tensions.* Select two opposing tensions in your life. They may be two contradictory urges or feelings, incompatible goals, two roles you are required to play, perhaps even two duties or responsibilities that conflict with each other. Some examples might be independence versus dependence, career versus family life, male versus female, freedom versus security and friendship versus solitude. Next, write down all the characteristics associated with each tension. Eliminate those shared by both. Then evaluate the remaining dissimilarities. These are the truly opposing forces in your personality. Explore your creativity. How can these contradictions be resolved? How can the tensions be allied? Keep in mind that there is often strength in diversity, but give some serious thought to how you can lessen some of the tension in the opposing forces in your life.

- *Try new things.* Learn how to accept and process criticism from your boss, clients, employers, friends and family members without becoming defensive and angry. Be open to new information about yourself. Play the devil's advocate by arguing the opposite side. Experiment more. Go to a new restaurant and order a dish you've never tried. Make your relationship more creative by surprising your partner with a small gift or favorite meal. Don't wait for a special occasion. Read an unusual book. Give those science fiction books you've been reading for the past eight years a rest and pick up an historical novel or pop psychology bestseller. As you become more comfortable adding unusual touches to your life, you will find life is more fun and rewarding.

- *Lose yourself in an enjoyable activity.* Jog, collect stamps, sing, dance, or write. Focus on the activity. Empty your mind of other things.

- *Devise your own ways of freeing creativity.* Learn to relax. Here are some suggestions to get started:

  - Invite friends over to brainstorm business options.

  - Ask your dreams for answers to a question before you go to sleep.

  - Meditate or keep a journal.

  - Change your routines; for example, write with your nondominant hand.

  - Play the devil's advocate at a business meeting by arguing the opposite side.

  - Take a course in a topic you've always wanted to try.

  - Play. Have a costume party, tell jokes, play games, paint. What can you do to make work more fun?

Androgyny

27 or higher: You appear to possess the best of both male and female strengths. Regardless of your gender and depending on the situation, you can be both nurturing and assertive, competitive and cooperative, confident and tender. You are tolerant, broad-minded, creative, autonomous and free from stereotyped thinking. You have probably selected an occupation and lifestyle that suits you and feels comfortable. You don't consider your work to be either a man's or a woman's job.

13 to 27: You have mixed feelings about what is appropriate for men and women. While you may tolerate some androgynous behavior, you may be more traditional about what constitutes acceptable gender-role standards. Back up. See which of your attitudes and behaviors are androgynous and which are traditional. Were the statements you scored low on related to assertiveness, achievement, confidence and intimacy, or to traditional beliefs and values about what constitutes appropriate male and female behaviors? As you become more aware of your feelings, attitudes and behaviors, you can take the first steps toward becoming a Quester.

12 or lower: You appear to have very traditional views about what is appropriate behavior for men and women. You probably scored low on other Quester characteristics such as intimacy, confidence, achievement, and growth. Your score here may also indicate rigid ideas about gender roles that could hurt your health and relationships. The energy you expend trying to deal with this conflict is incredible. Gender-role attitudes and behaviors are learned responses that can be unlearned.

Tips for Becoming More Androgynous
- *Take one step at a time.* Get to know your real self and learn to express this self in personal and work activities. Read over the suggestions for developing other Quester characteristics such as purpose, confidence, growth and creativity, and see where you can broaden your mind to free yourself from preconceived notions about yourself and others.

- *Learn to understand other people's values, rights, feelings and perceptions.* Being open-minded requires the ability to listen, to respond, to interact with people and to refrain from imposing value judgments on them. Try developing this quality by becoming more empathetic toward people. Empathy is the ability to get into other people's feelings and experiences, to walk in their shoes, and to let them know that you understand how they are feeling.

Strengthen empathy by listening. Start by practicing empathy with your partner or friends. People feel reassured, understood, when others pay attention to them. Listen to peoples' needs, priorities perspectives and problems. Summarize what you hear them say. Let them know you hear and understand their thoughts and feelings. Listen between the lines. What are the people feeling but not saying. Ask questions when you're unsure.

- *Try to put yourself in the other person's place.* A man who works in a traditionally male occupation, such as electrician, might try switching roles with a female colleague for a few days to identify subtle ways in which he might be discriminating against women. Acts that suggest discrimination could include passing over women for certain tasks, training or promotional opportunities. A man who believes household chores belong in the woman's domain could ask his partner how she feels about doing those tasks. He could then take responsibility for certain traditionally female chores, such as cooking, for a period of time.

  Women could do the same. Not all men like performing traditionally male chores such as mowing the lawn or fixing things around the house. A woman might discuss reassignment of responsibilities with her partner and take over some of the traditional male roles. She could also learn to be more assertive by saying what she means and feels without being offensive. First, practice being assertive in situations that feel less threatening, such as with family and friends. For example, tell that aunt who plans a three-week visit that a weekend visit would be better for everyone. Test your new assertive behavior at work, as well. With practice and time, you'll feel more comfortable.

- *Use the strength of both genders to make successful career transitions.* When making changes, women usually take more time than men to process feelings, understand themselves, explore options, and clarify goals. Men don't want to waste time. They dive right in. A balance between contemplation and action usually works best. Men could benefit from taking time to review their careers, and determining whether they're in the right niches. While self-appraisal is necessary, women shouldn't delay job search too long.

Both genders need time to express feelings and thoughts and reassess personal characteristics. They need to explore options, clarify goals and plan before acting.

Age seems to affect the values men and women bring to the decision-making process. The 20s are times when both genders build their careers. Climbing occupational ladders are important. During the 30s, women and some men begin placing more value on the quality of life. For women, the biological clock increases pressure to reevaluate family vs. career goals.

Women in their 40s are more willing than men to confront major life issues, honor important values and follow their dreams. Men often delay this process until they're 50 or older. Societal programming, family obligations or high career aspirations often influence men to focus on career advancement at the expense of psychological and spiritual development. Men who plunge ahead without reappraisal are susceptible to depression and illness. Poor health or retirement issues often precipitate men's reassessment of themselves and career goals.

Regardless of gender, periodically reassess your values and goals. Contemporary career development is a continuing quest to improve the fit between your developing career and evolving identity.

Since women put energy into *building relationships*, many expect nurturing work settings. Women look for positions that will enable them to balance personal, family and career obligations. Men are more concerned with career advancement. More strategic and objective, they view career changes as stepping stones to final career goals .

Before accepting positions, both genders should ensure the organization will meet desired criteria. Identify potential problems in prospective work environments. Know the company's mission. Talk with prospective associates. Learn about new products, markets, technology, systems and procedures.

Women tend to develop more lasting *networking contacts* than men. While primarily motivated to establish job leads, women are willing to share information, exchange ideas and help people. Men tend to use a network. They make contacts within their industries and job levels, get needed information and leave. Women often hesitate to ask for help from senior executives, but excel at follow up after meetings, sending thank you notes. Men tend to be less considerate about following up, and remove people from their networking lists when they have nothing to gain.

Adopt the strengths of the opposite gender. Expand your network. Seek opportunities to meet new people. Attend trade shows and professional meetings. Prepare an elevator speech. Exchange business cards. Volunteer for interesting projects. Learn about people's career needs, and find ways to help.

Risk Taking
37 or higher: Like most Questers, you tend to like adventure and risk taking. You appreciate original ideas, enjoy thrilling activities and delight in taking chances . You are also autonomous, like challenge, and are confident and flexible. However, if your score is over 48, your desire to risk may sometimes be extreme. Before embarking on a career-related adventure, do you research your options and develop an action plan?

15 to 36: You may be open to new experiences in some areas of your life (physical or social activities), but overly organized or rigid in others (economic or work activities). Or you may be reluctant to risk because of family commitments. If you want to enhance your willingness to risk, review your responses to the statements that measure risk. What changes can you make to help you become more risk-oriented?

14 or lower: You are definitely not a risk taker. You prefer to play it safe. You like a secure, well-ordered lifestyle. You don't like ambiguity or trying out new things, and you may fear failure. Change is scary, but if you want to grow and develop to your full potential, you may want to make some alterations.

Tips for Enhancing the Courage to Risk

*   *Identify activities you find risky.* Most of us are more conscious of the risks we avoid than those we take. That's why we don't think of ourselves as risk takers. Because we're aware of the risks we avoid, we assume that others take bigger risks -- but they may be avoiding risks we are taking. So risk, in this sense, is in the eye of the beholder. David has made three dramatic career shifts, but he does not see himself as a risk taker. For him, risk involves physical activities such as mountain climbing.

    Which of the following activities are risky for you?

    *   *Physical*—sky diving, skiing, taking drugs, having cosmetic surgery

    *   *Psychological/emotional*—staying in dissatisfying job, getting married or divorced

    *   *Social*—giving presentations, traveling solo in a foreign country

    *   *Intellectual*—taking a graduate course, chairing a high-level policy meeting

- *Economic*—investing in stocks, changing jobs, buying a home

- *Career*—any combination of the above.

Think about three successful risks you've taken. What did you do to make each turn out well? In which of the categories did the risks fall? What have you learned about yourself and your risk taking behavior?

Review your risk history. Make a long list of risks you've taken in your lifetime like learning to ride a bike or going on a blind date. Note what you've learned and how you grew from each risk.

- *Make small changes first.* This helps you develop confidence and trust. You can then move on to more risky ventures. Experiment with a different hairstyle or food. Change your daily routine. Take a bath instead of a shower, for example. At work, offer new ways of tackling a job. When you feel you are ready to take a bigger risk, such as changing your job, read over Chapters 8, 9 and 10 to learn how the Questers do it.

- *Set goals but don't write them in stone.* A risk without a clear purpose and goal can backfire. Balance tentativeness with commitment. Be open to new experiences. These may allow you to reach your destination using a different path. While you are on this path, you may come across some pleasant coincidences that entice you to modify your original goal.

- *Believe in yourself.* Affirm yourself. Replace negative thoughts and feelings with positive ones. Tell yourself, "I can do anything I want." "I am in charge of my life." (Or whatever you really want to be or do.) Avoid phrases that begin with, "I can't," or "I will never."

Describe the barriers that are blocking you from making a change. Personal barriers might include the fear of losing a secure income, fear of failure in a new job, fear of what others will think, fear of success and guilt that change might create family hardships. Societal barriers include old notions about career, outdated retirement policies, traditional gender roles, and blocks imposed by educational institutions, unions and professional associations.

- *Look upon something new, different, or unknown as exciting—an opportunity to challenge yourself and to grow.* If you don't try something new and different, how will you ever find out you can do it?

- *Complete this Fantasy Risk Exercise before you embark on your next adventure.* Write your answers down on a separate sheet of paper.

  1. Think of an important risk you would like to take soon, something that is within your control but that you are afraid to initiate. (Examples might include taking a credit course at a college, taking a short trip by yourself, applying for a sabbatical, changing your job, taking early retirement or moving to another part of the country.)

  2. What appeals to you about taking the risk? What would you gain from it? Be both objective and subjective about your response. Take into account economic, family, and other realities as well as your thoughts and feelings.

  3. What is frightening about the risk? What holds you back from taking it? What do you stand to lose if you don't take it?

  4. What's the worst thing that could happen if it turned out badly?

  5. If the worst thing happened, what would you do?

6. If you need information to pursue this risk, where can you go for it?

7. On whom can you count for support?

8. What could you do to make this less risky? What kind of measures could you build in to make it less urgent? Less irreversible? Less overwhelming?

9. If you broke the risk into small steps, what would the first step be? How soon could you take it? What would the second step be? How soon could you take it? Do this for each step.

10. Evaluate the outcome of the risk. Did it turn out as expected? If not, why? What have you learned for next time?

11. Celebrate your success. Give yourself credit for taking the risk, whether or not it turned out as expected. Gradually, you will see yourself as a risk taker.

Review the suggestions for developing other Quester characteristics such as confidence, growth, creativity and resilience. They will help you enhance your will to risk. Remember, taking risks gets easier each time. The more risks you take, the more courage you have to take more. Risk is like a muscle that strengthens with use.

Optimism
33 or higher: You hope for and expect the best. You see the glass as half-full. Because you think positively about what you want and learn from disappointments, you achieve happiness and success. You usually achieve your goals. Your vivid imaginings about desired outcomes help you attain your goals. You're healthy and will probably live to a ripe old age.

13 to 31: You appear to be moderately optimistic. You may be more optimistic with respect to some life components, such as social activities and relationships, and less optimistic in work-related activities, or vice versa. Review your responses to the Questionnaire statements to identify additional insights.

12 or lower: You tend to see the glass as half-empty. Your pessimism is robbing you of happiness. It may also be harming your health. This attitude can make it difficult for you to have good interpersonal relationships. What past experiences have made you feel this way? You can learn to become more optimistic by changing your attitudes and learning a new set of cognitive skills. If you want to change, practice some of the following exercises.

Tips for Becoming More Optimistic

* *Believe in yourself.* Have faith in your abilities. Without a humble but reasonable confidence in your own powers you can't be happy or successful. A sense of inferiority and inadequacy interfere with the attainment of your dreams, but self-confidence leads to self-realization and achievement.

  William James, the famous psychologist said: "Our belief at the beginning of a doubtful undertaking is the one thing that ensures the successful outcome of your venture" When you expect the best, you release a magnetic force in your mind, which by the law of attraction tends to bring the best to you. A sustained expectation of the best sets in motion forces which cause the best to materialize."

  Do not worship other people and try to copy them. Nobody can be you as efficiently as you. Remember also, most people despite their confident appearance and demeanor, are often scared and doubtful themselves.

* *Recognize that you create your own thoughts and have the power to change them.* Practice positive self-talk every day. Say, "I like myself because ... " "I can ... " "I will ... " Use positive statements about such things as being healthy, being in control, and being blessed. Don't criticize

or complain. Think of ways to improve the situation. Avoid phrases such as, "I can't," or "I'm too old." Write down affirmations that promote positive thinking. For example, "I can change ... "

- *Monitor your self-talk.* A crucial component to a happy and successful life is what we say to ourselves when we experience failure and disappointment. We learn to explain our setbacks in positive or negative styles during early childhood. For some people, an automatic response is, "It's going to last forever and undermine everything I do." But others are able to say and believe, "It was just circumstances, which I can overcome. Besides, there is so much more to life."

- *Concentrate on your successes.* Create a success collage using pictures that illustrate who you want to be and what you want to accomplish. Include the goal you want to attain, how you want to look, and the personal and professional image you want to project. Look at it every day to remind yourself that you are this successful person.

- *Eliminate negative thoughts and feelings.* Write down your negative thoughts and feelings. Indicate why you feel this way. For example, when adversity strikes, listen to your explanation. When it's pessimistic, dispute it. Use evidence, alternatives, implications, and usefulness as guides to challenge your negative thoughts. Replace negative thoughts with more positive ones. Each time you catch yourself using a negative phrase, say out loud, "Cancel, cancel."

Practice saying something positive about everything about which you have been talking negatively. Don't say, "'I'll never be able to do that.' Instead affirm, "With practice I will be able to do . . . ."

Never participate in negative conversations. Speak positively about people and events. By talking optimistically you can elevate the atmosphere and contribute to making others feel hopeful and happy.

- *View difficulties as challenges to be overcome.* If you lose your job, for example, consider it an opportunity to pursue your dream job or to start something better. Count your blessings. Get rid of any thoughts of defeat for as you think of defeat you tend to get it.

  Stamp indelibly in your mind a mental picture of yourself succeeding. Hold this picture. Never permit it to fade. Never think of yourself as failing. Whenever a negative thought concerning your personal powers comes to mind, cancel it out. Do not build obstacles in your imagination.

- *Take your mind off your problems or challenges.* Get involved in activities that let you focus your attention away from the problem. For example, go to a movie or a concert, meditate or pray, listen to music, or go out for dinner with a friend. Engage in physical activities to get energy moving in your body. Dance, play tennis or take walks.

- *Break the worry habit.* Worry is a destructive mental habit, and is related to physical diseases such as arthritis and high blood pressure. Practice emptying your mind daily before retiring at night to avoid the retention of worrisome thoughts in your consciousness while you sleep. Use creative imagination. Picture all worrisome thoughts flowing out of your mind as you would let water flow from a basin by removing the stopper. Repeat the affirmation: "I am now emptying my mind of all anxiety and insecurity." Believe this.

- *Learn to forgive.* Release negative feelings, the painful past and need for revenge. Forgiving someone is to agree within yourself to overlook the wrong they have committed against you and to move on with your life. Non-forgiveness keeps you in the struggle. The willingness to forgive can bring a sense of peace and well-being. It lifts anxiety and delivers you from depression. It can enhance your self-esteem and give you hope. Always remember that you are human. Sometimes people do and say hurtful things. It is important to focus on what you have learned from the experience.

- *Greet others with positive, cheerful statements.* Smile often. This generates enthusiasm, friendliness and good will. Associate with positive, happy people who will give you support and encouragement as you work toward your goals. Make other people feel important—and do it sincerely. Most of all, develop a sense of humor and learn to laugh at yourself.

- *Look for and expect good things to happen.* When you arise in the morning, you have two choices—to be happy or to be unhappy. Choose to be happy. Make a list of all things you have to be happy about and look at them every day. Read inspirational books and listen to positive message tapes. Do not affirm unhappy thoughts. By merely thinking about these you will help you make these happen.

  Success is 15 percent aptitude and 85 percent attitude. It's your attitude that will determine your success in your new venture. Fill your mind with happiness, positive and constructive thoughts, desired outcomes and helpful ideas. You are special and have unique talents to offer.

Growth

37 or higher: You know and accept yourself. You tend to seek growth in both your personal and your professional life by seeking new opportunities to develop yourself to the fullest. Your perception of reality is sound and you tolerate ambiguity fairly well. You can accept others as well as yourself. You are natural, spontaneous and innovative. You can also be altruistic. Self-fulfillment and achievement are important motivators for you. When you are no longer growing on a job, you move on to something else that will better satisfy y our needs for challenge, autonomy and self-expression. You tend to possess most of the other Quester qualities .

15 to 36: You are a potential Quester. You may enjoy challenge and be open to new experiences, but perhaps you can't take criticism. Or you may fear failure and have difficulty accepting your own limits. Look over *The Quester Questionnaire* statements again and note where y ou picked up low scores. If you want to develop to your full potential, consider making some modifications .

14 or lower: You probably like a very secure life with a not-too-difficult job. You may lack confidence, fear failure and be overly concerned with others' opinions. You don't need to change, but if you want to, start small. Try some of the following suggestions.

Tips for Facilitating Growth
*   *View growth as a journey rather than a destination.* Pursue your personal journey of self-discovery, self-improvement, reflection and renewal daily. The process requires personal investment and commitment. It needs moral foundation, hard work in character development, and knowledge of your strengths and limitations. Develop the other Queters qualities of autonom y, confidence, optimism, the will to r isk, resilience and pur pose.

    Have a deep understanding of y our own purpose and pursue it passionately. Your purpose should provide the motivation for you to engage in desired activities f or the love of these as opposed to prestige , power, money or pleasing others. If you are not inspired to liv e and work this way, now might be an appropr iate time to switch jobs, fields or companies. It may also be time to consider changes in other components of y our life.

*   *Be authentic.* Be your own person in every way. Your actions should be consistent with y our thoughts and

feelings. You must have the courage to commit to a process of personal transformation from the inside out. Authenticity involves making autonomous choices. Make decisions based on your personal needs values, interests and goals. Do not succumb to peer or family pressures.

Authenticity requires the courage to go outside your comfort zone. You must learn to be daring and honest, speak out to right wrongs, admit to personal weaknesses and own up to mistakes. You must also face challenges and unfamiliar situations head on.

Being congruent in words and deeds means being consistent with family, friends and neighbors as well as with colleagues and customers. As an authentic person, you serve as a role model for children and subordinates.

- *Practice self discipline.* Learn to manage emotions and negative thoughts and feelings. Restructure negative thoughts so they're more positive. Minimize fear by identifying worrisome issues and using appropriate information and resources. Live in the present. Don't worry about what might happen. When angry, take time out before acting. Go to a quiet place and breathe deeply, or wait a few days to cool down. Engage in physicals activities to reduce stress.

- *Develop trust.* Trust means people can rely on your word. Trust is built through honesty, integrity and consistency of relationships. Although it requires mutual commitment and effort, you can you can initiate and encourage trust.

  Behave consistently and predictably. Ensure that your words and subsequent actions are congruent and honor commitments. Integrity is reinforced to the extent that you do what you say you do. Communicate accurately, openly and transparently. Be explicit, direct and clear about your intentions and motives. State what you need and expect. Don't assume others know what to do. Tactfully air problems and seek win/win resolutions.

Show respect and concern for others. Demonstrate sensitivity to peoples' needs, desires and interests. Be genuine, open to people. Don't fear rejection or failure. Although you may be vulnerable to people who know your limitations, many will accept you for who you are.

Understand what trust means in different cultures. Get to know people better by engaging in social activities. This helps to strengthen common qualities and expose false stereotypes.

- *Build lasting and meaningful relationships.* Engage in intimate relationships with family, friends and co-workers. Be open, approachable. Know peoples' names, life stories, special strengths and celebrate their accomplishments. Develop "small talk" skills, and develop a social conscience. Volunteer for community service projects, cultivate mentoring relationships and understand the roots of discrimination. Get involved in hobbies that involve people interaction.

- *Continue to learn.* Learn how to learn. Know how to acquire new information, and translate that information into constructive experiences. Maintain professional competence and build knowledge in your discipline. Also take courses for sheer enjoyment. Often, you can get new perspectives or skills. Whatever course you choose— whether it's a new language, computer skills or art history of art—choose it because you are genuinely interested in learning more about the topic.

- *Express your creativity.* Take up painting, writing, macramé, singing, gourmet cooking, photography, woodworking or carpentry. Creative expression provides you with evidence of your creativity, which can inspire you to even greater performance.

- *Accept and encourage constructive feedback.* Don't take criticism personally. Listen to what your critics are saying, and then find out what you could do differently. If you think the criticism is unfair, say so, but only after you have listened carefully to your critic. Constructive feedback from people who have nothing to gain, and possibly something to lose, by offering suggestions enable you to grow.

- *Unlearn self-defeating attitudes and habits.* Review the suggestions offered under self-confidence, autonomy, achievement, creativity and risk. Learn how to accept compliments, relinquish your need for approval, depersonalize failure and learn to laugh at yourself. Be determined enough to achieve your goal, but flexible enough to change directions if necessary.

- *Take time to be silent.* Let yourself be guided by your intuition, rather than by externally imposed interpretations. Journal or meditate. Listen to your body, which expresses itself through signals of comfort and discomfort. Communicate with nature—take a walk in the woods or by the water, or find another setting away from the hustle and bustle of contemporary urban life.

Resilience

37 or higher: Like most Questers, you are resilient. You tend to be a purposeful energetic survivor. You thrive on challenge and change. You tend to be confident, creative and growth-oriented. You use both left-brain and right brain thinking styles and maintain optimism during tough times. Although you may experiment and make mistakes, you often create new ways of dealing with problems. Because you dislike regimentation, you may challenge authority or act without approval. However, if your score is *40 or higher* you may court perilous situations. Be careful for recklessness situations could be a danger factor in your life.

15 to 36: You may be resilient in some areas of your life but vulnerable in others. Like many human beings, you are reasonably competent to deal with stressful situations. Your cautious nature coupled with some flexibility would enable you to survive traumatic situations provided a great deal of initiative is not required of you. You have a greater inclination to follow rather than lead which works in some situation but not in others. To strengthen resilience, review your responses to the statements that measure resilience, and note changes you can make.

14 or lower: You are definitely not resilient. You don't seem to be well-adapted to survive catastrophes in your life. You are probably over-dependent, somewhat inflexible in your ideas and ways of behaving and rather fearful. However, a real catastrophe would probably bring out a strong urge for survival, and you may be better able to cope with these situations than you think. Part of the problem may be that you are rather hesitant to test yourself and your abilities because you fear failing. Try being a little bolder if you want to grow and develop to your full potential.

Tips for Developing Resilience

* *Learn to adapt quickly to new situations.* Your thoughts and attitudes can create either barriers or bridges to a better future. Identify positive aspects of the change such as exciting new opportunities, and abilities used. Write and talk about feelings to help overcome emotional trauma. Expect things to work out. Don't dwell on the negative or view yourself as a victim.

* *Note what you've learned from traumatic or stressful experiences.* Indicate how these have made you stronger, wiser, better. Identify early clues you ignored, and what you'll now do differently. Project into the future with "What if . . ." questions, and specify how you could resolve potential challenges. When talking about a difficult experience say, "It was challenging at first, but I'm glad it happened because ...."

    Use intuition and creativity. Set aside time for quiet contemplation. Attend to cues your body and mind are giving. Note physical bodily sensations (headaches), emotional feelings (fear, excitement), mental thoughts (ideas that pop into your head) and dreams. Practice active intuitive techniques such as asking for guidance before meditating.

Approach problems from different perspectives. Ask for feedback from people with different backgrounds. Take things out of their ordinary context and create new patterns for them. Notice the number of ways you can use eggs or milk cartons. Develop a playful, childlike curiosity. Ask questions, experiment. View mistakes as learning experiences.

- *Nurture a positive view of yourself.* Develop confidence in your ability to solve problems and trust your instincts. This allows you to take chances without approval from others, and be receptive to constructive criticism. Make a list of everything you like about yourself. Include personal traits and accomplishments. Obtain letters of appreciation from co-workers and superiors. Although it takes courage to ask for these, you'll be pleasantly surprised and moved by their appreciation of your strengths.

- *Be open to unexpected opportunities.* Review the fortunate experiences you've had over the past year and note those that were unexpected. Talk to others about their unanticipated opportunities. Identify strategies that appeared to facilitate good fortunes. Learn to risk. Look upon something new as an exciting adventure that will enable you to grow. Reduce risk by developing back-up plans. Take small risks daily.

- *Develop lifelong competence motivation.* Experts agree that learners who gain most from courses are self-motivated. Self-motivated learners take responsibility for learning, go within for additional strength and focus on aspects of situations they can control. Self motivation leads to competence, mastery and effectiveness in varied situations. Life-long, self-motivated learning is essential in a changing world.

Strengthen cognitive and social problem solving skills. Detect and dispute inaccurate thoughts and causal beliefs. Are you or your circumstances responsible for your beliefs? Are your beliefs based on fact or fallacy? Why or why not? Use positive self-talk and thought-stopping phrases to interrupt negative thoughts. "I can learn from this situation." Develop critical thinking skills. Ask questions. Compare and contrast, link ideas and evaluate.

Enhance interpersonal skills for conflict resolution, assertiveness and negotiation. See things through others' perspectives. Enhance empathy by listening to people's needs priorities, perspectives and problems.

- *Take care of yourself.* This helps keep your mind and body primed to deal with stressful situations. Attend to your own needs and feelings. Engage in enjoyable and relaxing activities. Exercise regularly, eat healthily and get at least seven hours of sleep daily.

  Let yourself experience strong emotions, and also realize when you may need to avoid experiencing them at times to continue functioning.

- *Monitor your exposure to violent media coverage.* Staying informed of current events is important. However, avoid over indulging yourself by hearing, seeing and reading the same horrific story over and over agan. This information is absorbed like a sponge by your subconscious mind which does not make a distinction between what you say and what others say.

- *Establish and maintain connections.* Good relationships with close family members, friends and others is important. Accepting help and support from those who care will strengthen resilience. Being active in civic groups, faith-based organizations, or other local groups provides social support and can help reclaim hope. As well, assisting others in their time of need can benefit the helper.

- *Don't view problems as impossible.* Act on adverse situations as much as possible. Take decisive actions, rather than detaching from them. After you have acted, step back to rest and reenergize yourself.

- *Accept change as part of life.* Certain goals may no longer be attainable as a result of adverse or changing circumstances. Accept circumstances you cannot change and focus on those you can change. Maintain a hopeful outlook. An optimistic outlook enables you to expect good things. Try visualizing what you want, rather than worrying about what you fear.

- *Set attainable goals daily.* Do something regularly -- even if it seems like a small accomplishment, which enables you to move forward and feel a sense of accomplishment. Ask yourself, "What can I accomplish today that will help me move in my desired direction?"

- *Keep things in perspective.* Avoid blowing events out of proportion. Don't predict the negative without considering other more likely outcomes. For example, I'll be so upset, I won't be able to function at all." When facing very stressful events, try to consider the situation in a broader context and keep a long-term perspective.

- *Engage in opportunities for self-discovery.* People often learn something about themselves, and find that they have grown in some respect as a result of loss . Many, who have experienced tragedies have reported better relationships, a greater sense of personal strength, an increased sense of self-worth, a more developed spirituality and heightened appreciation for life.

Start adapting to our new world today. Become competent, resilient and free.

Are You a Potential Quester?

352 or higher: You seem to be a Quester. The higher your overall score, the more closely you resemble the Questers. You probably attained high scores on the personality characteristics of intimacy, self-confidence, purpose, autonomy, achievement, creativity, androgyny, risk, growth and resilience. You also probably attained high scores on *The Job Satisfaction Questionnaire* and *The Job Involvement Questionnaire* (See Chapter 7).

171 to 351: You are a potential Quester, particularly if you agreed with statements 12, 24, 48 and 60, and disagreed with statements 36, 72, 84, 96 and 108. You may have scored high on some Quester characteristics and low on others, or you may have scored in the middle range on all of them. Low scores on *The Job Satisfaction Questionnaire* and *The Job Involvement Questionnaire*, and a high score on *The Burnout Questionnaire*, suggest that, for your physical and mental health, you should seriously consider a job change. (See Chapter 7 for these quizzes.) Chapters 8 and 9 should give you some ideas about how to accomplish this.

If you are engaged in serious self-assessment, your attitudes, values and goals may be shifting. You may be thinking about leaving a dissatisfying position or modifying another life component, such as a relationship that is no longer compatible with your developing personality. Read over those statements in *The Quester Questionnaire* again. They might provide you with some additional insights into yourself and your feelings about your career—and your life.

170 or lower: You seem to be a confirmed Traditionalist, at least for now. A high overall score on *The Job Satisfaction Questionnaire* suggests that you are probably a happy Traditionalist. If your score is low, consider exploring your career options or modifying another component of your life. This book and good career counseling can help you accomplish this.

Putting It All Together

You alone are responsible for your growth. You can choose to change your attitude and your situation, or you can complain. Everything you need to create your ideal work and life is around you. Through the act of creating, there is excitement, hope and the emergence of new opportunities leading to further learning and growth.

You have enormous power to change who you are and where you want to go. Learn to use that power. Take small steps first. Discard those old habits and attitudes that are holding you back, such as belittling yourself or taking unnecessary precautions. And if *The Quester Questionnaire* has shown that you are either a Quester or a potential Quester, don't ignore that discovery. Dare to take the next step.

Keep the following directives in mind as you clarify and pursue your goals:

- State what you really want, not what others think you should want.

- Write a paragraph outlining why you want what you want. State how your goal will benefit you and others.

- Be prepared to make tradeoffs, such as living on less while you return to school

- Work hard.

- Believe you will attain your goal.
  Think and act like you have already attained your goal.

- Develop a support group and associate with positive people.

- Be patient as you work toward your goal.

Chapter 4

Career Change: Up-Down-Sideways

What makes Questers different? Unlike most people, they ask themselves such questions such as, "What do I want out of life?" "What should I do next?" "Why am I here?" They have learned to do a little investigation into their needs, values and purpose. They get answers and then get going. Sounds impossible in today's job market? Not so. Many Questers have learned you can't put a price tag on happiness. They understand they alone are responsible for their career satisfaction and marketability. Most Questers have learned to monitor their careers and, when staleness or dissatisfaction starts to set in, they look for new opportunities. By remaining open to new alternatives, they actually enhance their ability to survive in tough job markets. You can do that too.

Questers tend to take care of their careers by evaluating their development, tuning into their feelings, and being aware of new opportunities. Questers see their careers as ongoing opportunities for personal and professional growth. Their next career assignment usually is lined up while they still have a job, not when they are faced with the stresses of being unemployed. Life is like a tree that branches out before them.

To Questers, the assumption that a job comes with an implicit social contract that guarantees work, status and income just isn't realistic. Their careers involve periodic assessments of who they are and where they want to go. Are you one of these people?

Finding excitement and satisfaction in a career requires understanding yourself—your needs, values, interests, skills, and purpose.

Finding excitement and satisfaction in a career requires understanding yourself—your purpose, needs, values, interests and skills. You may enjoy a variety of career directions in the same occupation, or maybe you want to explore different occupations, or perhaps you'd like to work for yourself. Questers feel free to move up or down what used to be called the career ladder. What matters is not what others think of their career direction or what is socially acceptable, but what feels right for them.

Life crises can profoundly influence the direction of your career. Questers face the same crises as everyone else: They go through divorces, experience deaths in the family, perhaps face job loss, job dissatisfaction, frustration with a boss or even the desire for financial independence. Major or minor, these determining events usually lead them to reassess their lives. Events like these can be catalysts for change.

Because of the influence of past generations—who typically trained for one occupation and stayed with it for life—many people today are not prepared for the idea of change. Indeed, many people fear change. But today career possibilities are almost endless. Not only are many traditional occupations still open but opportunities abound in emerging and growing fields like health care, computers, telecommunications, bioscience, business and finance, hospitality and service. Running your own business, working part-time in two different jobs and returning to school for retraining or upgrading are other options. Just stop and think about it. The world is full of opportunities.

Staying in the Same Field

Almost 60 percent of Questers who change jobs sta y in the same occupational field. Staying in a job that has a similar psychological climate, they move on to different work environments that provide them with new challenges and opportunities to grow. They relish the oppor tunity to learn something new; to try something different; to achieve greater challenge, responsibility, or authority; or to make a greater contribution to humankind.

Moving to a new position in the same field can be accomplished in many different ways. You can do similar w ork for a different organization. You can go from elementar y school teacher to special education teacher to school libr arian or art teacher. You can progress from rehabilitation counselor to social worker to college placement officer. Or how about from bank manager to hotel manager to hospital manager? Or bookkeeper to clerical supervisor to collection cler k? Why not from surgical nurse to special duty n urse to pediatric nurse?

People who stay in the same field often r ise to positions of greater responsibility, authority and autonomy, such as manager of a larger bank or hotel. With each move, they gain broader knowledge and experience. Questers who find new satisfaction and success in the same occupational fields often have fascinating stories to tell.

Helen is a physician who has found satisfaction by changing the focus of her attention in her or iginal profession. At 50, still slim and y outhful-looking, Helen is looking for answers to the mysteries of human pain. As head of her city's first palliative care unit (a hospice for the terminally ill), her quiet influence e xtends far beyond the hospital's walls. Helen has true compassion. She has tremendous kindness, energy and consideration for her patients. She listens and cares.

Caring for and helping people was Helen's goal when, fresh from a nursing program, she entered medical school in England. Her career was interrupted only once. At 30, she quit to have two children. Three years later, Helen moved with her husband and children to the United States. For seven years, she practiced family medicine in a Midwestern city. Then, at 40, hoping to learn more so she could better help her patients, she returned to school for specialized training in obstetrics and gynecology. As a woman and a mother, Helen already understood many of the concerns of her female patients. She enjoyed her work, and her patients enjoyed her care.

But Helen's true professional calling didn't emerge until she watched a dying cancer victim writhe in agony while giving birth. Helpless and indignant, Helen became determined to ensure that terminal patients could die in peace and dignity. Through the years, she gained a reputation for dealing sensitively with dying patients and their families. She also fought doggedly for a palliative care unit at her hospital. Helen had the ability and tenacity to see her ideas through. It wasn't always clear sailing. When financial problems and uncertain government funding threatened the establishment of the unit, she continued to be optimistic. Now, in addition to heading the palliative care unit, she conducts research into pain control. To promote palliative care, Helen schedules speaking engagements at least once a week. She also works actively to fulfill her patients' final wishes.

Helen changed jobs because she wanted to better serve her patients. She has all the qualities of a good physician: She's highly dedicated, selfless and self-disciplined. She is also healthy and can stand the pressure of working long days and nights and being on call. Helen's work gives her great satisfaction. In fact, her life is her work, although she also enjoys her family, regular swims, cooking and gardening. Helen has combined her career and family responsibilities in an enjoyable, rewarding lifestyle.

Len has changed jobs several times in the same occupational field. As a business administration student, he chose marketing. Marketing research helps companies make decisions by determining what motivates consumers to buy a company's products, how and when products are used, and how much people are willing to pay. "It was a dynamic field, not routine. I thought it would be a challenge."

Len is 55 now, and he still finds marketing challenging. By now, he's had several positions in the field. His first was with a large consumer food products corporation. He took it because he wanted to gain experience, learn about corporate life, and apply his knowledge. "I learned a lot about those things," Len remembers. "I also developed greater confidence and became better at speaking up about my ideas."

Five years later, Len moved on. He had mastered the job. Now, ready to explore other products and markets, he joined a large industrial marketing firm and stayed for 14 years. He was moved around sufficiently within the company so that he continued to enjoy both the new challenges and the opportunity for career growth. During the first four years, Len researched different products in the Midwestern regions. Then, he spent four years in a foreign country to open a marketing division. Heading up a training and consulting division in Canada followed that.

Len liked his job. but six years later, he was ready to move again. He was no longer growing, and the work had lost its challenge. If Len had stayed with the company, he might have been given the responsibility of heading a larger division. But the economy was uncertain, and he knew he'd have to wait his turn. Len decided not to wait. He was determined to take charge of his own career.

Doing so meant being responsible. Len knew he had to line up a new job before he could leave. That new job turned out to be general manager and marketing specialist for a medium-sized information systems firm in the United States. But after just four years, Len was feeling the itch to move again. The fact that he didn't agree with the philosophies of the other managers aided his decision. Len recalls being extremely unhappy; his co-workers were uncooperative and seldom agreed with him.

Len's next move was to his current position as general manager of special products for a medium-sized instruments distribution company. The work is exciting. More importantly, he is in tune with the philosophies and values of the other senior managers. Len has been with the company for four years now, and he still finds the work challenging. If he could start over, would he choose marketing again? "Very definitely!" Len asserts. "It's exciting and challenging."

That attitude explains why Len has been so successful in marketing. Both creative and detailed minded, he is well-suited to research. Len can see the big picture of shifting economic and social trends, political realities, and changing lifestyles. He also has the right temperament to cope with competition, uncertainty, pressure, constant change and long hours. Above all, he is extroverted and amiable. Colleagues get along well with him.

Len's personality is what makes him a good marketing person. He knows from experience that many of the most creative and lucrative positions in marketing are the least secure. Being responsible for important marketing decisions leaves him open to both praise and blame. As he says, "In parts of our business, you aren't considered good if you haven't been fired at least once. Because if you haven't been fired, you haven't had the guts to take the risks necessary to be successful." For talented, energetic and creative Questers like Len, marketing is a good career choice.

Chin Yong began his university education in an architecture program. By the third year, he had switched to civil engineering. It seemed more practical. He's glad he did. Today, Chin Yong is a structural engineer with a California consulting firm specializing in earthquake engineering. He analyzes construction plans and inspects building projects. He loves the challenge and creativity.

Chin Yong held two other civil engineering positions before be joined his present company. His first job was with a state department as a transportation engineer, planning, constructing, and maintaining roads, bridges and airports. That position lasted seven years, until he could no longer grow on the job. Then Chin Yong accepted a job in hydraulic engineering. He designed and supervised the construction of artificial canals and reservoirs and directed water-control projects. His second job also lasted seven years. When the challenge was gone again, he moved to the West Coast to specialize in soil research and earthquake engineering.

What does Chin Yong want to do in the future? "Perhaps become a free-lance consultant or learn more about environmental pollution control," he says. "I'm keeping my options open." Chin Yong does know that he wants to stay in civil and structural engineering. "I find it very creative. I enjoy seeing my work come to life."

Many Questers have turned hobbies and interests into rewarding careers.

At 31, *Linda* switched gears to turn her interest in carpentry into a full-time occupation. Linda's job as an interior designer had already given her an entry into carpentry. But successful as she was, she found herself much more fascinated by the carpenters' work than by her own. She began to dabble.

First, she built a deck and helped friends and neighbors

with odd jobs. Then, four years ago, pregnant with her second daughter, Linda got her first big carpentry job. The new addition to her family required a new addition to her home. As she and her husband worked on building an extra room, carpentry got into her blood. Soon, she was dreaming of building an entire house. Linda confided her wish to a neighbor. "I used to dream of things I wanted to do when I was young, too," he said, "but I didn't do them, and now I can't." Suddenly, Linda saw carpentry in a whole new light. Why should she only dream of the things she wanted to do? Why not do them, instead?

Determined to find a more satisfying occupation, Linda enrolled in a carpentry program. Coping with the demands of the program was easier than coping with the resistance she met from well-meaning but dubious relatives and some bigoted union officials. "First, I had to fight with my husband and my mother-in-law. All I heard was 'You should be home with your daughters.' But the more I fought, the more I knew what I wanted," says Linda.

Getting accepted into the union was another hurdle. Fortunately, a senior administrator of the apprenticeship program helped Linda get a job with a construction company as an apprentice carpenter. Linda now happily spends her days putting up walls, installing sheetrock and framing doors. Two nights a week, she attends school to complete her training as a journeyman carpenter. And she still manages to spend time with her daughters and husband.

Linda's pay is good, but the work is physically demanding. She ached all over for three months after starting her new job. "One day, we had to unload a whole truckload of sheetrock in the rain," she says. "I asked myself, 'Do I really want to do this?' Even then, the answer was 'Yes!'" Linda's mother and mother-in-law still don't approve of her occupation, but her husband now understands. He says she's more active and vibrant.

Linda is happy because she's doing a job she enjoys. Yet, carpentry isn't completely different from interior design. Both are in the technical crafts field and suited to Linda's interests. Without changing occupational fields, Linda has found a more satisfying and rewarding occupation.

Nick began his career as a sculptor and artist, struggling to discover himself. He followed that with a teaching stint in a local high school. When he was 31, he realized that art could actually help people suffering from emotional and social disturbances, physical handicaps, and neurological impairments. He entered a two-year graduate program in art therapy, then created his own job by telling state prison officials about the benefits of such therapy. He's elated about the new direction his career has taken.

These stories demonstrate that you don't have to make a drastic change to find satisfaction and success in your career. Many opportunities are available in your field or a similar one. Do you know what options are available to you?

Changing Occupational Fields

About 35 percent of job changers move to an entirely different occupational field. These people move to jobs that have a different psychological climate and often require distinct temperaments, needs, values, interests and abilities. They usually change for one of two reasons: Some find a poor match between their personality characteristics (such as interests, needs, values and abilities) and the requirements of their initial occupation; others realize they have outgrown their first occupational choice. Their beliefs or life experiences, which were initially compatible, have changed. Many Questers, who move to different occupational fields, prepare for their moves by returning to school full-or

About 35 percent of job changers move to an entirely different occupational field.

153

part-time, training on the job and/or conducting research about the new field on their own.

The Job No Longer Fits

Some Questers have jobs that no longer fit their developing personalities and goals. They may have chosen their first jobs wisely and carefully, been well suited to their positions, and been quite successful in them. But somewhere, over the years, they realized they had outgrown these initial choices.

Lynne became dissatisfied with her childhood career choice as she neared 30. As a little girl, Lynne wanted to be a librarian. Soon after college, she landed a job as a high school librarian. "I always questioned whether this field was a lifelong occupation, but I really never assessed my career goals," she recalls. Seven years later, at 29, Lynne realized she had to make a change. "It was like the seven-year itch," she says. Watching a play at a local theater, she was struck by the protagonist's rhetorical question, "What am I afraid of?" She realized she had to answer that question, too.

Lynne took a leave of absence from the library. Sometime during that year, she discovered the intrigue of the stock market. After investing her money for several years, she was ready to learn more. "When I read *The Wall Street Journal* or *Business Week,* I felt like I was reading a foreign language. But at the same time, the field fascinated me."

Lynne signed up for a securities course, but she began to wonder if she could find an entry point in what was then a male-dominated field. The idea of being in securities scared her somewhat. She wasn't used to taking risks. After working in a job with so much certainty, making such a radical move was difficult. "So I asked myself, what could stop me? Fear of failure or of trying something new? What did I really have to fear?"

Her first step was to talk to the brokers who had invested her money. A year later, she was ready to start work as a rookie stockbroker. "I knew I had to cross the line and give up security for growth," she reflects. While Lynne had enjoyed being a librarian, neither the routine nor working with teenagers really interested her anymore. These days, she fits a new baby and a job into a lifestyle that is "exciting and stimulating." Lynne's new position is well suited to her shift in needs, values, and goals. Like many successful brokers, Lynne thrives on the excitement, tension and more-than-moderate dose of uncertainty.

Learning to be a stockbroker isn't the only lesson Lynne mastered. She has learned to reevaluate her career choices regularly. She's thinking about her future now. "Maybe there is a third occupation out there for me, too. When you find out what you're afraid of, you can overcome anything."

Ed also had difficulty making the switch to a different occupational field. As a young boy, Ed thought he had his life carefully mapped out. Because he loved mechanics, deciding on an occupation wasn't hard. After high school, he entered a civil engineering program. His first job was with an engineering firm in the Midwest. Ed loved his work. But by the fifth year, his tasks began to seem too technical, detailed, and narrow. Ed started looking around. Finding a suitable job took almost a year. Hired in the operations department of a manufacturing firm at 31, he spent the next several years working his way up to head of his division. Ed liked the work, but not the new general manager. Their values and beliefs on policies and procedures just weren't compatible. Determined to leave before he was demoted or fired, Ed at 42 started looking around again.

Opportunities at Ed's managerial level weren't plentiful. He and his family liked the city they had lived in for so many years. Rather than move, Ed began considering a different line of work. Soul searching and research led him to real estate. The market was tight, and Ed knew he would have to take a cut in pay, but his children were self-sufficient and his wife was considering a part-time job. Armed with a clear option, Ed resigned, took a short real estate course, and joined a medium-sized real estate firm. He's happy he did. He says, "I enjoy making a sale, not so much for the money, but because I get a kick out of pleasing my customers."

Poor First Choice

While some Questers discover they have grown beyond the challenges of their first occupational choices, others were never suited to their first occupations. Many plunged into jobs without assessing their own personalities, the job requirements, or the work environments they had chosen. Making wise occupational choices requires time and understanding.

Bert is a good example. He went directly from high school into a university science program. He had always enjoyed science, and particularly research, so he thought, "Why not?" Hired as a lab assistant while still in his master's program, Bert discovered a new interest—teaching. So, with a year of graduate education behind him, he set off to teach science to high school seniors.

Making wise occupational choices requires time and understanding.

To his surprise, Bert discovered he really didn't like teaching. "I didn't like policing and being a baby-sitter to students who didn't want to learn," he recalls. But with a wife and young child to support, he could hardly resign. He bided his time while he searched for a more suitable position. He applied to a pharmacy program and was accepted, but after further thought, he decided he wasn't suited to the job. Then, he took some night courses in real estate, "But it really didn't appeal to me." Frustrated, Bert decided to try to make a go of teaching, after all.

Just when he was about ready to give up, Bert found a new interest. He enrolled in a computer programming course and realized he had found what he wanted to do with his life. Excited now, he studied by night and taught by day while he saved for the day he could study full-time. Two years later, with diploma in hand, Bert snapped up an offer from a small oil company to become a computer analyst. Within a year, he was working for a larger company at a higher salary. His new career offered challenge, learning opportunities, and a chance to keep ahead of the computer programming field. "I put up with the red tape because my job is challenging, never boring and there's always something new to learn," he says.

Surprisingly, Bert has also successfully managed to combine his new occupation with his old one. Teaching computer programming to adults helped him realize that he really did enjoy teaching, at least with students who wanted to learn. Now 41, Bert is very satisfied with his job and his lifestyle.

Jean discovered that dissatisfaction with a job exacts a high toll. Her break was more abrupt than Bert's. One day, Jean walked into her boss's office and quit her accounting and secretarial job on the spot. She knew career counselors usually advise against quitting one job before lining up another, but she also knew she'd never be motivated to change directions if she held on to her steady paycheck. "One day I thought, 'I'm not going to sit here grumbling anymore. I'm going to do something about it.'"

Jean spent the next 16 months discovering her real talents and interests and then searched for a job in which she could use them. Her first step was to sign up with a temporary employment agency so she could support herself. Then she went to the career counseling center at a local university. A battery of tests and inventories revealed a surprise: Jean's real aptitude wasn't in accounting; it was in language. She had always enjoyed writing, but she had no idea her skills w ere so advanced. This discovery was a real ego boost, b ut Jean still didn't know what she wanted to do. While she floundered, her temporary jobs led from typing pool to typing pool. Discouraged, she complained to the agency and ask ed for proofreading or editing assignments. The agency was reluctant to send her for a job in which she had no experience, but Jean insisted: "I can read, so I can proofread."

Her determination paid off. A two-week proofreading stint led to an eight-month editing assignment. Jean loved it. At the suggestion of a fr iend, she participated in a workshop on interviewing and job search techniques. She also got help with her resume. Finally, Jean made her first contact with an aerospace fir m. Although her lack of a college degree was a handicap, her persistence got her an interview and the oppor tunity to take an editing test. She passed with impressive skill, but it was several months and 40 phone calls later before she got the job.

That was three years ago. With a recent promotion to technical editor, Jean doesn't doubt for a minute that her efforts were worthwhile. "I'm getting paid for doing something I enjoy," she says with a smile.

Reentering the Workforce

Homemakers often change occupational fields when the y reenter the workforce. A few, like Edie, become Questers.

Edie graduated from a university on the West Coast with a science degree. Her first journey into the workforce was as a microbiology researcher. Shortly after her marriage five years later, she retired to raise children, run a house and do volunteer work. Twenty years later, the marriage was over, her children were growing up, and Edie was faced with the task of finding a satisfying job that w ould also support her and three children. She had to earn money, but she wanted more than just a salary. She wanted an exciting, people-oriented job. "Unfortunately, like many women, I thought I didn't have the right to please myself." At a women's career counseling center, Edie found encouragement to complete a master's degree in social work. At first, she was terrified at the prospect: "How could I support myself and my kids? What if I failed? How could I compete with younger people? What kind of a job could I get?"

Many married women who return to school or work have similar feelings and fears. Edie overcame hers. With child support from her ex-husband, a student loan and a part-time job as a salesclerk, she made it. Today, two years after graduation, Edie is doing excellent work as the executive director of a family social services bureau. She got the job because she had the personality, skills, experience and motivation to succeed. Some of those skills and experiences were learned as a homemaker and volunteer. A social work degree gave her the rest. Edie feels great.

Homemakers
Not all women want to return to the workforce, preferring homemaking to the stresses of corporate life. But some—like Verlynne, who was introduced in Chapter 1—feel pressured to do so by their friends, family or society.

Lashonda was a buyer of electronic equipment for a high tech company. On one of her business trips, she met an old friend at the airport where she was waiting for a connecting flight. The reunion led to a romance that led to marriage. Lashonda chose to quit her job and spend the next few years enjoying domestic pursuits, such as decorating her home and preparing gourmet meals. The change also gave her the time and energy to devote to caring for AIDS patients at a local hospice. Maybe, in a few years, she will return to her earlier profession. In the meantime, Lashonda is keeping her options open and following her passion. Both Verlynne and Lashonda are fortunate they can pursue activities they enjoy without having to worry about paying for the necessities of life. Not all women have that option.

Full-time homemaking is also an option for some men. For example, *Brad* prefers to stay at home doing household chores and looking after his two daughters, while his wife, Jan, works full-time to pay the family's bills. Being a househusband gives Brad time to devote to his passion— painting. This arrangement, which works well for Brad and Jan, is an option that an increasing number of Quester couples are choosing.

Questers like Verlynne, Lashonda and Brad find that homemaking, coupled with involvement in activities for which they have a passion, gives their lives meaning, purpose and direction. They prove that homemaking can be a viable alternative for some Questers.

Follow Your Dreams

Finding the right occupation is the key to succeeding in and enjoying your career. You shouldn't overlook your childhood dreams when you are contemplating an occupational move. But it isn't always easy to follow your dreams. Look at Jane's example.

A talented singer in high school, *Jane* grabbed the spotlight year after year at every musical festival in her area. She loved singing and acting. But when it came time to decide on an occupation, she listened not to her heart but to her parents' advice. They wanted her to seek a secure occupation, such as law.

For nine years, Jane practiced law, and she didn't really mind it, but singing was still her first love. She spent every spare moment singing in a nightclub production in her West Coast hometown. Then, it happened. One morning, as Jane rose to go to work, she realized she no longer wanted to practice law. Within two months, Jane was in New York, taking singing and acting lessons. The money she had saved from practicing law and from singing in nightclubs helped finance the lessons. Two years later, Jane has landed her first small part in a television series.

Will she make it big? Only time will tell. But, in the meantime, she is doing what she enjoys. She gave her childhood dream a chance.

Antonio also decided to pursue his dreams. He worked for 22 years as a chemical engineer with a multinational petrochemical organization. At the age of 42, when he recognized the company was downsizing, he decided to take his career into his own hands. So he took a course to help him identify what he wanted to do next and then researched his occupational options. Today, Antonio is working two jobs. He is a crop and sheep farmer and an environmental coordinator for his petrochemical company at a plant near his farm.

Antonio uses his engineering skills on the farm, and the skills and knowledge he's gained from farming apply to his engineering position. His associates agree that his diverse background makes him a superior problem-solver.

Antonio's decision to become a farmer required a significant investment of time and money. To many people, being a farmer means dropping several notches down the occupational prestige ladder. But Antonio is happy with his new work and lifestyle, and so is his family. His status on the career ladder is much less important to him than his health, peace of mind and job satisfaction. Antonio says, "I feel better mentally and physically, and I'm doing well financially. … My children love the country, and my relationship with my wife is better than it's ever been." Antonio has learned to be true to himself.

Running the Show

What do Questers do when they find there is no ready-made place in the market for their skills? Some go into business for themselves. Approximately a third of the Questers interviewed for this book have established their own businesses. They seem willing to go small in order to be in control of their lives and their careers.

Quester entrepreneurs typify the best spirit of Western culture. Inventive, bold, resolute and eager to meet new challenges, some become quite wealthy. Others find satisfaction in simply doing a job well. They prove it still is possible for someone with a dream to succeed. Entrepreneurial Questers have strong needs for autonomy and independence. Many are nonconformists who picture themselves as individualists and freethinkers. Their talents are broad, and they have a great desire for variety and flexibility. More than any other type of Questers, they are not afraid to take chances. Their ultimate satisfaction comes from seeing something they have created grow and develop; money is secondary.

Entrepreneurial Questers have the perseverance, self-discipline, energy, and stamina necessary to work 12-hour days and forgo weekends and holidays. Many, in fact, are workaholics. They take it for granted that one of the rewards of their efforts will be financial independence. Entrepreneurial Questers get along well with people. Not only do they motivate employees, they also like to solicit the support of customers and clients. Whether they work from home or out in the community, they do it with customary skill and enthusiasm.

Working from Home
Some entrepreneurial Questers operate their businesses from home. Here is what they have to say about it.

Eleanor started a children's discount clothing boutique

because she needed the money. A single parent with two young children to support, she returned to work after her divorce by selling clothing as a manufacturer's representative, a job she had held before her children were born. But housekeepers' salaries, upkeep on her house and commuting expenses left little from her paycheck. And her 10-hour workdays (including a three-hour round-trip commute) were a strain on both Eleanor and her children. When she tried to give needed time to her children, Eleanor was fired. Sometime during the six months while she collected unemployment benefits, Eleanor decided to start her own business.

The market for children's clothing was good, she had contacts in the fashion industry, and she wanted to be home with her children. So she opened a discount children's clothing boutique in the basement of her home.

"For the first time in my life," she says, "I'm independent. I'm available for my children, can go to the school play, take them on holidays, and, because I'm in a child-oriented business, it's okay for them to be here in the background when I'm talking on the phone with suppliers or customers."

In the first year, Eleanor's discount business broke even. She credits much of her success to her marketing strategy. By dressing her children in the clothing she sells, Eleanor finds new customers among friends and mothers of her children's classmates. Now thinking of expanding her boutique into a full retail store, Eleanor is talking like a Quester when she says, "Everyone dreams of having a successful business. I know I can do it."

At 34, *Ross* seemed to be a success. An accountant moving rapidly up the career ladder in a large firm, he had a promising future. But Ross was bored working with numbers. He really wanted to work with his hands. So, Ross decided to turn his hobby into his occupation. He began taking pottery courses during the evenings. He loved it. He was also very talented.

At first, Ross's wife wasn't pleased to hear about his plans and hopes. With two children to support and bills to pay, the couple had some heavy responsibilities. But she could see that his dissatisfaction was making Ross irritable and lethargic. So, they decided to compromise. Ross's wife took a part-time job to help pay the bills, and Ross stayed on part-time with the accounting firm. He devoted the rest of his time to pottery. Ross turned his basement into a workshop, bought a potter's wheel and built a walk-in kiln in his backyard.

Four years later, Ross is working full-time as a potter. Using his accounting skill to keep the books in order, Ross sells his wares to specialty shops, galleries, department stores and private clients. His pottery is so much in demand that he works long hours just to fill the orders. But he doesn't mind. He's happy with his work and his lifestyle. His relationship with his wife and children is better, too. Even though he is busy, Ross has more quality time to spend with them. Everyone has benefited from his career change.

Doing Business in the Community
Other businesses take entrepreneurial Questers away from home. But they still enjoy the benefits of working for themselves.

Decorating windows gave *Jennifer* the start she needed to set out on her own. A former occupational therapist, Jennifer went from a window-dressing job for a large department store to designing show suites for apartment complexes. When she couldn't find the clean, simple furniture she liked, she began designing her own. Her stark, uncluttered lines soon had people talking about the young designer, and she began getting commissions to design private homes.

Today Jennifer does freelance design and wholesales her ideas to other interior decorators. Her biggest success came while searching for a carpenter. She could hardly believe her luck when she discovered a top-notch furniture finisher and a first-class cabinetmaker. The three have been collaborating ever since.

Melvin demonstrates you can take a calculated risk and win. When he quit his senior management job, Melvin had $60 in the bank and a wife and two children to support. Quitting was not a spur-of-the-moment decision—Melvin had planned his moves—but illness forced him to resign earlier than he had intended.

Determined to market a little-known line of sportswear, Melvin put his convalescence to good use, researching his idea. He even researched bank managers, to find out who was the most liberal. Then, putting his idea on paper, Melvin approached the manager he thought would give him the best deal. His next move was to open a store. In four years, Melvin's business has expanded to 21 stores in eight cities. All smiles, Melvin still can't believe how quickly his idea caught on. He feels as if he's "in Disneyland. It's pure fantasy." Now he's researching a new venture, another specialty line.

Boredom, the desire to do something different, and following a long-time dream aren't the only reasons people start their own businesses. Some are forced into it. Being fired, laid off, or discovering that your skills are no longer in demand can be the impetus to starting a new business venture. If you take this path, you begin the process of learning new skills and expanding your options.

Involuntary Change

In recent years, downsizing, layoffs, mergers, company relocations, and bankruptcies have cost hundreds of thousands of people their jobs. People who had expected to sail into retirement have been suddenly cast adrift. Job loss due to a layoff or termination is much more traumatic than voluntary change. Because you have no choice in the matter, it can be a frightening and painful experience.

Often, business and professional women and men blame themselves for failing. They seek explanations by dredging up mistakes of the past. Some are vulnerable to clinical depression, sexual impotence or disinterest, and a variety of other physical ailments. Others vent their anger and frustration on spouses or children or abuse alcohol and drugs. For the most part, men in their 40s, 50s and 60s hold traditional values and attitudes about providing for their spouses and children. So, losing their breadwinner status is a crucial blow to their self-confidence.

Job loss due to layoff or termination is much more traumatic than involuntary change.

Dismissed employees typically go through five emotional stages, similar to the ones people experience when they face a terminal illness: shock, denial and disbelief; fear and anxiety; resistance, anger and blame; acceptance and exploration; and finally commitment. These stages are illustrated in the Transition Curve.

People often move back and forth between the stages, especially the first three. The pace of the healing process depends on the amount of introspection and "inner work" they have done prior to the loss. For example, those who have come to terms with their developmental issues (See Chapter 5), take less time to heal than those who have not.
Let's see how the five stages were experienced by Kent, a Quester who lost his job suddenly and unexpectedly.

Stage 1: Shock, Denial and Disbelief
Kent learned "out of the blue" that his engineering services were no longer required. He walked around numb for a week, asking himself, "What's wrong with me?

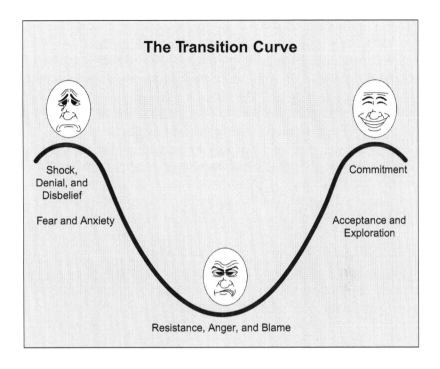

The Transition Curve

Shock,
Denial, and
Disbelief

Fear and Anxiety

Commitment

Acceptance and
Exploration

Resistance, Anger, and Blame

Are they challenging my competence? What did I do to deserve this?" He explained, "It's like getting dumped with a bucket of cold water."

The first reaction to sudden job loss is characterized by numbness and a general refusal to recognize what is happening. You might think, "This is not happening to me!" or "They don't really mean it." These kinds of reactions protect you from being overwhelmed. Many employees who are told they are targeted for layoffs continue their daily routines as if business will go on as usual, believing their dismissal is a mistake. The shock is particularly acute for people whose lives center primarily around work. When who we are is our job, we are vulnerable, because someone can take it away.

You should not make any major decisions during this stage. Instead, take time to process or absorb the injury until the hurt begins to recede. This is the time when you need a sympathetic listener—not necessarily someone to offer advice.

Stage 2: Fear and Anxiety

Kent felt terrible because he did not have a plan. He was embarrassed at what he imagined other people were thinking about him. He felt frustrated and out of control, and he wondered how his family was going to manage. He felt the need to regroup, to identify a goal, but he could not do it immediately. Instead, he walked around aimlessly. His short-term memory was poor for the first few weeks. He felt cold inside, his eyes appeared fixed and glazed. Because his goal was interrupted, he was overwhelmed. At night, he had horrible nightmares in which he had no destination, no home, no safety.

In the second stage, you wonder how you are going to manage. You may feel out of control, asking yourself questions such as, "How am I going to pay for the mortgage and the medical insurance? What am I going to do next?" Fear can escalate to unmanageable levels as you wonder, "What if I never work again?"

You are mourning the past and resisting change. You don't want to be disturbed. Letting go of your old way of life is like confronting a death in the family. We often resist change because our sense of security is threatened. We feel out of control, powerless, afraid of looking foolish. Kent felt the need for some closure so that he could start healing. He had to create his own closure, which he did by retreating and not talking to anyone about his situation for a while.

It's important that you not allow your fear to get out of control or refuse to acknowledge it. This can cause panic, which can prevent you from acting altogether. Acknowledge your fear. Identify exactly what you're afraid of. Are you afraid of the loss of material things? Rejection? The unknown?

The key to managing your fear is to start living in the present. Don't spend time worrying about what might happen; instead, do what you can to explore the possibilities that lie ahead. This is your opportunity to pursue that job you may have dreamed about for a long time.

Stage 3: Resistance, Anger and Blame

> For awhile, Kent blamed his supervisor and his company for his dismissal. "It was the way it was done. ... I was not involved in any decision making. They could have done it in a nicer way. ... I was not even told why I was being let go."

As long as it is a passing stage , anger is healthy, because it means you value yourself. Not everyone is angry, but it is common to complain and to blame someone or something. While blame is the first explanation of events, it is rarely the full explanation. Blaming is finding someone or something we can hold responsible for our painful predicament.

In addition to anger, you may feel physical, emotional or mental pain. You may doubt your ability to survive the change. This low ebb in the process is often followed by grief and depression.

Anger must be dealt with. Acknowledging your feelings helps you progress more quickly to the next stage. Talking about your feelings with a trusted friend, family member or professional will help dispel some of the negative emotions. Another way to vent emotions is to write them down. For example, you can write about the trauma and explore questions like, "Why me? What is the meaning of and the positive potential in this loss? How can this anger and resentment be transformed into life-affirming energy? What dreams, long put off, can I now pursue?"

Translating the events into words tends to diminish the stress and increase your self-understanding. This will also enable you to present yourself more favorably to others, for example, in prospective job interviews. Writing forces you to address your emotions, cognitively reappraise your situation, and come to terms with your predicament.

Exercising regularly, punching a bag, listening to music, participating in community and trade activities, relaxing in a hot tub, praying and meditating are other activities that might help you get through this tricky transition.

Stage 4: Acceptance and Exploration

When Kent began to let go of the loss, to make the best of his predicament, he was able to breathe more easily. He decided he was not going to let the dismissal ruin his life. He convinced himself he was a competent worker and decided to use the opportunity to pursue his long-time goal of writing. As he explored opportunities in the field, Kent felt on top of the situation. His goals were now more in tune with his inner desires. His energy level was high, and he started to be friendlier with others.

After the period of inner conflict, people usually shift into a more positive, future-focused phase. You realize at this stage that you are going to make it! You begin looking forward to and exploring new possibilities. You feel and sleep better. You have more energy to discover and explore new opportunities. You start clarifying goals and are motivated to swing into action. Your creativity is high. You realize you have the ability to move forward.

Remember, though, you shouldn't try to complete the exploration stage too soon or settle for something less than what you really want. Take time to explore and pursue your passion now. If necessary, you can take a survival job while you explore and prepare to pursue your dream.

Stage 5: Commitment

After exploring options that would allow him to combine his engineering skills with his interest of writing, Kent decided to pursue a certificate program in technical writing at a local college. Today, he is optimistic and excited about his future.

Commitment involves focusing on a new course of action and adapting to a new situation. You pursue your vision and make a commitment to finding a new job, starting a business, or going back to school. You have grown and adapted. The future is bright.

Fortunately, 60 to 85 percent of people who lose their jobs find new positions within three to 10 months. It may take older individuals a little longer because they face subtle and not-so-subtle age discrimination. Many large companies prefer to hire younger workers, who command less pay, are more willing to relocate, and are easier to mold into the company image. Mature workers usually find their expertise is highly valued in middle- or smaller-sized companies.

Fortunately. 60 to 85 percent of people who lose their jobs find new positions within 3 to 10 months.

Regardless of age, people who have positive attitudes, work hard, and follow their hearts usually come out ahead. The crisis provides them with a stronger sense of themselves, greater control over their careers and lives, and opportunities to pursue their dreams or positions that offer greater personal and professional satisfaction. Some (although not all) end up earning higher salaries, as well.

With the help of a therapist, *Gunter,* 50, converted his feelings of anger and frustration into positive energy and action when he lost his job. He began to see the crisis as an opportunity to move in a new direction. A computer technician for 15 years, Gunter had been bored with his job but afraid to do anything about it. A blessing in disguise, his layoff forced him to come to terms with what he really wanted to do with the rest of his life.

Gunter attended a career workshop, which helped him to clarify his dreams, values, needs, interests, skills, and goals. He also continued pursuing his leisure interest in photography and took skill-building courses to enhance his proficiency. He began subscribing to magazines and newsletters about photography and layout design and initiated a network of contacts. Within four months, Gunter had landed an exciting position as a photographer with a growing technical magazine.

Carol headed a learning center at a Midwestern university. But when the center closed, she w as forced to find a new job. As she searched, Carol tur ned a hobby into her sole means of support, operating a catering business from home. She explains, "I didn't anticipate what a dr astic change it would be to go from Carol-the-academic to Carol-the-cook."

When the business became too big for her home, she rented space in a large w arehouse and hired four assistants. Fortunately for Carol, a bad experience turned into a positive one. She never did return to the academic world. "Starting over was the best thing that ever happened to me," she reflects.

Many Questers who face a job loss lear n that the best protection may be to lead a more balanced lif e. They learn to depend less on the organization and to seek reinf orcement of their self-images through a variety of activities and institutions. These may include family and social relationships, spiritual practices, leisure and community activities, and fraternal and religious societies. They also discover that life doesn't end with a pink slip; it can have happy, new beginnings. Personal dreams, long put off, can now be pursued!

Turning a crisis into an oppor tunity requires knowing yourself, developing a positive attitude, and believing in yourself and in your goals. Through hard work and persistence, each challenge you successfully master will help y ou to take more responsibility for your life.

A dismissed employee reflecting on her experiences with involuntary change shared the following thoughts. "Change is an irreversible force that sometimes reshapes our liv es, bringing new challenges and goals, new commitments to be made. You can use change to y our advantage by letting it move you to a new wonderful place you would never have thought to go."

To help you manage your transition, refer to the suggestions offered below.

Action Steps to Respond to a Change

- *Assess your financial status and develop a budget.* If necessary, make some changes in your lifestyle.

- *Get your feelings out.* Talk to family members or close friends about your concerns, fears and plans. Write about the situation and explore questions you want to address. If necessary, seek professional help.

- *Accept the fact that you lost the job.* Don't lie about it to yourself, your friends or your family.

- *Join a support group for people who are facing the same challenge.* If such a group does not exist, consider starting one of your own. Meeting once a week provides ideas, a sounding board, networking opportunities and positive feedback

- *Seek advice and assistance from professionals.*

- *Develop a positive outlook.* Your attitude about yourself will determine how others see you.

- *Schedule periods of rest*, so you can begin the renewal process and handle the stress.

- *Schedule some quiet time to think and reassess.* You need time to consider what you really want to do with the rest of your life.

- *Create a routine and stick to it.* A predictable schedule, particularly in your home life, will help reduce stress.

- *Learn, practice and use body-stress relievers that work for you.* These might include taking a short nap, breathing deeply, exercising, walking, receiving massages, meditating and listening to music.

- *Pay attention to your sleep patterns and diet.* Eating a healthy diet will keep your energy level high. Avoid alcohol, which acts as a depressant.

> - *Exercise regularly.* This will help you recharge your body.
>
> - *Make your job search a full-time job.*

Growing in Your Current Job

Not all Questers change jobs to get their needs met. Some, like Eva, create their own opportunities for growth in their current positions.

Eva has been a staff development officer in a large government department for 14 years. During this time she has initiated several progressive policy changes and implemented several innovative staff development programs. She has a knack for identifying both employee and employer needs, and she keeps abreast of new developments in the human resources field.

What can you do to grow in your current job and get your work needs met? First of all, you need to know exactly what you find satisfying or dissatisfying about your position. *The Job Satisfaction Questionnaire* in Chapter 7 will help you identify the needs that are important to you. List these needs and ask yourself if you ever got them met in your job. Review your job history with the company. What was there about your job that made you feel good? Is there anything you can do now to regain that feeling?

Eva has strong needs for challenge, autonomy and personal and professional growth. She continually signs up for professional development courses. Any time she wants to initiate a new program or policy, Eva presents a well-researched proposal to her superior, demonstrating the need for the program and documenting how she intends to implement it. Most of her proposals are accepted, and everyone in the department ultimately benefits—employees, superiors and Eva.

There are several ways you can grow in your job. Look over the suggestions below, and incorporate them into your work situation.

- *Identify colleagues and friends who are satisfied with their positions and have more control over their work.* What are they doing differently from you? Are they taking more initiative? Volunteering for new assignments? Being more assertive at meetings? Being more politically astute? Are you feeling out of control? What is this telling you?

- *Explore ways to creatively redesign your job.* What can you do to derive more input and challenge? Propose suggestions to your boss. Include examples of ways you can work more effectively and efficiently. Show how your changes will affect the company's bottom line.

- *Take the initiative.* Look for jobs you would like in your company. Identify the project manager, research ways you can enhance the project, and offer help and suggestions. Volunteer for special projects and challenges. Offer to take charge of a newsletter, social activity or community relations project.

- *Become more assertive.* Speak out for what you need, believe in, and deserve. Constructively question policies and take the initiative. Offer help and participate in new assignments.

- *Become a team member.* Work toward the success of a project. Help the company meet its deadlines and bottom lines. What can you do to make your boss more successful? Offer recommendations for making the company's products or services better. Show that you're committed to your team's success.

- *Network.* Find out what's happening in the company. Communicate regularly with superiors and colleagues. Attend meetings, participate in social activities and read the company newsletter.

- *Become an expert in your field.* Continue to learn by attending seminars, reading professional journals and attending professional meetings. Share your knowledge and skills. Create a demand for your expertise.

- *Learn to manage stress.* Develop interests outside of work. Make family and leisure time fun. Find hobbies and volunteer work that will provide challenge and help you to feel good about yourself.

If you've tried most of these suggestions and they're not improving your work situation, consider changing to a new department, a different employer or another field. Or take some time out to think about what you really want to do.

Stress

Many people who are not suited to their occupational choices experience stress symptoms because their personal traits are not compatible with their occupational environments. Some of these individuals become Questers.

Terrie, a 48-year-old sales manager, had long been dissatisfied with her job. She stayed because she was convinced she couldn't afford to switch jobs. "To be truthful, I was afraid to," she says. Then, she developed a strange illness, in which abnormal lumps formed all over her body. Terrie's doctor could find no physical cause for her malady, and so referred her to a psychologist.

Testing and career counseling revealed that Terrie was more suited to literary arts than to sales. She decided to pursue a library science degree, although history also interested her. Returning to school was intimidating, but a scholarship and her savings saw her through. Now 53, Terrie has been working as a librarian for two years. She loves her work, and her health "has never been better." She is also researching and writing an historical novel. Terrie is beginning to sound a lot like a Quester.

Ray developed Irritable Bowel Syndrome (IBS) when he switched from one civil engineering job to another. Career counseling and introspection finally revealed that he was in the wrong occupation. Ray had an average aptitude for engineering but little real interest in the field. He also had highly developed literary, artistic, and creative abilities, which made him well suited to advertising. The stresses he faces now as creative director of an advertising agency are far greater than any he faced as an engineer, but his IBS is under control because, for Ray, it's positive stress.

Up or Down?

Does it really matter which way you are headed on the organizational career ladder? Not to most Questers. When they change jobs, better social status, prestige and income are seldom the first issues on their minds. What Questers really seek are satisfying positions that are more compatible with their developing personalities—positions that offer opportunities for personal and professional growth; for service to others; and for greater challenge, autonomy and use of skills. Of course, some do end up with more status, prestige and money. Others don't.

Don is a quiet, sensitive physician who, at 40, dropped several notches on the career ladder when he moved from medicine to education. A caring and successful pediatrician, Don found that after 11 years of medical practice he wasn't happy anymore. He felt hurt seeing children and adolescents suffer as he stood by, sometimes unable to alleviate their pain.

The death of his father made Don realize that life is too short to spend in an occupation he didn't enjoy. Despite reminders from colleagues that he had spent thousands of dollars building up his specialty, Don decided to go back to school to study education. Today, Don is in his third year of teaching biology to teenagers. He is still

177

working with adolescents, but these kids are not sick and suffering. He has discovered that teaching suits his temperament better than medicine.

For many, abandoning a medical practice to become a teacher seems like a drastic drop in career status. But as a newly emerged Quester, Don is happy with his new occupation and lifestyle, even though he took a substantial pay cut. When Don decides teaching is no longer right for him, he will probably change occupations again. His status on the prestige ladder will be m uch less important to him than his health, peace of mind and job satisfaction.

Interestingly, occupational prestige studies rank physicians among the top 5th percentile. Public school teachers, on the other hand, rank between the 25th and 40th percentile, depending on the study. At the bottom are shoe shiners, clothes pressers, waitresses, street sweepers and garbage collectors. But at least two people interviewed for this book moved from high-status professions to the very bottom of the occupational prestige scale, and are happier today because of it.

Until two years ago, *Dwight* was a lawyer with a prominent international law firm. These days, he can be found decked out in badly soiled khaki pants and a g rimy army jacket. Since last July, Dwight and 35-year-old Timothy, a former administrative assistant to a senior go vernment official, have been driving a garbage removal truck in a town about 80 miles nor thwest of a large Easter n city. Unlike many young people who are forced to make drastic career changes, these two are in an unpopular job b y choice.

Why did Dwight leave law? He explains, "I was getting pretty bored with being surrounded b y so many high-powered lawyers working on legal refinements. It just wasn't challenging anymore, and I had to w onder how much value I was really contributing to society. I don't want to give the impression that there is more social utility in garbage than in law, but I'm satisfied with what I'm doing now. I wasn't before."

Dwight and Timothy are intrigued by the possibility of expanding the garbage removal business into garbage disposal and recycling. After eight hours of guiding a nine-ton truck without power steering along the wooded roads that twist around the town, Dwight's body aches all over. "But I don't feel the strain of the long hours as I used to when I worked at the law firm all day."

When Dwight and Timothy decided to buy the garbage removal company, Dwight and his wife gave up their downtown apartment and moved into an average-looking house near the business. Timothy, a bachelor, bought a townhouse. Both have taken substantial pay cuts—Dwight by 40 percent, Timothy by half that. Despite his smaller salary, Dwight says he has much greater peace of mind. "If you're traveling on a superhighway but going in the wrong direction, you feel insecure. But if you're on a mud road and it's going the right way, that's security."

That's how Questers differ from ordinary folks. Few move up the career ladder simply for prestige or money. Instead, they change jobs for the opportunity to grow and develop in satisfying careers.

The Choice Is Yours

Would it surprise you to learn that approximately half of all employees experience significant job stress? Stressed workers report that their job stress interferes with their relationships, health and ability to perform their work. You probably know many such people;

Approximately half of all employees experience significant job stress.

maybe you are among them. They are the ones who are exuberant on Friday afternoon and depressed on Sunday evening. As a matter of fact, the number one risk for heart disease is job stress and/or job dissatisfaction; more people die on Monday morning than at any other day or time of the week.

Why, then, do people stay in jobs that are unrewarding and damaging to their health? For many, it's simply a fear of change. They find it easier to stay in comfortable ruts and collect gold watches at retirement. Unfortunately, while their comfortable lifestyles may be materially rewarding, they don't always reflect what people believe is important in their emotional and spiritual lives. Even if you're surrounded by every symbol of the good life, you may be suffering from malaise and deep-rooted dissatisfaction. That malaise sets in because many of us have never been encouraged to stop and ask ourselves, "Am I doing what I want?"

You are suited to just as many occupations as you are wrong for. You can change to a more suitable job if you have outgrown your position. Even while you're still employed, you can be planning your escape. Remember, this isn't just a job change—this is your life!

Finding the right organizational fit is important, too. Companies' personalities are just as different as people's. Your company's structure may be rigid or relaxed; it may treasure hard work and reliability, or new ideas and flexibility; it may insist on strict adherence to the hierarchy or form committees that include several levels of employees. In any case, checking out a company is just as important as checking out a job.

Deciding how radical a change you want, and what that change requires, is vital before you even begin to make a career shift. You need to examine your needs, values, interests, and purpose, as well as any transferable skills you already have. For example, ministers or teachers looking for personnel work may be able to transfer many of the skills they have already developed (such as advising, mentoring, communicating, teaching, motivating, supporting, arbitrating, problem solving, organizing, scheduling, delegating and planning). But an artist who decides to become a banker needs a lot of additional training and may have incompatible needs and interests. The unstructured, free-flowing creative skills of the artist typically don't translate into the analytical, highly structured skills required of a banker.

Companies' personalities are just as different as peoples. Finding the right organizational fit is important.

Before leaving a job or investing time or money in further education, think over your career change carefully. Give yourself time to make a well-reasoned decision. Find out if you are, in fact, a Quester. Find out if you could become one.

Chapter 5

The Career Cycle
Meets the Life Cycle

Adulthood is not a plateau. It is a time of change. Adults
continue to grow throughout life—mentally, psychologically, and
spiritually. Recent research describes adult growth and
development as a cycle that follows an underlying, universal
path. Many influences along the way shape this course. They
may produce alternate routes or detours, they may speed up or
slow down the timetable, or they may stop the developmental
journey altogether. This journey continues as long as you live,
following a basic sequence of stages, issues and concerns.
This is called life cycle theory, and it assumes you will pass
through the stages as long as you continue to realize your
potential. But the theory cannot predict how you will deal with
your developmental issues. The career stages—Beginning
Career, Developing Career, Maturing Career and Continuing
Career—are inextricably linked to the developmental stages of
other components of your life cycle. They are described in this
Chapter.

Life Cycle Basics

Your personality or identity is formed by many external and
internal influences. Your culture, occupation, social class,

family, interpersonal relationships, leisure activities, social roles, image and participation in the world and global events constitute the external forces. Your internal realm is composed of your spiritual origins and genetic makeup which includes, body build, intelligence, temperament and vulnerability. Throughout life, these two systems interact to influence your identity and personality. As events in the external system are interpreted by the internal system, crucial shifts in needs and values can throw you off balance. These are signals telling you to change and move on to the next stage. These shifts occur throughout life. Sadly, however, many people refuse to recognize them.

For each external system, you have a corresponding inner sub-identity. Your identity is made up of several such sub-identities, which represent your various life roles. You have an occupational identity, a family identity, a social identity, an interpersonal identity, a leisure identity and a spiritual identity. Each plays a different role in your life. Some people have large occupational and family identities, with smaller leisure, social, and spiritual identities. For others, the balance is reversed. Still others have sub-identities that are completely balanced. Moreover, the size of your identities changes as you mature. Parents with small children typically have larger family identities in their late 20s and early 30s than they did before they had children; and when their children leave the nest, their family identities will become smaller again.

As the life cycle progresses, you move through alternating developmental and transitional stages. Each stage presents a unique set of tasks you must master and problems to solve.

Between each developmental period you'll experience transitional periods that allow you to question who you are and where you are going. These transitional periods give you time to reexamine your needs and values, to take another look at your external life systems, to explore and evaluate your options, and to make decisions to either deepen or alter your earlier commitments. Each transition takes from three to five years. And each developmental period can take from five to eight years.

Transitional periods are times of disequilibrium and anxiety. Dangers arise both in moving and in staying put. If you stay with a life component after you have outgrown it, you may betray yourself and limit your possibilities; if you break out, you impose burdens on yourself and may fail to find what you seek. Either way, you face dangers and losses as well as gains. If you are growing, almost half of your adult life is spent in modifying that life.

Every initiation involves a termination of what came before. The developmental periods are necessary for stability; the transitional periods are necessary for growth. This process represents the overriding polarity you must integrate in your life—the polarity of change versus continuity, the problem of how to maintain a continuous sense of yourself while growing.

Developmental periods are just as important as transitional periods. If your life contained nothing but transitions, you would feel as though you were being whirled in a centrifuge. If it contained only developmental periods, you would experience yourself as an inert lump. At one pole, you risk anxiety; at the other, depression. Your life must move between the two as you try to combine solidity with forward movement, security with risk.

Often significant positive or negative experiences cause us to reexamine our lives and come to terms with developmental issues. These experiences include marriage, the birth of a child, the death of a parent, serious illness, travel, the loss of a job, and divorce. Any of these may cause a shift in values and goals.

Adults in transition may be every bit as miserable as adolescents. But those who face up to the agonizing self-evaluation and go about setting future goals develop healthier, happier, and more mature identities. Failure to resolve the

Adults in transition may be every bit as miserable as adolescents. But those who face up to the self-evaluation will develop a healthier, happier and more mature identity.

difficulties of transitions can lead to severe severe physical and emotional problems, including high blood pressure, heart attacks, alcoholism, depression and even suicide.

Many problems and issues adults must deal with appear and reappear in new forms throughout the life cycle. They are not the exclusive property of any age group. Issues of intimacy and occupation, for example, haunt us forever. We find compromises for a while, then must renegotiate them. And so it goes.

You may face five, six or more transitional periods: at adolescence, age 30, age 40, 50, 60, 70 and other times. Of course, you may not face them exactly on schedule. Although the phases are normal, not everyone passes through all of them. Some people get fixated at one particular stage and spend the rest of their lives making futile attempts to work it through. Those who have difficulty making transitions often resort to familiar, earlier behavior patterns. A three-year-old adjusting to a new baby in the family may forget toilet training or refuse to speak. A man in his late 30s may resume the dating behavior (now extramarital) of earlier years to avoid the pain of advancing to another developmental level.

While some adults fail to adjust to new stages, those who weather transitions often do so by finding new meaning in their work and other parts of their lives. They may accomplish this by making some change, such as leaving a dissatisfying job, returning to school, getting married, seeing a marriage counselor or leaving an unhappy marriage.

Having realistic expectations about impending crises and transitions can help you ease the stress and pain of their arrival. If you do some thinking about your life transitions and prepare for them, you will be better able to manage them. The following chart provides an overview of the career and life stages and the major career tasks all growing people experience throughout the life cycle.

Career and Life Stages

The Beginning Career
Adolescent Transition completed (approximately ages 17–23)

The Beginning Career Advances
Age-20 Developmental Period

- First full-time job is assumed.
- Needs for expansion, career mastery and self-motivation prevail.
- Little self-evaluation occurs.
- Lifelong patterns may be established.

The Developing Career
Age-30 Transition (approximately ages 28–33)

The Developing Career Expands
Age-30 Developmental Period

- Values, priorities, and goals shift; a more balanced life is valued.
- Short- and long-range goals are pursued.
- Productivity, fulfillment, excitement and creativity are enjoyed.
- Occupational and/or job changes may occur.

The Maturing Career
Age-40 Transition (approximately ages 37–45)

The Maturing Career Grows
Age-40 Developmental Period

- Need for job satisfaction heightens.
- Creative leadership peaks.
- Interest in guiding the young blossoms.

Age-50 Transition (approximately ages 48–53)

The Maturing Career Strengthens
Age–50 Developmental Period

- Needs for job satisfaction and a balanced life deepen.
- Innovative leadership and mentoring activities continue.

The Continuing Career
Age-60 Transition (approximately ages 58-63)

The Continuing Career Flourishes
Age-60 Developmental Period

- Career options (including retirement) are explored and evaluated.
- Continuing opportunities for purpose, meaning, direction, and growth are identified and pursued.

- Another occupational cycle is completed.

Age-70 Transition (approximately ages 68–73)

The Continuing Career Continues to Flourish
Age-70 Developmental Period

- Decisions to continue paid employment, engage in volunteer activities, or pursue a more leisurely lifestyle are contemplated.
- Choices are made and plans implemented to pursue activities that offer opportunities for continuing purpose, meaning, and growth.

Age-80 Transition (approximately ages 78–83)

The Continuing Career Reevaluates
Age-80 Developmental Period

- Decisions are made with respect to continued work, volunteer activities, or pursuit of a more leisurely lifestyle.
- Continued desire to be involved in activities that provide a sense of purpose, meaning , and direction.

Age-90 Transition (approximately ages 88-93)

The Continuing Career Continues to Reevaluate
Age-90 Developmental Period

- Decisions are continuing to be made with respect to work, volunteer activities or pursuit of a more leisurely lifestyle.
- Health and living arrangements are addressed.
- Continued desire to be involved in activities that provide a

sense of purpose, meaning and direction.

Age-100 Transition (approximately ages 98-103)

The Career Cycle: Entry, Mastery and Disengagement

Your occupational identity is part of your overall sense of who you are. If you are growing as a person and developing in your job, you will have several occupational identities throughout your career cycle.

A healthy, vital occupational identity has three stages: entry, mastery and disengagement. During the *entry stage*, you make a commitment to a job, become involved and develop the skills and personal meaning that make up your occupational identity.

In the mastery stage, you work hard to achieve excellence, acquire experience, and achieve a sense of accomplishment, enjoyment, challenge and purpose. This is the most productive stage for both employees and their bosses. You gain enjoyment and fulfillment; your boss gains a satisfied and productive employee. You are confident and energetic.

If your job loses its challenge (because your employer cannot or will not alter or expand your tasks, or if you cannot or will not move into another position), the quality of your performance will start to deteriorate. You may begin to disconnect from your work. In this disengagement stage you stop using your skills enthusiastically because you are no longer getting the perks you earlier enjoyed. The challenge, meaning and fulfillment are gone. Your enthusiasm, energy and confidence plummet.

Forming your career identity is a lifelong process. If, like a Quester, you are growing and developing, you will enter, master and disengage from several positions. These positions may be sequential, each building on the other in a logical sequence of increasing skills and responsibilities: For example, one might advance from teacher to department head to supervisor to principal. Or the positions may be entirely unrelated: For example, one might move from construction worker to teacher to accountant to musician to police officer. You develop a healthy occupational identity when you commit yourself fully to a set of work tasks and master them. When the job is no longer rewarding, you move on. You move while your identity is still healthy.

Forming your career identity is a lifelong process.

Remember *Kathy* from earlier chapters? Her first full-time job was with a large insurance firm. At first, Kathy was enthusiastic about the position, but four years later, her feelings began to change. She no longer felt alert and enthusiastic. She had moved from the entry to the mastery to the disengagement stage of her job in just four years.

If she had been able to move to another position in which she was learning new tasks, Kathy would have continued growing. She would have been in the entry stage of another occupational cycle. If her employer had expanded her tasks, she might have stayed in the mastery stage for several more years. But Kathy left the company after working in the same position for seven years. She was in the disengagement stage for four of those years. Today, as an enthusiastic law student, she is in the entry stage of her second occupational cycle.

The Cyclical Pattern

Questers tend to reorganize themselves, their lifestyles and their career goals every five to ten years. Staying in one job for five to ten years seems to be the norm. When they no longer derive desired rewards from their jobs, they tend to leave.

Most Questers set their own rhythm of change.

Throughout their lives, they continue the process of entry, mastery and disengagement. Most Questers set their own rhythm of change.

The length of your occupational cycles depends on your occupation; the strength of your intrinsic job needs, such as challenge and growth; and where you are in the life cycle. Many Questers in middle management have occupational cycles of four to eight years. Questers in occupations such as teaching and air traffic control have similar occupational cycles. However, Quester hairdressers who work for others generally change jobs every three years. Many nurses and others who want to take advantage of better advancement opportunities or higher salaries also change positions every two or three years. Examining the career paths of all these workers, however, reveals a cyclical career pattern. The rhythm of change is apparently related to events occurring in other components of the workers' lives—and the transition periods of their life cycles.

This cyclical pattern of movement is not the same as the changes made by entry-level employees and recent college graduates in the Beginning Career. These young adults, who are still exploring the fit between their personal qualities and occupations or organizations, may stay in jobs for only a few months to a few years as they learn more about themselves and the work world. Some change jobs several times before finding the right fit.

Questers who are in senior management or professional jobs may remain in their positions for ten or more years. Because these Questers continually create greater challenges and growth opportunities for themselves, they maintain their feelings of mastery, competence and confidence. Self-employed people can similarly continue to grow in their careers. However, workers who don't receive challenge, autonomy, and other desired career rewards tend to become bored and lack enthusiasm and confidence These disengaged people may remain in their jobs for their entire working lives.

Some refer to them as "shelf-sitters" or "deadwood." Whom do you resemble?

Interaction of the Career and Life Cycles

The career cycles of Questers often imitate their lif e cycles. When they are in the occupationally disengaged stages , they are usually also facing transition stages of their life cycles. Let's look at the Questers to see ho w their career and life cycles intertwine.

Kathy left her management job dur ing her Age-30 Transition. The self-assessment she did dur ing this transition was influenced by her growing job dissatisfaction. Feelings of depression o ver her father's death also affected her. As she looked more closely at her values and goals, she came to ter ms with the major issue of her Age-30 Transition—changing occupations.

Vern's occupational cycles also coincided with his lif e cycle transitions. Vern started work as an ambulance attendant and loved it. Six years later, his enthusiasm gone, he decided to disengage. He knew that neither he nor his patients would benefit if he stayed put. Vern returned to school to study ph ysiotherapy. Soon after, he married. His decisions to marry and to change his occupation resulted from the self-evaluation he did dur ing his Age-30 Transition.

Vern liked working as a physiotherapist in a hospital. Initially, he derived the job perks he wanted—challenge, variety, scope and autonomy. But during his fourth year, he became increasingly fr ustrated and tense because he had little input into decisions aff ecting his job. Three years later, he decided to tak e a year off to sor t things out.

Vern's time-out was part of his Age-40 Transition and was closely tied to his disengagement from his ph ysiotherapy position. A year off helped him put his life into perspective. He returned to school to get some upgrading in physical therapy and then established his own consulting business. Vern, now 47, is in the developmental period of his 40s and the entry stage of his third occupational cycle, a physiotherapy consultant.

Today, a number of managerial and professional workers are becoming more involved in cyclical careers. Many top executives set themselves time horizons of three to ten years to tackle the tasks, see the results, and then then move on. Both the executives and their organizations benefit. The executive has the excitement and challenge of accomplishing a difficult set of tasks and maintaining his or her flexibility. The organization has an enthusiastic, innovative manager who can bring fresh new ideas into the company.

It's sad to see so many workers stay 30 or 40 years in jobs in which they are psychologically disengaged, watching the clock as the days and weeks pass. With prestige or financial rewards their jailer, they abandon reality, living unfulfilled lives because the thought of starting anew seems humiliating, degrading, or frightening.

The Beginning Career

Your first developmental period begins with a commitment to your first full-time job. This is a critical time. As you take hold of the adult world, you must make decisions, commit yourself to a new set of roles, and perform tasks that will strongly influence your later life. The lifestyle and occupation you pursue in early adulthood is the framework for experiences throughout your life. But before we look at the Age-20 Developmental period, let's backtrack to review the adolescent transition, so we can better understand the transition that marks entry into adulthood.

The Adolescent Transition

Late adolescence, which occurs from ages 17 or 18 to ages 22 or 23, is an critical period. Many decisions you make about career and life goals will affect your growth potential during adulthood. Remember when so many changes were taking place in your inner and outer worlds? Physical growth and sexual maturity were accompanied by maturation of your thinking capability. Your ability to think in abstract terms multiplied as you struggled with problems, devised solutions, evaluated experiences, and reconsidered your values. You looked at reality from many angles and considered the implications of your decisions. As you finished high school, you wondered what to do next: travel, continue your education or begin working?

Making decisions about a career and other life roles, such as family and sex roles, are the major psychological tasks of adolescence. Erik Erikson, one of the pioneers of life cycle theory, called this the search for identity.

According to psychologist James Marcia, two factors are essential in attaining a mature identity. First, adolescents must explore several options before choosing among life's alternatives. Trying on different roles, they struggle to make decisions about occupations, values and lifestyles. Second, adolescents must finally commit to investing themselves in their choices. They may be in one of four identity states: *moratorium, identity achieved, identity foreclosed* or *identity confused.* Not all adolescents achieve a mature identity, nor do all achieve identity states at the same speed.

As you made the adolescent transition to greater maturity, you probably experienced confusion and depression. The task of bringing the pieces of your life into a coordinated and clear self-identity is difficult and time-consuming. Those who can consciously explore their options and make commitments to desired values and goals at this point typically emerge stronger and in control of their destinies.

Your identity is never static. Of course, your identity is never static. Each time you complete a transition phase and reevaluate your values and goals, you are reformulating your identity. An identity foreclosed young adult may become an identity achieved adult—a Quester—as he or she comes to terms with the career decisions made dur ing the Age-30, Age-40 or later-life transitions. How you deal with the transitions in your life determine whether you become a Quester.

Choosing an occupation is a cr ucial step. Work can be a source of pleasure, self-esteem and goal fulfillment, or it can contribute to disappointment and feelings of failure. Many adolescents are anxious about career decisions . They are afraid of making a mistak e. But decisions we make during adolescence are not irreversible. We can contin ually reinvent ourselves and change or modify aspects of our careers and our lives. No learning or experience is ever wasted. We can innovatively combine the knowledge and experience we gain in varied life situations to create our next career adventures.

Four Identity States of Adolescents

• *Moratorium.* In this "time-out" period, adolescents have not yet made commitments or invested much of themselves in others; they are still vague about their own values. Even while delaying their commitments, however, they are actively struggling to find the right roles. Experimenting by "playing the field" with the opposite sex, working at odd jobs, or trying different courses in their first few years at college, they search for roles that fit them. Ideally, adult demands can be put on hold so that the y are free to experiment. Most young people in this state are v ague about what they want to do.

Kathy was in a mor atorium before she committed herself to an insurance job. She tried on several jobs and then went for career counseling before she decided on an occupation.

Vince also had went through a moratorium when when he dropped out of his first y ear of college to travel in Europe for two years. When he returned home, he committed himself to a five-year geology program. Kathy and Vince were lucky. Their parents helped with the finances.

• *Identity achieved.* Those who have reached the state of identity achievement have explored their options and made commitments to desired values and goals. They know who they are and what they want to do. They have developed strong, healthy identities by experimenting, carefully evaluating alternatives, and making their own decisions. Their efforts to resolve questions of identity may have taken them onto paths of overzealous commitment, emotional involvement, alienation or playful wandering. Flexible and inner-directed, they set realistic goals and are unlikely to subscribe to authoritarian values. They are committed, at least for a while, to occupational goals. Having successfully worked through a moratorium, they are more mature than adolescents in the other groups.

• *Identity foreclosed.* Young adults in the identity foreclosed group have made commitments without exploring their options. They seem very sure of what they want to be.

> *James,* a fourth-year medical student, studied hard to get good grades in college so that he could enter medical school. His parents thought medicine was a good profession for him; it paid well, had prestige, and provided financial and job security.

> *Judy,* the daughter of a prominent banker, attended finishing school and then a prestigious women's college because that was the "family destiny." (Often, the family destiny will define value as striving toward intellectual achievement, independence, power and status, or societal contribution.)

James, Judy, and other adolescents like them make commitments without exploring their options. They passively accept the identities their parents or significant others cut out for them without seriously evaluating their own goals and values. People with foreclosed identities are generally more brittle, authoritarian, and conventional than those in any other group. They have not yet broken loose from the significant adults in their lives. They are "locked in." Until recently, most young women in our culture were part of this group.

• *Identity confused.* Adolescents in this group have not yet consciously explored their options, nor have they made commitments. Instead, they have retreated from the task of defining who they are or what they want to do. They may perform well in school and social roles, but they feel like misfits. They tend to opt out of situations to avoid commitment. Often, in early attempts to define themselves, they become immobilized by feelings of inferiority. But, unlike those in a moratorium, they don't seem compelled to do much about it. Some young people in their early 20s who seem to live in a world of suspended animation are actually in a confused state. They can't bring themselves to make career commitments—or any extended plans for that matter.

If you explored your occupational and educational options during adolescence and then made a commitment to a desired program of studies or occupation based on your research, then you were an identity achieved young adult. You probably made a sound career decision. If you think you didn't make a good choice, however, all is not lost. You can still make changes to your career.

Below, we'll look at some of the basic characteristics and tasks of young adults entering the adult work world.

The Beginning Career Advances
Your need to expand and your career drive are likely to take precedence during the Beginning Career. Young people are busily engaged in the increasing responsibilities of career, marriage or relationships, and acquiring knowledge. The road ahead is exhilarating, conflicting, and sometimes overwhelming—it doesn't leave much time for self-evaluation. But most young people are certain they have what it takes to overcome any challenge. They are eager to shape a dream, create a lifestyle, and make something out of their lives. Career plays an important part in realizing their vision, but young people must also strike a balance among work, love and leisure.

As always, two impulses are at work now. One is the need to build a firm, safe lifestyle for the future by making strong commitments. The other is the urge to explore and experiment, to create structures that are easily reversible, to satisfy the cravings of the riskier self. Both of these needs can easily be taken to extremes. Like the identity confused group, young people who are too tentative tend to be transient and unstable. They spend their 20s hopping from one job to the next, and from one personal encounter to another. On the other hand, young people who commit themselves too strongly (like those in the identity foreclosed group) tend to be fearful, rigid adults who cling too tightly to their first choices. To maintain occupational flexibility and adaptability, you must strike a balance between tentativeness and commitment. You need to explore your alternatives, keep your options open, avoid strong commitments, and not blindly hang on to choices.

The Beginning Career is more stable than the transitions that lead to and from it. It begins with a commitment to a full-time job to prepare for a life of work. For many, the process starts in the early 20s and ends with the Age-30 Transition. However, given permission to experiment, prolonged schooling, and ample time out, it is not unusual for some Questers to be nearly 30 before they start on their Beginning Careers.

The Beginning Career is a mastery stage when young people gain positive feedback, achieve competence, and become self-motivated.

The Beginning Career is a mastery stage when young people gain positive feedback, achieve competence and become self-motivated. The positive feelings that flow toward them fill them with self-confidence.

Devlin, a 25-year-old middle manager, says of his career goals, "Success and greater responsibility provide me with greater motivation to reach my career goals with my employer. … I'm interested in obtaining more efficiency in all aspects of my personal and business dealings."

The future path of your career starts with

the Beginning Career. Patterns that affect your future lifestyle often begin here. Many older Questers in the Maturing or the Continuing Career started here. But these patterns can be changed. Some current Questers were Traditionalists or Self-Seekers in the Beginning Career but moved to the Quester track as they gained knowledge experience, and the courage to risk.

Most Questers in the Beginning Career have already confronted the challenges of the adolescent transition. They have committed themselves to occupational goals and are working on implementing these. They have struck a balance between tentativeness and commitment. They have committed themselves to a career, but they know that technology and their own development will one day change the pace of their lives. Both Kathy and Vern are young Questers who recognize the need to be tentative.

A number of Beginning Career Questers may seem a lot like their Traditionalist and Self-Seeker peers, but they have been through many broadening experiences. They may endorse several values, but personal and career development matter most. They want positive rewards from their jobs, such as autonomy, challenge and opportunities for self-expression. They also want quality from other life components. They are not afraid to work hard for what they want. Many put in long hours on weekends to achieve their goals. They also may make many material sacrifices to reach these goals.

> *Jose's* goal is to own a jewelry store. To get enough money and experience to set out on his own, Jose has taken a job as a management trainee with a large retail chain; at the same time, he works evenings sorting mail. On the weekends, Jose throws all his energy into designing jewelry. His wife doesn't mind. Designing and making jewelry is one of her hobbies, too.

> *Rob* is another Beginning Quester who sees work as a major source of satisfaction. After trying out a variety of

courses and programs at college, Rob wound up in physical engineering. He likes his first full-time job as an engineer for a large consulting firm. He enjoys the challenge, is involved in his work, and relishes the positive feedback. Working gives him a sense of competence and confidence.

Unlike many of his Traditionalist colleagues, Rob's sense of competence is inner-directed. Money and promotions come second to the feelings of accomplishment he gets from completing a challenging task. Moreover, he is less concerned with socializing simply to get ahead. For him, the status, affiliations and external guideposts many rely on don't count. He places more value on a self-defined lifestyle and career goals. To Rob, a job is an "opportunity for challenge, freedom, a sense of identity, autonomy, involvement or creativity." His career goals are open-ended. He wants "to learn, to experience, to grow."

Petite, attractive, 27-year-old *Susan* is another young Quester with similar values and goals. A journalist for three years, she is happily involved in her work and has also managed to combine work and marriage successfully. Susan and her husband of two years have worked out a system of sharing domestic responsibilities. And like many young women approaching their late 20s who have postponed having children or decided against parenthood, Susan is more satisfied with her life than most of her Traditionalist contemporaries. Late motherhood is a bona-fide pattern among many female Questers under 30.

Beginning Career Questers who have been in the same jobs for four or five years may begin to feel stale or bored. Company policies incompatible with their values may trouble them. A few years earlier, they simply didn't care. But now, the excitement, romance and challenge that made their jobs special begin to disappear. Questers who feel this way are in the late mastery or early disengagement stages of their first occupational cycle. A series of jolts in other areas of their lives may begin to wean them from earlier illusions. Their experiences with a career, marriage or the death of a parent are prepar ing them for the Age-30 Transition. At the same time, their feelings, needs, and values are beginning to change. So the Beginning Career ends.

The Developing Career

The Age-30 Transition

The Age-30 Transition ushers in the De veloping Career. Many people begin to question their past decisions . They may realize they have ignored impor tant needs, interests, and desires. Now, new choices must be made and commitments altered or deepened in all major areas of lif e. For some, this period is marked by turmoil and confusion. For others, it involves an intellectual inquiry into the past.

As you progress through this tr ansition, you may feel confused, sluggish and dissatisfied. The desire to tr y new things begins to take precedence over safety needs. Apparent restrictions you face are the outg rowth of decisions you made in your late teens or ear ly 20s, choices that w ere perfectly appropriate at the time. Now, however, the fit feels wrong. This dissatisfaction may make itself felt suddenly, emphatically, sometimes precipitated by an external event. Often, however, the need to change begins slo wly, with a vague but persistent sense of w anting to do and be something more.

Often the need to change begins slowly, with a vague but persistent sense of wanting to do or be something more.

Remember *Al,* the farmer in Chapter 1? As he approached the Age-30 Transition, Al began to feel that his life and his job no longer had pur pose and meaning. Al's Age-30 Transition was tied to his occupational cycle. At 28, after working in computers for five years, he was in the ear ly disengagement stage of his job. The meaning and excitement had disappeared. This, coupled with the birth of his first child, pushed him to reassess his life and career goals.

You may discover a change in how you look at time. You become aware that your life is finite. Death is still just an abstract fear, however; you still have time to do it all. New experiences are waiting. You are impatient to get on with your life, but the desire is not yet urgent.

The severity of the transition phase is reflected in the moratorium of one or more years many Questers take at this point.

Adrian, a happy entrepreneur, "walked away from the world" during his transition. He needed time to rethink the direction of his life. Adrian was particularly restless as he approached 30. While he performed his management tasks dutifully, he was in the disengagement stage of his occupational cycle. His job seemed frustrating and restricting.

Adrian emerged from his moratorium with greater self-understanding and renewed confidence to move forward in his new, self-determined career. He and his wife became partners in a variety of entrepreneurial projects. Today, Adrian describes his job passionately: "It represents a future; it gives me an economic base to pursue my own lifestyle." Now 34, Adrian is working on the goals he set during the transition. When he is no longer challenged, he will probably seek greater challenges.

Janet also experienced a moratorium. A creative and assertive young woman, she quit her job as a news photographer to travel in Europe for a year. She had no definite future plans. Even though she liked her colleagues, she no longer felt challenged at work. The marital problems she was experiencing aggravated her depression and lethargy. Counseling sessions with a psychologist gave Janet the necessary support and courage to "get away from everything for a while."

"While in Europe, I smiled for the first time in years. I returned home a different person. I felt happier, more at peace with myself, than I had felt in a long time." Janet changed both her job and her marital status. But it was a difficult process. "When I was in Europe, I prayed for help in making the right decision about my marriage in every church I visited as a tourist … and there were plenty of them!"

Questers who take time-out periods show it can be helpful. They typically emerge from their breaks with greater self-understanding, renewed confidence, and the courage to move forward in their self-determined careers and lifestyles.

Roman is a potential Quester. Currently, he's recovering from surgery. He has a four-year business degree and has worked as a manager for the past seven years. Roman has some hard decisions to make about his career and life goals. Until now, he has been doing what everyone around him told him to do. That's probably why he's ill. Not feeling good about your job carries high physical costs. You only deceive yourself if you think it doesn't.

Many Traditionalists in their late 20s or early 30s experience similar thoughts and feelings as Questers. But instead of making the changes they need, they simply modify their lives to place higher value on family and leisure, building directly on the past and making few real changes.

Men may feel anxious about making it through the Age-30 Transition, but women face an even more turbulent time. Women have more options and, therefore, more decisions to consider. The "biological clock" increases the pressure they face to make decisions about when and if they want a family. For some, occupational change means dropping out of the work world to have children and stay home with them. Many say they would like to return to work in a few years. A few feel they have had enough.

Most women Questers marry later than their Traditionalist contemporaries and have fewer children—on the average, only one. Those who wait are usually happy and enjoy a balance of marriage, career and motherhood. They relish love, family and work. Many are willing to spend extra time on their work, but they are not willing to allow their love or family relationships to disintegrate for the sake of professional or business success.

> *Beverly* is a good example. She spent the married years of her early 20s as a graduate student engaged in occasional research projects. Her Age-30 Transition brought a strong desire to trade career for family. For the next seven years, Beverly was deeply engaged in domestic life. Then, at 37, she began to think about returning to work full-time. She felt she was "getting narrow." That's part of the complexity of women's development.

Clearly, the passage into the 30s stimulates a psychological change of gears on all fronts. For Questers, this transition brings the desire to broaden their lives and make some changes. Many tear up the part of the lives they spent most of their 20s so carefully building. Those who have been in corporate slots feel narrow and restricted. Some decide to open their own businesses. Others return to school to prepare for new occupations. Still others decide to enjoy life by traveling for a while. If they have been in training, such as graduate study, now they eagerly look forward to starting a new job. If they have been single, they long for marriage and emotional attachments. Women who have been pursuing a career may decide to have children and become more domestic.

Moreover, self-assessment is often linked to other life crises, such as divorce or job dissatisfaction. As experiences snowball, self-evaluation, a necessary prerequisite to passing successfully through the transition, takes place.

Transition challenges occur whether people are entering or leaving jobs. But the solution most Questers find is constant. They are willing to listen to their inner voices and willing to risk. Even if they take no overt action during the Age-30 Transition, they experience an unseen shift, a change in the way they feel about life that will likely lead to later changes. The equilibrium regained by reaching the other side of 30 enables people to reexamine their origins and to acknowledge parts of themselves that were left out by earlier choices.

The Developing Career Expands

For the Questers who remain in the work world, the decision to make a commitment to another position marks an entry into the developmental period of their 30s, and the entry stage of another occupational cycle. This is a productive, fulfilling, exciting and creative time. Both their personal and occupational lives seem fuller and richer. During the Developing Career, most Questers deepen their commitments and invest more of themselves in their work, family and other valued interests. They pursue their short- and long-range plans and goals.

During the Developing Career, most Questers deepen their commitments and invest more of themselves in their work, family, and other valued interests.

The reappraisal of the Age-30 Transition leads many adults to shift their values, priorities and goals. They become more self-aware and more interested in sharing their understanding of themselves and others. They place higher value on the quality of life. Leading a more balanced life, becoming more family-oriented, and developing relationships may take priority. Job satisfaction suddenly becomes more important than climbing a corporate ladder or earning higher wages.

Questers also become more aware of their strong needs to become self-fulfilled, to derive challenge and independence from their jobs, and to make use of their skills. They have outgrown their earlier choices. All of them want to avoid stagnation. Their reappraisals often help them make the decision to leave jobs when they feel stagnant. The Age-30 Transition is usually interrelated with a job transition. Many Questers have completed one occupational cycle and are eager to get started in another. But their decisions do not come easily.

Tall and well built, *Mark* has blond hair and brown eyes. He is good-looking and well liked by his peers. Mark completed his college degree at 22 and entered a management training program with an international banking firm in a large Western city. His decision was largely influenced by family history: His father was the president and major shareholder of a large manufacturing firm, and his older brother was a successful executive in the family operation. Mark's goal was to become a senior executive. He enjoyed his work, especially the contact with his colleagues and subordinates. But over the next seven years, he gradually came to realize he just wasn't cut out to be a manager.

Mark explains: "Two factors influenced my self-appraisal and consequent decision to leave management—the breakdown of my marriage and the fact that my father, who was in his mid-50s, was struck with two heart attacks. These events helped me realize that I wasn't going to live forever, and that if I only had one life to live, I shouldn't be wasting it. I should be involved in doing something I enjoy."

Then 31, Mark decided to enter broadcasting, a longtime love and hobby. The only experience he had was at his college radio station, years before. Combined with some initiative and a willingness to take a salary cut and change his life–style, that was enough. He got his foot in the door in a small town 100 miles from his hometown. Now a disc jockey and part-time announcer, Mark loves his work.

We can see evidence that Quester qualities can be strengthened at any age. Some Traditionalists become Questers during their Age-30 Transition.

Talking about the changes in her values and lifestyle over the past few years, new Quester *Alice* says, "Position, status, and power were extremely important to me in my 20s. Now I'm different. I'm more self-aware and I'm more interested in the quality of life, work, and leisure. I also know that I need a job that gives me autonomy, scope, and challenge. ... I have taken steps to do something about changing my status. I've made plans to enter a profession."

Brian is also in the mastery stage of his second occupational cycle. He dropped out of high school at the end of his sophomore year for a job doing office work for a railway company. He did well. Promoted to supervisor and then to management, Brian completed his high school diploma at night school. His first job lasted 13 years. Then, he began to feel restless. He remembers feeling trapped as he rounded the corner to his 28th birthday: "I wanted to do something different ... something I felt better about. Helping people meant more to me than financial rewards."

But Brian had a wife and two children to support. Could he do it? The deciding factor came suddenly, with the death of his mother two years later. "Life is too short not to do what I want to do," he thought. So, at age 31, Brian quit his job and went back to school to get a degree in occupational health and safety. "My wife was great about it," he says. A former dietitian, she went back to work to support the family. By taking extra courses at night, on weekends, and during the summers, Brian completed his degree in three years.

Two years into his new occupation, Brian loves his job: "I feel very good about life in general. I understand myself better, I'm a better person, and I think I've become more broad-minded and liberal. ... We have more conversations as a family, and I know where the children are coming from now."

Far from being vagabonds, most Questers who set out to find more satisfying careers need roots. Questers who tore up the structure of their 20s are particularly keen to build a solid base in their 30s. As he decorates his new apartment, Mark, the disc jockey who moved to a new town, says, "I want to feel I'm a very stable citizen." Many Questers aren't bothered much by work pressures. They don't feel helpless in the face of continuing distress. Questers often feel a sense of exhilaration from a challenging job well done. They feel in control of their work and lives.

Bill, a Quester who is currently disengaging from his second occupational cycle, is a good example. A sensitive, reflective, diplomatic man who describes himself as "a loner and a lover of people," Bill worked in a government department after completing his master's degree in forestry. He was promoted up the ladder at regular intervals but more slowly than he would have liked. Gradually, Bill became bored, disinterested, and disenchanted with his job and lifestyle. When he received an offer to teach forestry at a two-year college, he willingly accepted. "Teaching was something I had always wanted to do. I thought it would provide me with more meaning, interest and freedom than the government job, and it does."

Four years later, Bill was still teaching, but he was thinking that in the future he might like to devote his time to writing. He had been married for 12 years, but was not particularly happy. Bill and his wife had been through two separations, and it looked as though their relationship might not survive.

Questers often feel a sense of exhileration from a challenging job well done.

Bill is in the process of disengaging himself from both his marriage and his second occupational cycle. The unhappy marriage and his desire to tr y something new are precipitating and aiding the self-assessment that accompanies a transition. For Bill, it will be the Age-40 Transition.

Many Questers who have been involved in their new occupations for three to four years are also making transitions. They are beginning to think about what the y want to do next. They have mastered their second set of tasks and are enthusiastically looking forward to conquering new ones. Bill, for example, is still interested in wr iting. Others, like Melvin, are pondering expanding their businesses. Still others are considering returning to school to make more dramatic occupational shifts.

The Maturing Career

While many people dislike the term, mid-life is our most creative and productive time. Our careers kick into high gear, and real career advancement can occur.

Our perceptions of mid-life vary with our age. Forty-year-olds perceive mid-life to begin at 50; those in their 50s perceive it to be older. However we look at it, increased longevity has extended our middle years. The Maturing Career today spans the years from about 40 to 60. It starts with the Age-40 Transition and includes the Age-40 De velopmental period, the Age-50 Transition and the Age-50 Developmental period.

Trends suggest that distinctions between Maturing Career and Continuing Career will continually become more blurred and of little consequence. Nevertheless, the characteristics and developmental tasks that distinguish these stages help us to better understand our life-long career development.

The Age-40 Transition

The Age-40 Transition acts as a link between the Developing Career and the Maturing Career. The transition can occur anytime between ages 37 and 45, depending on when your earlier transitions began and ended, how many life crises you have faced, how you dealt with them, and where you are in your existing occupational cycle.

During this transition, we become aware of our advancing age and death. Time seems scarce. We begin to think about the time we have left to live, rather than the time we've already lived. We become aware of our lost youth and our faltering physical powers. We question the stereotyped roles we have adopted, and we realize we do not have all the answers. We may wonder, "Is this all there is to life?"

Our source of identity moves from outside to inside. This switch causes both men and women to switch from one set of goals in their 20s to a different set by their 40s. We begin to notice previously hidden masculine and feminine aspects of our nature. Men often are caught by surprise as a more tender, feeling side emerges. And many women are amazed to discover a more aggressive, rational side surfacing. We become aware of developing an ethical self. An old part of us is dying—and we are troubled.

During this transition, we may question every part of our lives. To pass through this authenticity crisis, we must listen to our inner voices and critically evaluate ourselves and our goals. We must identify and accept our suppressed and unwanted parts and integrate them into our real selves. Now we must shelve the phony selves we created simply to please others. We must master other tasks, as well: committing ourselves to goals that have meaning and value to us, coming to grips with our bodies' decline and our eventual mortality, and feeling free to express what we previously considered foreign.

Psychologists and psychiatrists who investigate adult development assert that the difficulties of the Age-40

Transition help explain the high rates of alcoholism, depression and suicide that occur during this period. These difficulties also explain why many creative and industrious people burn out in their mid-30s, while others blossom only after that age. Quite often, people who considered themselves successful during young adulthood become disenchanted with their work, spouses or lifestyles at this time. Many question how important and fulfilling their work really is, realizing that career stages that required compliance might have interfered with the development of an achieved identity.

If you have been in a job for 10 or more years without promotions or lateral moves, you are probably already in the disengagement stage. You may be feeling stale, tired, anxious, unattractive, restless, old, burdened or even unappreciated. You may be thinking of getting back to your original career dream after being nudged away from it through earlier career or family demands. Depression, anxiety and other emotional problems may be taking a toll.

Being in charge of your life and your career is increasingly important at this time. You want to produce something lasting and worthwhile. Many who did nothing about their careers in their early 30s may feel panicky now. "This is my last chance!" they cry. Some are forced out of their jobs by obsolescence or technological change. Others flee from well-established bases such as marriage. Still others decide their lives are just fine as they are. Any of these alternatives is okay, if it feels right for you.

> *You must evaluate your life, not by external symbols of success, but by feelings of accomplishment or peace of mind.*

Psychologist Daniel Levinson and his colleagues point out that this is a time of paradox. They describe the dilemma a man faces when he realizes that, if he doesn't make a switch, he will never become his own person; but, if he does, he risks hurting the people he loves by failing. "Having made his bed (marital, occupational, or other), he cannot continue to lie in it. Yet to change is to tear the very fabric of his life, to destroy much that he has built over the last 10 or 15 years".

At this stage you realize that you must evaluate your life, not by external symbols of success such as a prestigious job or a big house, but by internal symbols such as feelings of accomplishment or peace of mind.

> *Bertrand* 41, is thinking of changing jobs again. For the past six years, he's been teaching law at a Midwestern university. Bertrand likes his job. It provides independence and variety. But he's feeling stale and restless. He is thinking about starting a business, something he can be enthusiastic about. A creative man, Bertrand's needs for challenge and growth are stronger than many others feel. Because he understands himself, Bertrand knows he must change soon to keep his occupational identity healthy.

Sometimes ill health or misfortune forces people in this transition to make changes that push them to become Questers.

> *Kit,* a brilliant man of 42, was the controller of a large corporation. He had worked his way up with a master's degree in accounting. Kit's position, salary, and lifestyle were the stuff of which dreams are made. He had a beautiful wife, well-behaved children, a large home with a swimming pool and sauna and luxurious vacations. But he was frustrated and uneasy. His doctor referred him to a career counselor. It soon became apparent that at least some of Kit's frustrations were related to his career. He was in a figures-and-paper job. He belonged in a selling-and-people-persuading position. Kit was lucky. He could ask for a move to a sales department, where he could use his accounting skills. By night, he studied marketing techniques and strategies. Two years later, he was a sales manager.

Martha has a similar story. A married woman of 38 with three children, she was feeling "out of sorts" and didn't know why. The feelings came on gradually. Night after night, she lay awake. Her relationships with her husband and children faltered. She thought she had everything she needed—a loving husband, well-behaved children, a nice home, and enough money to buy the things she needed. Then she let a friend talk her into counseling. It was a wise move.

During her counseling sessions, Martha realized she was putting her own needs second to what she thought her husband and children wanted. Martha's whole world revolved around her family. She gave them her time and even sacrificed many pleasures for them. A year later, Martha had the courage to talk about her feelings. To her surprise, her family understood her needs and encouraged her to pursue a longtime goal to become a dietitian. Soon after, Martha began following her dream. Today, Martha is in the final year of her college program. She is talking like a Quester. She feels great.

For many adults, the Age-40 Transition is so difficult that they fail to make a smooth transition. A long process of frustration and failure follows. A woman whose children no longer seem to need her may become depressed or decide to have another baby. To bring back the excitement of years long past, many men try to reassert their masculine prowess through vigorous physical activity or risky stock ventures. Alcohol and the Internet can become escape routes leading nowhere. Many of these problems are a result of job dissatisfaction and disengagement. Staying on the job physically, while far removed from it intellectually and emotionally, causes many dissatisfied workers to wither. Those adults who weather the crisis often do it by finding new meaning and purpose in more satisfying work or leisure activities.

The Maturing Career Grows
For many Questers, the Maturing Career begins after the

Age-40 Transition. Relatively stable and contented, they understand themselves better. They are in tune with their needs. They are more real, happy, warm and mellow. They feel alive! Their families are still important to them, and so are their friends. But having some time to themselves is becoming more important, too.

During this Age-40 Developmental period, Questers are in the mastery stage of their next occupational cycle. Their job satisfaction is high. So is their productivity. They are creative, but their creativity is more "sculptured" than in earlier years. They form and fashion a product, work and rework the material, act and react to what they are making. In place of the intense, spontaneous and often unconscious creativity of the 20s and early 30s, the creative process now is more deliberate, conscious and analytical. It may continue for years. The creativity of leadership heightens during the Maturing Career. Leadership abilities in education, law and industry are at their highest among those in their 40s, 50s and 60s.

Along with leadership ability, the need to make a lasting and significant contribution to a profession or organization is strongest in middle age. Because developing a future generation of leaders is a significant and highly satisfying contribution, interest in guiding the young blossoms now.

> *Betty,* a Quester politician, radiates star quality that belies her age of 46. She refused entreaties to run for public office a seat in the Senate because, as she said, "I want to be a mentor rather than a power broker." Betty and other Questers like her often become role models to the young women who will succeed them.

Men and women in the Maturing Career may also become interested in people-related work. Adults in people-oriented occupations such as teaching, social work, sales and politics find immense satisfaction in helping others.

Erik Erikson called adults who have dealt with the mid-life

crises *generative.* They are nurturing, protective, productive and creative in a new sense. They feel voluntarily committed to guiding new generations as parents, as business mentors, and as members of society. In contrast, those who haven't dealt with these crises successfully tend to be egocentric, nonproductive, self-indulgent and depressed; they lack the ability to truly care for others.

> *Peter* left his senior management position to teach accounting in a two-year college. He traded a plush office with deep pile rug, a brown leather sofa, windows overlooking a lake and a private secretary for a cubbyhole with no windows, no rug and a secretary shared with seven others. He made the decision to leave his career of seven years quite suddenly, when he spotted an ad for a business administration instructor. He felt no hesitation when he was offered the job a few days later. "I was ready for a move," Peter explains. "I was beginning to feel stale in my position. Even though I liked and respected my colleagues, I couldn't see myself spending the next 20 years of my life there." Now 45, Peter is in the mastery stage of his teaching job. Like a typical Quester, he is keeping his options open.
>
> *Evelynne,* whom you met earlier, is another 45-year-old Quester who is keeping her options open. Evelynne made the decision to start over during the self-appraisal she did at 40. Today, in the mastery stage of her entrepreneurial cycle, Evelynne is thinking about getting involved in something new a few years from now.

By the time Betty, Evelynne, Peter and other Questers in their mid-40s reach their 50th birthdays, they will probably modify or change their plans again if they feel they are no longer growing. These career shifts probably will be associated with their Age-50 Transitions.

The Age-50 Transition
During the Age-50 Transition, many adults come to grips with

issues they didn't resolve in earlier transitions or face new tasks. Recurring issues such as those related to work, family and faltering relationships reappear.

During this transition, *Murray,* 51, came to terms with his growing job dissatisfaction, something he didn't face earlier. As principal of a junior high school, Murray was tired of political hassles. Art and interior design had been longtime hobbies, and for many years he had dreamed of spending more time on his leisure activities. So he decided to open a furniture store in the suburbs of a Midwestern city. At last, Murray could put his interests and knowledge of art and interior design to use. The management and people-related skills he developed and used as a principal were invaluable in his new venture. A Quester throughout his working life, Murray found his occupational disengagements always coincided with his life cycle transitions.

Brady's career followed a similar patern. At 47, he left his dentistry practice to travel the world for a year. When he returned home, he took a lower-paying but more challenging job as a researcher. Brady felt he needed to expand personally and professionally. "I feel more alive now, and believe I am a better husband and person. I'm also more productive as a professional." His family and colleagues agree. Brady is a good example of the growing number of professionals in their late 40s and 50s who leave secure positions to pursue new interests.

For Traditionalists, the period from age-40 to retirement is often called the *maintenance period.* Established in their careers, they enter a plateau. Usually holding their own at work, they try to maintain what they have already achieved. However, in an economy characterized by downsizing, layoffs, mergers, company relocations and bankruptcies, they may not be able to stay in their comfortable ruts.

The Maturing Career Strengthens

Women in the Maturing Career

Many women in Maturing Career are anxious to return to work after staying home with their children. Studies of North American women between the ages of 40 and 60 indicate that they feel extraordinarily good about themselves, their lives and their futures. These feelings are shared by women in all kinds of roles, from homemakers to executives. Some are just now becoming Questers.

Many women are the beneficiaies of a new social climate created by the women's movement. Not so long ago, the common perception was that women 50 or older were over the hill and unemployable. Today, the numbers alone challenge the old stereotype. Women in their 50s and 60s are frequently regarded as glamorous and desirable. Those such as Tina Turner, Lauren Hutton, Diane Sawyer, Jane Fonda, Suzanne Sommers, Cher and Susan Sarandon have popularized the appeal of "older" women.

> *Many women in Maturing Career are anxious to return to work after staying home with their children.*

Many women in their 50s or older return to school and quite literally start new lives. *Kate,* a mother of six, began studying economics at 50 and now works in the trade department of the federal government. *Anne* is also returning to school. The 50s can be a special time for working women, too. *Oprah Winfrey,* the American multiple Emmy Award winning host of The Oprah Winfrey Show, is, according to some assessments, the most influential woman in the world. *Shirley MacLaine* won her first Oscar for Terms of Endearment when she was 50, *Dame Helen Mirren* won her first Oscar for the Queen at 61, and *Helen Tandy* won an Oscar for Driving Miss Daisy at 80. Shirley MacLaine, Dame Mirren, Jane Fonda, Martha Stewart and many other women in their 60s and 70s are setting goals they hope to realize over the next 20 years.

These women know that age has a lot to do with one's state of mind. Studies show that women who are homemakers tend to be physiologically 10 years older than women in the workforce. It's not the work. It's the lack of control, dignity, respect, stimulation and company often associated with being a homemaker.

Today, diet and exercise are changing the way women look and feel about themselves. Nowadays, your only limits are your energy level, drive, motivation and goals. At 50, you've just begun to come into the knowledge and experience you've spent a lifetime piecing together. Many women over 50 experience a new sense of independence and strength. They feel good because they're doing the kind of work they want to do. They are keeping themselves young. That such changes are commonplace even into the 70s and 80s surprises many younger women. Yet, this bloom in the middle and later years of the female life cycle is a signal that it's never too late to find wholeness.

The career patterns of reentry women often resemble those of young adults in the Beginning Career. Women who have been out of the workforce for a while tend to have strong needs for career expansion and mastery. They are making up for lost time. At the same time, many of their husbands want to slow down and lead more balanced lives.

Looking for jobs to replace the outlived job of mothering is particularly difficult for middle-aged women of today. Their generation was never adequately prepared, emotionally or educationally, for the reality that paid work is central to the self-confidence of middle-aged women. And, yet, they rally. All at once, a sense of accomplishment becomes vitally important. Middle-aged women today are modeling new career attitudes and behaviors for younger women to follow. Mobilizing their strengths and pouring their energies into work outside the home is one way of handling stress. This sudden, strong emphasis on achieving something worthwhile brings exhilaration and a renewed sense of purpose and confidence.

Most Traditionalist women don't do much about achieving their identities until after their mid-40s. Now, however, they begin to establish a firm sense of their own identities for the first time. Many women, who have weathered the crises of the Age-40 and Age-50 Transitions, see their 50s, 60s and 70s as the happiest times of their lives.

Men in the Maturing Career
It has traditionally been assumed that age is kinder to men than to women. However, recent research has revealed surprising results: Many men over 40 have a harder time making a satisfying passage into the second half of their lives. Why? The reasons are varied.

First, while most women feel sad over losing their youth, many men feel dread. Also, women in middle life reach out and form intricate webs of nurturance. As their youthful competition for men is replaced by the conviviality of shared experience, their friendships multiply and deepen. The opposite seems true for men in middle life. They rarely make new friends and may become emotionally dependent on their wives.

Additionally, many men are terrified of losing their strength and control. They rarely stop to reexamine where they have been or where they want to go on their life journey. Few nurture their spirits or are willing to risk deeper intimacy that will offer them a buffer against the inevitable losses of middle and later life. Rather, they plunge ahead to the next stage, unaware that events such as layoffs, loss of social status, the departure of grown children, and sudden deaths of friends are portents of pending physical problems.

Many Traditionalist men feel stuck. Some plunge into depression or succumb to heart disease before making a move. And yet, there's so much more to live for. With 30 or more years to live after mid-life, there is ample time to reinvent yourself. The second half of life—whether you think it starts at 40, 50 or 60—can be the most exciting and deeply meaningful of all.

Some Traditionalist men become Questers by learning to let go and asking for help. They listen to what their bodies are telling them, nourish their spiritual sides, and learn to redevelop intimacy. They also know that exercise is the single most potent anti-aging medication known to humankind. The developmental period of the 50s comes to an end when we begin wondering what to do about retirement. Should we work full-time or part-time if we have the choice? Or should we disengage ourselves completely from the marketplace?

The Continuing Career

The Age-60 Transition

The Age-60 Transition marks the boundary between the Maturing Career and the Continuing Career. As we progress through this transition into late adulthood, we again question and explore our inner selves in relation to our external world, examine our careers and other options, and settle on a course that will give us opportunities for continuing growth and revitalization. If you can come to terms with issues that lie before you now, you will acquire a clearer and fuller sense of who you are. You will develop greater inner strength and become more capable of pursuing your goals.

One issue almost all of us must deal with is whether or not we will accept the compulsory retirement included in the employer-employee contract of a number of organizations.

New attitudes toward aging, improved diet and exercise programs, and medical advances have prolonged life expectancy dramatically in the Western world. In 1900, only 1 American in 25 was over 65. In 2000, 1 in 5 was 65 or older; and by the middle of the 21st Century, 1 in 4 will be 65 or older. During the 20th Century, we have gained 25 years of life expectancy. Life expectancy will continue to increase in the 21st Century. In fact, experts predict that life expectancy will increase to 120 years by 2030.

Despite all these advances, many people and organizations still cling to outdated ideas about retirement and aging. For example, they believe that retirement at age 65 or younger is an effective and efficient use of human resources. Interestingly, 65 was the retirement age set by German chancellor Otto von Bismarck in 1881, when few Germans lived much beyond that age.

Now, although mandatory retirement is usually 65-70, many healthy and productive individuals in their 50s or younger are being "retired" early due to mergers, new technology or other factors. It is doubtful whether this practice will continue as the baby boomers remain productive well beyond their 50s and 60s and 70s.

Today, retirement means different things to different people. For some, loss of work means losing part of themselves; they feel as if a piece of their inner selves has disappeared. Retirement raises the specter of unwelcome inactivity. To others, retirement means escape from a dreary and frustrating job and the freedom to do things they had no time for before. Still others consider retirement as escape from suffocating pressures. Decisions about your post-retirement life may be related to how long you want to live. Research shows that individuals who remain active and involved in their work or leisure activities during their middle and later years are healthier, happier and live longer.

Individuals who remain active and involved in their work or leisure activities during their middle and later years are healthier, happier, and live longer.

For many Questers, "retirement" brings continued growth and revitalization. During the Age-60 Transition, many are in the late mastery or early disengagement stage of their fifth, sixth or seventh occupational cycles. Some cycles have been sequential, a logical succession of increasing skills and responsibilities.

Others have been as unrelated as athlete, artist and mechanics teacher. Older Questers are continuing to find work in which they can grow. Fortunately, at the same time, some Traditionalists are becoming Questers at this stage, as well.

> *Wally* worked for the same bank for 40 years until recently, when he began to think like a Quester. His retirement plans are still tentative, but he can hardly wait to get started. Wally believes retirement will give him the chance to do something different, to be more flexible and autonomous. For Wally, compulsory retirement doesn't mean disengagement or diminished activity. It means greater challenge, scope and freedom.

In fact, today many people who seem to be Traditionalists are retiring from their jobs early to embark on exciting, new ventures. For example, look at Cliff's story.

> *Cliff* spent his adult life in a blue-collar world as a building custodian. He decided to retire early and enter an entirely different field. Cliff took courses to help prepare for his new occupation—selling real estate. "One of my strengths is that I'm a creative person, and that type of individual always searches for new experiences," he says.

For most Traditionalists, however, retirement is difficult because it requires dramatic changes. Finding out you have nothing to do, or that you are just in the way, can be devastating when you have been a good provider or wage earner for 35 years. Death rates increase dramatically for retired men and women. So do illnesses that have no physiological causes.

Once you toss out the traditional view of retirement, you have the option of creating the kind of paid or unpaid work and lifestyle you really want. You can design meaningful activities by working full- or part-time, studying, traveling, establishing your own business, restructuring or modifying your current position, doing volunteer work, or pursuing leisure activities that give you a sense of accomplishment and usefulness . And you don't have to do any of these at a given age. Whether you're 50, 65 or 85 you have control over at least some of your circumstances. Success in the changing world means adapting to the new rules and confronting the risks and opportunities it provides. Here's how some Questers do it.

The Continuing Career Flourishes

When many Traditionalists are retiring, most Questers are in the entry or early mastery stage of their next occupational cycles, which may coincide with the developmental periods in their 60s, 70s or 80s.

> *Phil* is a good-looking man with a spring in his step. Now 70, he has had an amazingly diverse career. Phil dropped out of school after repeating the 10th g rade and managed to get a job as a photographer's assistant with a local newspaper. From there, he moved to newspaper reporting. During the Age-30 Transition, he went back to school. Phil earned his education degree and got married in the same year. He taught school for six years, then became principal of a school in the same city . At 45, he was off to work as editor of a newspaper and then a magazine. By age 60, when most men are planning f or retirement, Phil ran successfully for public office in state elections. He left politics at 67 to focus on writing and producing television programs.
>
> When Phil is asked which job he enjoyed the most, he replies, "I enjoyed them all. I enjoyed whatever I was doing when I was doing it. My various positions have a common thread running through them. … I need to work with people and to communicate to others."
>
> Phil has some regrets, however. Most involve interpersonal relations: "I have been so immersed in what I'm doing that I have neglected friendships and family at times. Much of my success is due to the energies that I ha ve put into the work at hand. … I have sometimes wondered why I work with

such single-mindedness. It is not for the financial rewards, nor is it for the renown. If there has been a dominant drive, it has been a deep need for challenge ... for variety, scope ... for personal satisfaction. However, I would lead a similar life if I had my life to live over again."

Phil has this to say about his career goals. "I am by no means certain what I will do next. I will certainly continue to write." Like many Questers, Phil's career goals are still open-ended.

Growing old is not a death warrant for mental activity. Many outstanding people did not reach their prime until long after 50. *Pablo Picasso* was still painting at 91, *Grandma Moses* at 101. *Arturo Toscanini* gave his last performance at 87, and *Giuseppe Verdi* composed "Falstaff" at 80. *Konrad Adenauer* was chancellor of West Germany at 87. *Artur Rubinstein* excited audiences with his piano artistry well into his 90s. So did the late centenarian *Eubie Blake. Paul Newman,* Academy Award-winner and salad dressing king, who has a passion for speed, is actively competing in auto racing at 83. *John Glenn* returned to space at 77; and *Barbara McClintock,* who won the Nobel Prize at 81, continued her research until her death at 90. *Art Linkletter,* cultural and TV icon, continues to write, speak and model his youthful attitude at 95.

Growing old is not a death warrant for mental activity.

Sociologists say that with more people living active, youthful lives well past 70, public perceptions of later adulthood are changing. College students fresh from high school share the classroom with 80-year-old coeds. Gray-haired athletes enter marathons. Retired workers become entrepreneurs. Artists become world travelers. "A few years ago," laughs one fashion expert, "the sight of a woman over 40 dressing in jeans and riding a motorcycle was thought bizarre, or at least inappropriate. Now women are expected to be fit into their 70s, and jeans have become haute couture."

Nowadays, who would we tell to "act your age?" The rhythm of life has changed in other ways, too. A man and woman can become parents again at the same time they become grandparents. Puberty arrives earlier and menopause later. Grandparents are getting younger and living longer. You truly are "as old as you feel."

Attitudes are going through immense changes, and people have many new and interesting alternatives.

Kay was a principal until she retired at 65. Everyone was amazed at her energy level and wondered how she managed to find time for skiing, singing, and other projects on top of her heavy work schedule. When she retired, Kay and her husband spent a year traveling around the world. Six months later, however, Kay was bored and restless. To keep challenge and meaning in her life, she approached the school board and asked for a job. Her first project was to coordinate a group to attack the problems of inner-city schools. This was followed by a stint evaluating private schools. Now 72, Kay is still working on educational projects. She also has time for social activities. She is feeling great and hopes to continue with her present lifestyle.

Frank worked for the railway for 42 years, first as a mechanical apprentice, next as a tradesman, then as a supervisor. He climbed the organizational ladder until he was in his mid-50s. Then his career reached a plateau. To keep involved and enthusiastic, Frank volunteered to do First Aid with the Red Cross in his spare time. At 61, he retired early to become a full-time First-Aid worker. When most of his railway friends were retiring, Frank opened a practice in reflexology (a form of therapy based on manipulation, anesthetization or cauterization). Now 75, Frank is still a vital man. "Age," he says, "is a matter of attitude more than years." Frank plays tennis and skis during his spare time. He is also remarrying.

Questers like Frank and Kay, who continue to maintain their curiosity and interests and desire to lear n and master new skills, develop into fresh, healthy, exciting 90-year-olds. They trust themselves, and are open to the boundless, unforeseen opportunities of the 21st Centur y. The richness of their past is a source of strength and wisdom, r ather than nostalgia, which often acts as anesthesia to living. And, although they enjoy their scrapbooks, they continue to par ticipate in our amazing new world.

Questers tend to think about ho w to pursue their passions and use their brains. There is no significant loss of br ain cells in the brains of people who are living health y, normal lives— all the way into old age. Brain cells tend to shr ink or grow dormant not from old age itself, but from lack of stimulation and challenge. If we introduce vigorous mental stim ulation daily, even an older, developed brain can grow—sprouting new neural foliage and making new connections.

Questers also seek out spir itual fulfillment and n urture intimacy. In addition to pursuing a passion, the strongest link with survival, particularly male sur vival, is the n urturing love provided in a happy marriage or other intimate, loving relationship.

Contemporary career development is a contin uing quest to improve the fit between your developing career and y our evolving personality. Only you can establish your rhythm of change. Remember it's never too late!

Chapter 6

Job Satisfiers

The rewards Questers get from their jobs depend on their personalities. But most are seeking higher-level needs such as freedom, growth, independence, challenge, achievement, variety, involvement and altruism, plus a sense of pur pose and identity. They tend to enjoy their jobs, describing them as fun, exciting and pleasurable.

Phyl, the energetic 70-year-old now in his seventh occupational cycle, said it best: "There is nothing more thrilling than creating something out of y ourself. To follow a strong drive toward a goal and find y ourself, to work at what you want to do and do it successfully, to risk everything when the chances for success seem so small, to giv e everything to your work and get everything back from it, this is the ultimate satisfaction."

How different Questers are from many Traditionalists. *Lorne,* a 50-year-old writer in the civil ser vice, is thoughtful when he considers why he works. Then he says, "For bread and butter. It's a necessity, a way of making a systematic lif e for me in that it gives me a place to go, even though it's no longer fulfilling because it is no longer challenging. I'm not learning anything. I'm not reaching." Lorne acknowledges that he misses the challenge and stimulation his career used to provide. Now in the disengagement stage of his occupational cycle, he has, quite simply, outgrown his job.

The sense of resignation in Lorne's voice is echoed when we hear *Jessica* describe her job. A 40-year-old bookkeeper and former homemaker, Jessica sees her work as "an escape from housework and doing routine tasks." Her job may be more rewarding than housework, but she's far from satisfied.

Unfortunately, while a number of Traditionalists derive a sense of identity and sometimes challenge from their work, their careers tend to satisfy little more than lower-level needs for money, security, prestige and something to do. Many Traditionalists are missing the intense feelings of satisfaction that drive Questers to further challenges. Ultimately, they will pay for it.

How Satisfied Are You?

Because your job needs are dynamic, they usually reflect your reactions to your current work environment. For example, as you gain competence, a job that at first seemed challenging may become boring.

Why, then, do some people seem satisfied doing the same work over and over again, day in and day out, without complaint? Their need hierarchies may be very different from those of most Questers. Less important needs can be satisfied much more easily than higher-level needs. So, for instance, if you have a high need for social contact and your job gives you many opportunities to satisfy that need (assuming other important high-level needs are also met), you will have a high level of job satisfaction. If, on the other hand, you took a job that offered few chances to make social contacts, you would be very dissatisfied.

As you grow and develop, your needs constantly jockey for position. As a result, in middle age you may seriously consider changing the direction of your career. A young person with a job that demands extensive travel may be quite satisfied. But once that person is married and has children, being away from home may become so displeasing that he or she seeks a new job with limited travel demands. Whether or not you're satisfied with your job depends on the degree to which it meets your needs.

A look at the job satisfiers many Questers seek will give you a better idea of where your career fits into your need hierarchy. What follows is a summary of the items many Questers consider when they look for satisfying careers.

Emerging Identity

Part of the search for career satisfaction is finding an occupation that fits your personality and self-image. Your career is a statement about you. Knowing who you are and who you want to become and receiving recognition from your work are essential to job satisfaction. The desire for self-awareness and recognition will last throughout your life.

Your career plays a major part in how you represent yourself to society. The recognition you get from your job is an important part of your life. A career charts your path in the human community. Asked who they are, many people will respond by telling what they do. Children also face this. Who among us hasn't been asked, "What do you want to be when you grow up?" The proper answer, of course, is a doctor or a police officer or an astronaut. A more appropriate question is, "What kind of person do you want to become?" The expectations of others tend to encourage most people to emphasize the *work they do* rather than *who they are.*

The importance of a job to one's sense of identity is evident when you speak to the unemployed. Many feel worthless without a job.

Grace, an assistant vocational rehabilitation counselor, was depressed to find herself out of work, even though she puts her husband, her 12-year-old son, and her home before any job. "When I was working, my husband was proud of me, my son was proud, and then all of a sudden I had nothing," she recalls. "Though I never really blamed myself, I felt emotionally worthless. There's more to life than staying home, and it's bad when getting your unemployment check is your big day out."

Who among us hasn't been asked, "What do you want to be when you grow up?" ... A more appropriate question is, "What kind of person do you want to become?"

In our society, you are judged not only by what you do, but also by the industry in which you do it, your responsibilities, and your company's reputation. A person who craves responsibility might be quite happy working in a small company. But someone who identifies with prestige and status may accept a much lower-paying position just to join a large, renowned company in a prestigious industry. Much job dissatisfaction can be traced to the mismatch between a worker's identity needs and his or her employer.

Of course, as you grow and develop, your identity changes, too. In fact, most Questers are constantly reshaping their identities. They commit themselves to occupations only as long as the jobs fit their personalities.

Finding Purpose in Work

Everyone needs something to believe in. People who know they have a reason to exist are healthier, happier and live longer. Your career can give you a sense of purpose. Your purpose may be the same throughout your life, or it may be modified as you grow. Having a sense of purpose means being open to and accepting change. It also means being honest with yourself. Questers periodically ask themselves, "Who am I? Who do I want to become? What do I really want to do with my life?" They also want to know how they can better guide, teach or help others, as well as how to make useful products.

Everyone needs something to believe in.

Most people want to improve themselves or some aspects of their lives, but many are afraid of letting go of the status quo. They are too dependent on security, money, prestige and power. This dependency results in a sense of meaninglessness, frustration and anxiety. By contrast, Questers typically seek higher level rewards such as meaning, purpose, love, altruism, joy, harmony, growth, beauty and truth. They strive and struggle to reach the goals that will help them attain these rewards.

> *Brock* exudes happiness, a sense of inner peace, and good health. A politician now, the 55-year-old Quester has been an actor, salesman, market research analyst and stockbroker. He thought he'd take early retirement, but he just couldn't do it. After a year of being idle, Brock decided he preferred to work, even though he didn't need the money. "After a year, I felt parasitic and indolent. I have to be involved in something I can believe in, can enjoy, can commit to, and from which I can be of use to humankind. To energize myself, I needed something that would make me push myself to the limits." Brock moved into politics, and now he feels he is making his country a better place to live. "It's a wonderful feeling to be involved in something you love," he says earnestly after being elected to public office. "It gives you a sense of purpose and meaning— and of feeling needed."

> *Kim,* a 30-year-old human resources consultant, says, "My mission is to learn and to teach." Kim says she knew this as a young child, but lost her passion to pursue these goals when she was raped at the age of 10. A workshop she attended recently helped Kim "reconnect with my inner child, to reclaim my purpose and commit myself to this dream."

As a child, you might have known what you wanted to do. But as you grew, various experiences such as traumas and learned belief systems disconnected you from your inner self. By breaking down the barriers and asking yourself specific questions, you can reconnect with your life goal. This gives you the courage to believe in yourself and to commit yourself to pursuing activities that give your life meaning. Kim describes purpose "as a rough diamond. As you become more and more in tune with it, you can make it shine more brightly. This will give you the strength to follow your dream."

The Need for Challenge

Questers usually need more challenge than other people. As soon as they master one challenge, they are off to tame yet another. Why? Differences in genetic makeup and early socialization experiences give some people a greater thirst for challenge. But the workplace can also play a big part.

The Work Environment
Learning new tasks, having control over your work, and being responsible for decisions all involve mental challenge. But what happens when your work doesn't provide enough challenge or opportunities for mastery and achievement? The result is usually boredom. Employees who enjoy sufficiently challenging jobs are enthusiastic and involved. Those who feel responsible for the actions and outcomes of their work strive harder, because their total personalities are involved. Coping with challenge also requires effort and commitment to your goals in life.

Challenge, of course, is dynamic. Once you have mastered a difficult task, you need new challenges. The quest for challenge corresponds to a growing person's occupational cycle.

Achieving Psychological Success
You can get a better understanding of the cyclical

relationships between challenge, achievement, involvement, self-confidence, goal attainment and job factors from the diagram below. Achieving your goals creates feelings of psychological success. The prerequisites for feeling good about your job are listed below:

- Challenging work

- Autonomy

- Support from others

- Feedback

As mastering each task pushes you to new levels of competence, your satisfaction increases—and so does self-confidence. As a result, your involvement in your job probably increases, too. These increased feelings of success, confidence, involvement and commitment usually lead you to set more difficult goals. When this cycle is occurring, you feel turned on by your work.

To set work goals, you need a healthy degree of autonomy. Close supervision may make you feel that your performance reflects more on your supervisor than on your own efforts. However, getting support when you try a difficult task

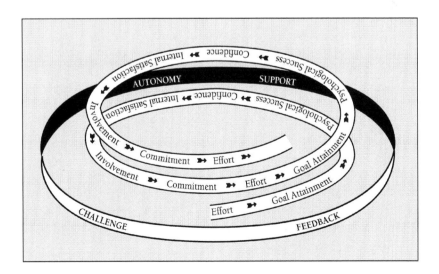

(regardless of whether you succeed or fail) spurs you on; it also helps develop your creativity. Feedback is necessary to help you evaluate your performance. This tends to give you feelings of accomplishment.

> *Glen* is a good example of what happens when an employee receives support and encouragement. As an accountant for a meat-packing plant, Glen persuaded his boss to allow him to plan and install a new management information system. He researched his plan thoroughly, and its success was overwhelming. Glen's confidence was bolstered by this success and by the discovery of a whole new set of skills. As a result, he asked for a transfer so he could develop his management potential. Now general manager of a division, Glen is again happily involved in the entry stage of a new occupational cycle.

The good feelings of success and satisfaction that Glen and other Questers derive from their jobs come because they tend to have challenging positions that are interesting and meaningful. They are able to set their own goals, work independently to achieve them, gain support from supervisors, and get useful feedback about their performance. Because of this, Questers are satisfied they are doing good work.

Different Strokes for Different Folks
Of course, challenge comes in many forms. At one end of the stimulation spectrum is the commodities broker who makes potentially disastrous trades every minute. At the other end is the product researcher who may develop a new product only once or twice a year. Both are challenged—with different timing.

Just as too little challenge can cause dissatisfaction, so can too much. If the level of challenge is so great you can't cope with it, you are in the wrong job. Moderate challenges, which make success difficult but possible, will give you the most pleasure and satisfaction.

Questers, who understand how to match their needs for stimulation to the right job, can find challenge in many different occupations. What do you need to find challenge? And how much is right for you?

Variety Adds Spice to Life

Questers tend to enjoy work that allows them to accomplish many different tasks. They appreciate jobs that require some thought, have some unexpected challenges, and let them use their own ingenuity.

Sandy gets plenty of variety in the Peace Corps. A broad range of experiences, skills and interests prepared her to succeed at this often frustrating job. Before she married, Sandy, now 51, was an agricultural agent. While she gave up her career for motherhood and marriage, Sandy kept busy with volunteer work. She headed a political campaign, lobbied successfully for a home for battered women, developed a youth employment center, and chaired many committees that worked for better facilities for the mentally challenged. "I love challenge and variety. I want to help others."

When her husband died Sandy was just 49, and she needed a job to support herself. She was well qualified for the Peace Corps. Although her position as a director is often difficult, she treasures the variety. "Every minute, every hour is different. I get to work for world peace, travel, meet people from all walks of life, and help with all kinds of projects in agriculture, education, social work and medical care. I even answer phones for the African relief hotline."

The Need to Achieve

Understanding why many Questers are so involved in their work requires understanding the need for achievement. People who derive feelings of accomplishment from completing a difficult task feel satisfied and proud. How successfully they cope with a task deter mines how competent and proud they feel. Psychological growth occurs only when there is opportunity for achievement.

Psychological growth occurs only when there is opportunity for achievement.

To see how important achievement really is, you must meet *Omar.* He raised $275,000 to start his own Italian ice cream store, the first of its kind in a large Eastern city. The store drew 160,000 customers in just six months. Strange as it may sound, Omar didn't really care ho w much money he made or how famous he became, or even whether he could beat the competition. What he cared about was his product. "I had a product that I lo ved and believed in, and I wanted a perfect gelato store that looked attractive and authentic and gave people something wonderful." To achieve that, he was willing to pay his employees well.

Persistence Is the Mother of In vention

Inner toughness, the ability to stic k with a dream or an ambition even when it's not going well, sets Questers apar t from many Traditionalists and Self-Seekers. Instead of panicking and packing it in when their dreams seem about to fall apart, they size up their problems and figure out alternative solutions. As they have discovered, the paths to success are many and varied.

Shawna learned that when she decided to go to college . Divorced and with two children to support, she worked day and night just to make it through her program. By the time she had earned her bachelor's degree, she had to face facts. She was just too poor to afford her longtime dream of becoming a doctor. So she took a job as a junior biologist, then as a technical writer, moving from a computer company to a small medical electronics firm. While she seemed to be dr ifting, Shawna was actually questing, constantly fine-tuning her abilities.

By 1995, Shawna had saved enough money to start her own

company making electrosurgical equipment, the same product her former employer had specialized in, only better. Her company's best-seller, a high-tech scalpel, made her rich. Shawna's interest in medicine had finally paid off, but in a much different way than she had envisioned.

Hard Work Is Energizing

The accomplishments of many Questers take a tremendous amount of hard work. Omar held a full-time job at an investment firm while working nights to research gelato recipes. His new position still keeps him going day and night. Shawna went to night school and studied weekends. Getting ahead as they did without succumbing to exhaustion or self-doubt takes enormous determination and single-mindedness.

But hard work can be very energizing. And hard work has other rewards, such as positive feedback and the feelings of satisfaction that accompany a sense of accomplishment. Like many Questers, as you gain competence and become more fulfilled and involved, you will also gain energy. You may even learn to approach your job with verve, as if you are playing an exhilarating, although serious, game.

Successful activity, no matter how intense, leaves you with comparatively few scars; it causes stress, but little distress. Work wears you out mainly through the frustration of failure or boredom. Many of the hardest workers in almost any field live long and happy lives.

Information Is Power

If a Quester doesn't know something, he or she tends to find out, pronto! As Omar tells his employees, "There's no such word as can't." While some salesclerks sit around waiting for customers, Quester salesclerks might hound their bosses to teach them how the businesses operate.

Questers know that every bit of know-how they pick up only helps to make them more resourceful.

"There's no such word as can't."

When they're not studying, most Questers are e valuating what they've learned. This thirst for information heightens their chances for succeeding when taking risks. Omar found market research invaluable when he approached possible financiers. While the banks had a million facts and figures to show why another ice cream store wouldn't make it, Omar had the research to prove it would. "I might have stopped right there, but I had done my own research, and I just had a feeling that gelato would go."

Confronting Fear of Failure

Questers seldom risk their resources on impossible dreams. While they take chances, their actions are based on sound knowledge of the facts plus planning and intuitive feelings. Omar's friends were appalled when he left his w ell-paying position. But he had done his homework so well that opening the store felt like the next step in a well-conceived plan.

Of course, risk takers must confront the fear of failure. Losing job security and possibly your pride along with it is risky, indeed. Questers tend to deal with this by waiting until the signs look good—and then by plunging ahead. They work out their anxieties by acting, not agonizing. Because setbacks are inevitable, Questers train themselves to look at reversals as learning opportunities, not as signs of personal inadequacy. "Failure is good for you," Bernadette says confidently. "It's a kind of bruise that makes you tougher. If I've done my absolute best and still goof, I say, 'Okay, I'm human.' I forgive myself. Then I sit down and take a look at what went wrong."

Enhancing Your Potential

How can you develop your achievement potential? Begin by setting personal and professional goals, and then start realizing them one step at a time. For example, start and stick with a training or savings program. At work, figure out how long a

When you are generous with your own talents and time, your efforts are usally rewarded many times over.

240

single project will take you to complete, then try to do it 10 minutes faster, then 20 minutes faster. Not only will your increased efficiency raise your feelings of competence, it could prompt your boss to give you even more responsibility and challenge.

While you are raising your own sense of competence, try to avoid competing with the experts around you. Instead, enlist their help and support. Many Questers are backed by efficient and loyal support teams. When you are generous with your own talents and time, your efforts are usually rewarded many times over.

Self-Confidence Is Empowering

Confident people stand out. They seem so comfortable and in control of their lives. But self-confidence often is the result of accomplishing something. It also stems from learning to accept one's negative qualities.

Most Questers don't feel rejected for long if they have been passed up for a promotion or some other form of recognition. Because they are self-confident, they tend to have the courage to move on to occupations that do satisfy their needs. Their confidence gives them the courage to take other risks, leading toward goals that are important to them. Studies in the workplace have found that most managers and professionals select "feeling that my work is worth doing" as the most important factor contributing to their sense of self-confidence and self-respect. Other contributing factors are listed here:

- An equitable salary.

- A sense of accomplishment.

- Growth opportunities, such as freedom, independence, authority and creativity.

- Sufficient feedback and recognition.

- The ability to advance within the company.

- Two-way communication.

- Enjoyable work.

- Company security.

Highly self-confident employees get more pleasure from succeeding at their work than from any other factor. They are more likely to:

- Value challenging tasks.

- Find the pleasure of achievement to be intense and enduring.

- Want promotions for reasons of justice.

- Desire responsibility over status.

These workers are less likely to:

- Value prestige, approval and verbal recognition as sources of self-assurance.

- Be emotionally affected by criticism.

- Experience conflicts and feelings of anxiety on the job.

- Be defensive and employ defense mechanisms. (Less confident employees often project their failures onto other people or circumstances.)

How do Questers become self-confident? They develop their confidence through hard work, practice, determination, and achievement. You can develop your own self-confidence in the same way. Start by realizing that at your core is an inner strength that you alone have the power to bring to the surface. The ability to tap that resource is what long-distance runners call *digging down.* Once you've grabbed hold of your own power and felt the magical quality you possess, you'll see that self-confidence can truly turn your world around.

Bette learned that lesson while she was young. A shy,

quiet little girl, she stayed pretty much to herself. "If you had known me then, you would have said that I was one of the most unassuming and unambitious children you ever met." But Bette had a secret. While other kids were outside playing, she was poring over her mother's magazines and trying to copy the high fashion togs on her sewing machine. "I wasn't too successful at the time," she remembers. "But I knew somewhere deep down inside me that as long as I could play 'dress up' in my life, I would be happy. As I look back on it, I realize that even then my career was growing inside of me."

Bette's interest in sewing was translated into the desire to become a dress designer. "Not to say it was a piece of cake. It wasn't!" She studied and worked hard. Though still just a frightened little girl at heart, she traveled to Paris and New York to learn her trade. And she took risks. "But the important thing is that once I made my decision to work toward this goal, I gave myself every opportunity to achieve it."

These days, when she recalls her past insecurities, Bette thinks that she, like the legendary glass of water, was half full, not half empty. "Now, I design dresses that other little girls dream about!"

Bette didn't acquire self-confidence overnight, and neither will you. Self-confidence develops as you work on and achieve small goals. Like learning a foreign language, developing self-confidence may sometimes leave you feeling awkward and uncomfortable. You will make silly mistakes, and you will feel as though it's someone else, not you, doing those things. But the more you practice, the easier it becomes and the more natural you feel.

Ultimately, you alone are responsible for the decisions you make. The final results—self-confidence, knowledge, and success—are the results of those choices. To become more like the Questers, you will have to act like the Questers.

Autonomy Is Being in Control

Questers tend to have a strong desire to control their own work. They perform best at jobs in which they have the freedom to use their own ideas and knowledge, to pioneer new procedures, to take responsibility, and to prove their competence. Questers need the freedom to persist, to take risks, and to fail without fear of being reproached or fired.

You alone are responsible for the decisions you make.

Few large organizations today provide employees with the opportunity to be autonomous. That's why so many Questers go into business for themselves or work for small companies. A National Science Foundation study showed that small firms produce about four times as many innovations for each research development dollar as medium-sized firms, and about 24 times as many as large companies.

Mauro, now 55, owns one of these small companies, a factory that manufactures statues, fountains and tombstones. During his career, he's been a copywriter, salesman and middle manager for a large manufacturing firm. He left the last position because he was frustrated by the bureaucracy. Unable to use his own ideas, he felt stifled. He explains, "I had little input into decisions affecting my job and little creative input. The position was becoming really watered-down." Feeling emotionally drained and physically ill from his lack of power, he soon developed ulcers. "I felt like I was wearing a straight jacket."

When Mauro decided he couldn't take feeling powerlessness anymore, he left. Friends who knew him when he worked for his old employer are startled by the way he changed. His wife, Sandra, is happy with the new Mauro, saying, "Mauro is more relaxed now. He was an old man 10 years ago. Now, he's young again." In control of his life and his health, Mauro feels good about himself again.

Nothing breeds success like success, and nothing blocks it more effectively than frustration. Frustration caused by a lack of work autonomy can lead to serious consequences. Unrelieved tension or distress, usually accompanied by feelings of helplessness, can pose a threat to your personality and your self-confidence. Ongoing frustration can weaken the body's immune system, resulting in physical and psychosocial illnesses such as migraines, high blood pressure and back pain. Low self-confidence, job dissatisfaction, lack of creativity and low aspirations usually accompany the feelings of general ill health and malaise associated with lack of autonomy.

For employers, the cost is measured in high turnover, dissatisfied employees with low levels of motivation and morale, reduced productivity and creativity, and ineffective management. That's why some organizations today are trying harder to involve their employees in decision making and providing human relations training. Employees are taught to alleviate frustration and stress through relaxation exercises. They are also encouraged to talk to a trusted friend, counselor or relative when they feel tense.

Frustration caused by a lack of work autonomy can lead to serious consequences.

Fitting In

Corporations often have a hard time tolerating the very creative employees who are the force behind many innovations. In an organization's eyes, these highly creative people may seem impatient, egotistical, obnoxious and even a bit irrational. As a result, some Questers have a difficult time convincing prospective employers to hire them. If hired, they may not be promoted or rewarded. The frustration of seeing their creative efforts ignored is what prompts a number of Questers to move on.

Fortunately, some Questers can continue to be themselves and find autonomy in large companies. A few organizations give their employees plenty of autonomy. These companies encourage workers to take practical risks—and, even if they fail, support good efforts. They know that many employees must be allowed to experiment and even fail. The companies have learned that energized employees can accomplish miracles. By creating small, independent divisions that give managers control over hiring, firing, finances and purchasing, these organizations breed loyal, dedicated managers who make better decisions than centralized departments ever could. The absence of paperwork and overplanning is as conspicuous as the internal competition. Unlike many organizations, managers who take on additional responsibilities outside their own divisions are rewarded, not punished.

Jack is a bright, young Quester who works for a progressive company. Encouraged to take risks, he has the freedom to persist and the freedom to fail. At 32, this enthusiastic chemical engineer developed a new medical adhesive product. Supporting and protecting Jack in the development of his product, his manager sympathized with Jack's occasional failures and celebrated his frequent successes. Jack appreciates the support he has received, noting, "Without the freedom to persist and fail, I never would have discovered the product." Now developed, the product has been so successful that Jack's employers have given him even more autonomy and incentives to promote further development and marketing.

Coping with Forced Autonomy

Not all Questers find a company they can fit into neatly. That's why unemployment has motivated many a Quester to become more independent and autonomous.

Carol, the educator-turned-caterer, is just one Quester who had to learn to cope with forced autonomy. Today, these Questers are adamant that they will never again let someone else control their careers. Simone, the manager of an insurance agency, is another Quester who learned coping mechanisms in the face of unemployment.

Five years ago, *Simone* found herself suddenly unemployed when her insurance company folded after she had advanced from policy typist to branch supervisor. It didn't take long for Simone to turn a crisis into an opportunity. "I realized there were only two ways to do things: work for somebody else or work for myself." She decided to open her own agency. She had already prepared for the change by taking night courses. Like most Questers, she had thought ahead long before fate pushed her to move on.

The yearning for independence is a familiar feeling among Questers. Hasn't everyone, at least once, dreamed of owning a business? These dreams come true more frequently now as the economy and job frustrations prompt more and more employees to strike out on their own. But can you really do it? Of course you can, *if you're willing to put in the time and work and to take the risks involved.* Most Questers have—and very successfully, too. Why can't you?

Involvement Is Excitement

Questers are generally very involved in their jobs. Psychologically, they identify closely with their work. They take their positions seriously, and their moods and feelings are significantly affected by their work experiences. Their jobs must satisfy the needs and values that are important to them. People who are highly involved in their jobs are likely to feel either extremely satisfied or extremely dissatisfied, depending on what's happening at work. On the other hand, uninvolved employees tend to have less extreme emotional reactions to the same job experiences. If carried to extremes, such job involvement can become a neurotic compulsion. Although wise Questers want to immerse and enjoy themselves in their work, they also learn to balance their jobs with the many other dimensions of their lives.

247

Job involvement is closely related to job satisfaction. Some experts say the orientation to work is learned early in childhood and is hard to change; others think it may be related to biological makeup. But most agree that, while work orientation can be developed, it is also related to certain personality characteristics and work environments. As discussed earlier, a person's work orientation can be modified by providing opportunities for psychological success (challenge, autonomy, support and feedback).

Enthusiasm Is Good for You

Involved employees have an infectious enthusiasm about their work that employers can't help but admire. One company president remarked that he'd forgive just about any mistake, at least once, that was made out of enthusiasm. This president came away from his first meeting with the new company lawyer (a woman chosen after much hesitation) glowing with admiration. As it turned out, the company was involved in a legal battle it was almost certain to lose. Did this new lawyer tell him he could win? "No," he said. "I know better than that, and if she had, I'd have fired her. What she did do is to outline all the steps she could take to limit our loss and all the ways she could press the other side to settle. She was so enthusiastic about it that I came out of our meeting feeling pretty good about the whole thing. Any lawyer who can make me feel good about losing a million-dollar case is unusual. Given a case she can win, this lady is going to be a real tiger!"

The excitement of being involved in your job affects other people, too. Joyce, the schoolteacher from Chapter 2 who left her job to become a principal, moved on because she was no longer enthusiastic about what she was doing. "Enthusiasm is catching," she explains. "If I can't be enthusiastic about what I'm teaching, neither can my students." The intensity of high-energy performers and actors comes from their deep involvement in their work. They *can't* be boring. They're too interested in what they're doing.

Enthusiasm is no less valuable in your private life. More love affairs and marriages die from lack of enthusiasm than from any other cause. Nothing is more wounding than indifference or boredom. Even in the bedroom, the amount of energy or interest you put into a relationship pretty m uch determines how much pleasure you get out of it. Sex is a need just like other needs, and often it is treated only as such. But the real, physical need for sex can be fulfilled by masturbation or routine intercourse. An interesting, fulfilling sex life requires people to share their feelings, energy and passion. It's surprising what a satisfying sex life can do for your image. And why not? The better you feel about yourself and your life, the better your image becomes. The same principle applies to your job. The real secret of having an exciting image is enjoying what you do.

Passion Provides Perspective

Passionate involvement in their work helps many Questers to deal with any problems that arise. Indeed, for many Questers, work itself is a passion.

Gerald, the eye specialist you met in Chapter 2, calls himself a work addict, but a happy one. "I love my work," he remarks. "Helping people see is rewarding. On occasion, I've met my wife at a party at six in the evening when I've been working since six in the morning. I haven't had time to wash or change to black tie, even if that's what all the other men are wearing. I might be completely exhausted, but when I think of what I did with my day, I feel good inside."

Gerald says that even if he starts the day feeling sick or out of sorts, he forgets about it once he gets to work. "When you are working at your best, you forget your negative feelings. At that moment, nothing else exists."

Money Is a Byproduct

Financial rewards are often the result of a growth process that begins with a real interest in your work and a love of accomplishment for its own sake. After all, earning power is

Financially successful people are involved in occupations they like and value.

simply the byproduct of doing a good job. Even in today's turbulent society, many people without family money or social connections are growing rich on their own initiative. They are not hotshot investors, intellectual geniuses, money-grubbers or ruthless competitors. In fact, personality studies of financially successful people claim that these traits actually impede moneymaking potential. Financially successful people are involved in occupations they like and value.

Andrea, the vice-president of a Western investment firm, was divorced and unemployed with two children to support when she discovered her life's work. From secretary to administrative assistant for a financial services company, she has blossomed into a six-figure employee. Andrea used her position as a springboard to learning what was previously foreign to her: finance. Studying largely on her own, she borrowed money for night courses that helped her earn a broker's license. "I learned a lesson that I wanted to get across to other women whose husbands had left them," Andrea says, with determination in her voice. "When you're on your own, you can't afford to be a financial sleeping beauty." Andrea's financial planning series for women is an ongoing success.

The Joy of Helping

Financial rewards and prestige are not the primary motivators for Questers. What they do value most is an occupation that gives them opportunities to contribute to the welfare of others. Feelings of altruism or concern for others' well-being usually develop around the Age-40 Transition. Most middle-aged people become more committed to being mentors—to guiding and helping others. Many Questers seem to develop the need to be altruistic early in life, and they look to their work to satisfy this need.

Take *Christopher.* Until two years ago, this 31-year-old lawyer was doing quite well working for a large insurance company in a Midwestern city. Then, suddenly, he quit his job and took time off to do some wandering and put his life into perspective. He turned up two years later in a storefront legal office funded by the Office of Economic Opportunity.

Christopher explains that his insurance position, which involved defending the company against plaintiffs who had been struck by cars, was the first rung on the career ladder. His next move would have been as a personal injury lawyer. Had he stayed with the company for the usual ("heaven forbid!") 25 years, Christopher could have retired with nearly $400,000 in profit-sharing receipts. He laughs now, "Once the novelty wore off, spending 10 hours a day defending an insurance company was a waste of time. With the education I've got, I might as well do something useful."

Today, Christopher is satisfied that he is doing something useful. He's still a lawyer, but now his clients include single parents, senior citizens, immigrants and people struggling with landlord-tenant disputes. He represents juveniles in trouble, minorities abused by the police, inmates caught in the state penitentiary system, and people dumped into the streets because of overcrowding in state hospitals. Happily involved in a challenging new position, Christopher charges one-tenth of the going legal fee. "Every day is different," he says with real pleasure. "I can work four days straight, 16 hours a day, and never feel tired. Until my eyes start falling out … then I know I have to go to bed."

Unlike his new position, his post at the insurance company was all about competition. "Everyone was trying to push the other guy down and crawl all over him to move up. If you didn't, you knew he was going to do it to you. God, the days dragged! I'd have a stack of 100 files on my desk, and all I could do w as make checkmarks or go into court and make the same motions, day after day. And why? To save the company money."

Legal problems aren't the only ones that concer n Christopher these days. If a client has an emotional problem, Christopher calls a psychologist. If the problem is a lack of job skills, he encourages the client to go bac k to school. "They're so pushed down, so depressed. You get to know them intimately. I call them by their first names. We've been to each other' s homes. After five o'clock, I never even saw the people I worked with at the insurance company. I would never have shared my thoughts with those people. But I would with my clients."

These days, money and fame are the fur thest things from Christopher's mind. Helping his clients is reward enough. But he also realizes the immensity of his task. At times, he feels overcommitted, overextended and powerless. Still, Christopher has few regrets.

Many Questers feel the same way Christopher does and happily commit themselves to helping others. Some are even able to work contentedly within the bureaucratic constraints that Christopher finds so frustrating. For example, look at Meagan.

Soft-spoken *Meagan* has been called the Indiana Jones of her state's child welfare system. Each day, she slashes through a jungle of red tape to saf eguard the rights of her government wards. Why did this former political scientist abandon a prestigious consulting career to become a community social worker? "I think, more than anything else, for the challenge of developing something new that might have a chance of helping depr ived children," she says thoughtfully.

Tigers Rarely Reach the Top
Popular myths aside, wealth and success don't ha ve to be

achieved at the expense of others. Wealthy and successful Questers don't simply claw their way to the top, heedless of whom they hurt along the way. Indeed, many make their contributions through inspiring others, promoting teamwork, and developing other people's abilities. Of course, Questers must be competitive to succeed. Those who own businesses know the importance of being acutely aware of how their products and services stack up to those of their competitors. But most Questers are less intent on getting ahead at the expense of others than they are on achieving.

> This is what *Ryan,* a factory owner, has to say about competition: "I know what my competitors are doing, and I keep 10 steps ahead of them. I can meet them any way they want. But not to cut their hearts out. We all have to make a living." Other more ruthless competitors have come and gone during his career, but Ryan is still in business.

Growing on the Job

Whether or not a job rewards you depends on what you want from it. For most Questers, this equation is easy: They seek occupations in which they can thrive, develop and mature. They want to develop their own personalities, to exploit their own talents, to innovate, to get the job done without having to follow rigid regulations. A Quester's drive for growth is closely related to such other job satisfiers as challenge and autonomy.

> Like other Questers, *Nicole* has left several jobs that didn't offer the rewards she wanted. Petite, vivacious, with expressive brown eyes, Nicole at 38 is a magazine editor. Before that, she was a staff writer for an institution that published health care literature. And long before Nicole began her writing career, she was an elementary school teacher.

Loved by her fourth-grade students, Nicole was flattered by the power she wielded as a teacher. "But I felt I wasn't really using enough of me," she recalls. So she took a writing job. And as much as she loved reading and writing, that job just wasn't right for her either. "When I first got my job, I came in early and stayed late," she says. "I would work a project to death and get it really done right, and then ask for more. But I found I was out of place. No one else was devoting as much passion to their jobs as I was, and they didn't want to be reminded of it."

So, she settled down and conformed, divorcing her mind and spirit from her work. Like her colleagues, who were just as capable as she was, Nicole simply ceased to care. "I played cards for three hours at lunch or went sunbathing or shopping," she says. "It was a very comfortable job, and it was despicable."

Because Nicole's company expected less than she offered, she felt she was forced to play the game by its rules. "But I couldn't. At the end of the day, I felt that I had not accomplished anything. I was furious. I felt humiliated and used." Predictably, it wasn't long before she quit.

The difference between her last position and her new one shows in Nicole's face. Blossoming as an editor, she is delighted that her new job offers her the freedom to develop her writing, editing and other skills. The magazine's readership has doubled since she became editor, but Nicole is constantly concerned with improving its quality.

Always highly independent and innovative, Nicole will change jobs again, if necessary, to avoid stagnating. Like many Questers, she is more concerned with having a position and a lifestyle that matches her purpose, interests, needs, abilities and goals than with seeking material rewards.

Brad satisfied his love of challenge by opening his own business. His success story started with a belt and a buckle. During his second year of college, Brad received a beautiful belt buckle as a gift. Intrigued by the possibility of designing his own belt, Brad splurged $50 on leather-working tools and materials. Soon, he was selling his unusual, handmade belts to friends. "The business really snowballed from there," he remembers fondly.

As his belts began selling at local art shows, Brad expanded his work to include caps, wallets, key cases and other small leather products. Suddenly, Brad realized that he could be a business success doing what he enjoyed. "The more involved I became in running the business, the more I realized how much I enjoyed the challenge." Today, he has 25 stores and is a multimillionaire.

Persistence Pays

Genius and natural talent (such as Brad's) aren't the only prerequisites for success. The word persistence crops up again and again when Questers talk about their accomplishments.

Ryan is a 64-year-old entrepreneurial Quester who, like Brad, loves to innovate. He has kept expanding his business for the sheer joy of seeing it grow. From a newly built factory on the outskirts of a large industrial city, Ryan manufactures coin and vending machines, vending machine parts, and video games. He's thinking of expanding into computers. It wasn't always a sure thing, however.

Ryan borrowed $500 from a bank to start his first business, a pinball game parts factory. As he kept adding new products, his business developed into a successful enterprise. Ryan admits he's not an engineer, but he does love to create mechanical parts and products. "I love to see a piece of iron do some work," he says, with a sparkle in his eyes. "I have an idea, and then I see if I can make it work. I love what I do," he continues. "I persist, and I keep on top of things."

Creativity Is Action

Questers possess the kind of creativity that enables them to bring ideas to life. While there is no shortage of potentially creative people, there is a shortage of people who have the courage to attain results. Creative Questers have the know-how, energy, daring and staying power to venture beyond convention. They may—and, indeed, usually do—fail somewhere along the road to success. But their determination drives them on to bigger and better projects, and eventually they succeed. They are not geniuses. They are merely persistent.

Keeping Your Options Open

Having the ability to succeed is one thing; deliberately setting out to do so is another. Questers tend to achieve because they set career goals related to their purpose, needs, values, interests and abilities. They also listen to their inner feelings. Careful to keep their options open, they have the freedom to develop and to find challenge. Their career goals may range from open-ended goals to five- or seven-year plans. But all represent an active and independent commitment to career management. Questers are in control of their lives. Most will eventually move on to new goals that better satisfy their developing personalities. Having made at least one occupational move, they are not afraid to make others when they are no longer growing.

A good many Questers, aware that they might be approaching a dead end, have searched for and found a new road. They are usually adept at anticipation—imagining future bends in the road and preparing to shift gears in advance.

This willingness to manage their own careers and to anticipate their future needs is what separates most Questers from many Traditionalists. Questers learn to maintain a balance between tentativeness and commitment. Committing yourself to and becoming actively involved in a job that satisfies your goals is admirable. But Questers are usually the masters, and not the slaves, of their commitments. With a clear understanding of their own needs and goals, they can balance the two with skill as they travel along the sometimes rocky road toward career satisfaction.

Having the ability to succeed is one thing; deliberately setting out to do so is another.

In today's economic climate, being flexible, resilient and open to change are your best protections against obsolescence. Most Questers have learned to ignore the dangers and focus on the opportunities. Open-ended career goals permit them to react quickly to the changing marketplace.

Having a satisfying career and life isn't always easy. But to most Questers, the easy life is not worth living. Consider your own career and lifestyle. What kind of life are you leading?

Chapter 7

Rate Your Job Satisfaction

Are you satisfied with your job, or does it make you feel moody, depressed, and discouraged? It's normal to experience career ups and downs, but if your lows become much more frequent or last much longer than your highs, you probably need to give serious thought to whether you are in the right position. You can find out by asking yourself specific questions about your job and work habits. The three questionnaires in this chapter—*The Job Satisfaction Questionnaire, The Job Involvement Questionnaire* and *The Burnout Questionnaire*—will help you do just that. These questionnaires also will help you determine whether your work attitudes and habits are leading you to burnout, and what you can do about it. Directions, scoring procedures, interpretations and suggestions are provided

As you read the items in each questionnaire, think through them carefully. The more honest you are, the more you will benefit. Let your feelings be your guide.

The Job Satisfaction Questionnaire

Each of the 44 items in this Questionnaire evaluates one job facet. Understanding how well your job satisfies these facets can give you a good picture of your overall degree of job satisfaction.

For each facet, circle:

+2 if you are very satisfied (VS)

+1 if you are satisfied (S)

0 if you are not sure whether that facet is present in or appropriate to your job (N/A)

-1 if you are dissatisfied (D)

-2 if you are very dissatisfied (VD)

Grade each facet with your present job in mind. Scoring directions and an analysis of your responses follow the

The Job SatisfactionQuestionnaire

	RATINGS				
	VS	**S**	**N/A**	**D**	**VD**
1. Personal development	+2	+1	0	-1	-2
2. Growth	+2	+1	0	-1	-2
3. Security	+2	+1	0	-1	-2
4. Appropriate salary level	+2	+1	0	-1	-2
5. Self-esteem or self-respect	+2	+1	0	-1	-2
6. Participating in decision making	+2	+1	0	-1	-2
7. Accomplishing something worthwhile	+2	+1	0	-1	-2
8. Having authority	+2	+1	0	-1	-2
9. Assisting others	+2	+1	0	-1	-2
10. Social status and prestige	+2	+1	0	-1	-2
11. Time to pursue leisure activities	+2	+1	0	-1	-2

	+2	+1	0	-1	-2
12. Money to pursue leisure activities	+2	+1	0	-1	-2
13. Desirable locale	+2	+1	0	-1	-2
14. Opportunity to develop friendships	+2	+1	0	-1	-2
15. Varied responsibilities	+2	+1	0	-1	-2
16. Professional development	+2	+1	0	-1	-2
17. Seeing work results	+2	+1	0	-1	-2
18. Feedback on performance	+2	+1	0	-1	-2
19. Fringe benefits	+2	+1	0	-1	-2
20. Merit promotion	+2	+1	0	-1	-2
21. Paid study leaves and/or time off for courses	+2	+1	0	-1	-2
22. Opportunity to change jobs within organization	+2	+1	0	-1	-2
23. Use of special skills or abilities	+2	+1	0	-1	-2
24. Respect and support form subordinates	+2	+1	0	-1	-2
25. Compatibility of personal goals and values to those of organization	+2	+1	0	-1	-2
26. Resources to do an adequate job	+2	+1	0	-1	-2
27. Respect, fair treatment, and support from superiors	+2	+1	0	-1	-2
28. Physical surroundings	+2	+1	0	-1	-2
29. Interesting work	+2	+1	0	-1	-2
30. Amount of pressure	+2	+1	0	-1	-2
31. Relocation possibilities	+2	+1	0	-1	-2
32. Aesthetic contributions	+2	+1	0	-1	-2
33. Using own ideas	+2	+1	0	-1	-2
34. Time to spend with family	+2	+1	0	-1	-2
35. Amount of job involvement	+2	+1	0	-1	-2
36. Amount of unrelated/clerical work	+2	+1	0	-1	-2
37. Ability to organize work	+2	+1	0	-1	-2
38. Clients' and/or customers' appreciation	+2	+1	0	-1	-2
39. Challenging work	+2	+1	0	-1	-2
40. Work hours	+2	+1	0	-1	-2

41. Using creativity	+2	+1	0	-1	-2
42. Having a sense of purpose	+2	+1	0	-1	-2
43. Having autonomy	+2	+1	0	-1	-2
44. Having a sense of identity	+2	+1	0	-1	-2
45. Other	+2	+1	0	-1	-2
Subtotals	___	___	___	___	___
Total Satisfaction Score	_____				
Total Dissatisfaction Score	_____				
Overall Job Satisfaction Score *(Satisfaction + Dissatisfaction)*	_____				

Questionnaire.

Scoring

To determine your job satisfaction score, follow the steps below:

1. Add your subtotals for your VS, S, D and VD scores, and write them in the space provided under *Subtotals*.

2. Determine your Total Satisfaction Score (add the VS and S ratings) and your Total Dissatisfaction Score (add the VD and the D ratings), and write these in the spaces provided.

3. Determine your *Overall Job Satisfaction Score* by adding your Total Satisfaction Score and your Total Dissatisfaction Score.

The highest possible score you can receive is 88. The lowest possible score is -88. The higher your score, the more satisfied you are with your job. The lower your score, the more discontented you are.

Interpreting Your Score

50 or higher: If your needs and values are being met

thoroughly in each job facet, your Overall Job Satisfaction Score will be 88. (This rarely happens.) If your score is over 50, you are quite satisfied. However, there may be some aspects of your job you could improve. Find out what these are by reviewing your low scores. Think about how you could better satisfy those needs.

20 to 49: You seem moderately satisfied with your position. However, your job situation is in need of some changes. Can you improve the facets for which you got negative scores? If not, you need to assess your current job in relation to your desired career goals. Consider exploring other career options in your current or another organization. Try viewing your work as a continuing opportunity for growth and development. Some jobs are good; they are regenerative. The longer you keep them, the more they increase your value. Other jobs diminish your value; they are repetitious. The longer you do them, the older you get, the more you lose your flexibility and opportunity to grow, and the more easily you can be replaced by someone who is younger and cheaper.

20 to10: It's likely you are tolerating a number of on-the-job conditions that make you unhappy. Perhaps you should consider moving on. Don't remain in a deadening work situation. Circumstances often force people to take jobs that are incompatible with their needs and abilities. Choosing a job out of economic necessity is understandable, but choosing to remain year after year in a blind alley is detrimental to your health and well-being. Don't put off your resolve to do something about this situation. If you do, you might end up in the next category within a few months.

The key to an ever-evolving career is to monitor your own career development and stay attuned to new opportunities.

11 or lower: You scored yourself "D" for most job facets, indicating that you find many of your job conditions dis-satisfying. You probably have a serious case of the job blues. Obviously, you need a change, perhaps even a dramatic shift to a totally new field. Considering that you have so few satisfiers in your position, it's amazing you can even motivate yourself to go to work. Your position may be affecting your health. If you think you would have answered this quiz in a similar way six months or even a year ago, you may also be a procrastinator who is waiting for someone to force you to make a move. Wait no longer. Put your career back into your own hands.

What did completing *The Job Satisfaction Questionnaire* tell you about your job needs? What are your highest and lowest needs? What needs are currently being satisfied? What needs are not? What needs do you want your ideal position to satisfy?

Appraising your job satisfaction should be an ongoing process. You should do it whenever you need to clarify where you are in your career and what you want your next step to be. You can also do it to get to know yourself better, or to get ahead. The key to an ever-evolving career is to monitor your own career development and stay attuned to new opportunities.

Further Considerations
The Job Satisfaction Questionnaire should help you pin down your major sources of job satisfaction and frustration. Now you have to decide what to do with this information.

Many employees hope their discontent will go away on its own. But it rarely does. Others throw themselves into their work in an attempt to compensate for their feelings of self-doubt. Some distance themselves from their work, which can lead to poor job performance and problems with the boss. All of these reactions to job dissatisfaction are part of a survival mentality. Too many people put up with unhappiness at work that they wouldn't tolerate in other areas of life. Rather than trying something new, they adjust to the old. They don't select, they settle. As they age, these people may regret that they never even tried to find out what might have been right for them.

This is the big question. You might tolerate your work because it pays the bills. You might even like it because it's familiar and easy. *But is it what you want to be doing years from now?* As you reach the end of your life, will you have regrets about how you managed your career?

The Job Involvement Questionnaire

Do you identify closely with your job? Are you absorbed in it? Does it give you a sense of purpose? Are your moods and feelings significantly affected by your work? To find out, complete *The Job Involvement Questionnaire*.

Answer the statements below by circling either *Yes* or *No*. If you are uncertain about a question, check the response that most closely describes your feelings. Once you have completed the Questionnaire, add up your scores. Scoring procedures and an interpretation follow.

The Job Involvement Questionnaire

1.	The most important things that happen to me involves my job.	Yes	No
2.	I am a perfectionist in my work.	Yes	No
3.	Most things in life are more important than my work.	Yes	No
4.	My work is one of the most rewarding and fulfilling parts of my life.	Yes	No
5.	I would probably work just as hard as I do now even if I did not have to support myself and my family.	Yes	No
6.	Most of my friends would probably agree that I usually have a great deal of energy, and get much of my energy from my work.	Yes	No

7.	I never work on weekends and holidays.	Yes	No
8.	I rarely find time for vacations.	Yes	No
9.	I would never think of breaking a date or canceling an appointment to get more work done.	Yes	No
10.	Most of my interests are centered around my job.	Yes	No
11.	My involvement in work doesn't cause problems for my family and friends.	Yes	No
12.	Most of my goals are not job-related	Yes	No
13.	I often do extra work for my job that isn't required.	Yes	No
14.	Even though I'm efficient, I work harder than most people doing similar work.	Yes	No
15.	I live, eat, and breathe my job.	Yes	No
16.	I feel depressed when I fail at something connected with my job.	Yes	No
17.	I'll stay overtime to finish a task, even if I'm not paid for it.	Yes	No
18.	For me, mornings at work just fly by.	Yes	No
19.	How well I work does not affect the way I feel about myself.	Yes	No
20.	Sometimes, I'd like to kick myself for mistakes I've made at work.	Yes	No

Scoring

Give yourself one point for each *Yes* responses to statements 1, 2, 4, 5, 6, 8, 10, 13, 14, 15, 16, 17, 18 and 20.

Give yourself one point for each *No* response to statements 3, 7, 9, 11, 12 and 19.

Now add up your points.   *Total points:* ____

Interpreting Your Score

The maximum possible score is 20. The higher your score, the more involved you are in your work. A low score suggests a lack of involvement

13 or higher: You seem to be very involved in your work, and probably enjoy it. You also appear to be good at your job. It may be central to your identity. You take your work seriously, and your moods and feelings are affected by work experiences. Some people may call you a "workaholic." Happy workaholics tend to:

- Have families that support their work habits.

- Have autonomy at work.

- Have work that provides sufficient challenge and variety.

- Get enough recognition, support and feedback from their supervisors and coworkers.

- Have jobs that make them feel good about themselves.

- Have jobs that enable them to express their needs, values, interests and skills.

- Are in good health.

- Avoid drug abuse.

- Take time out for fun.

- Organize and manage time.

- Set realistic work goals.

- See friends outside their work situations.

- Have regular exercise programs.

- Control their own lives.

- Thirst for novelty and challenge.

- Have work that gives them a sense of purpose.

If you can answer yes to most of the forgoing, you are probably a happy workaholic. You generally feel good about yourself. You're independent, growth-oriented and enjoy intrinsic rewards. Your position satisfies your needs and values and gives you a sense of purpose. You may have an infectious enthusiasm about your work that communicates to others.

The word workaholic has negative connotations, but fortunate indeed are those who are passionate about their work.

The term workaholic has negative connotations for some people, but fortunate indeed are those who are passionate about their work. After all, you will spend at least a third of your adult life on the job or commuting to and from it. The label workaholic, for those who are happily involved in their positions, is a positive, not a negative, term.

But do learn to relax. Make time for fun. Fun leads to creativity. Spend more quality time with your friends, family, leisure pursuits, and yourself. People who are happily involved in their work usually are flexible and can cut loose to enjoy the many other dimensions of their lives.

There is a distinction, of course, between happy job involvement and neurotic compulsion. If you disagreed with more than half of the forgoing statement you may be driven by a neurotic compulsion. Neurotic workaholics don't enjoy leisure pursuits that differ from their work routines and often feel uncomfortable in social settings. You may feel distressed, anxious and dissatisfied when you are not working. Your family life and other relationships may be crumbling.

If this is the case for you, consider getting more involved in leisure, social, family or spiritual activities. These will not only add more spice to your life but also enable you to approach your work with renewed vigor and creativity. If your work is always with you, you are constantly tired, irritable and withdrawn, and you feel that you lack control over your life; you may be headed for burnout. Complete *The Burnout Questionnaire* and follow the suggestions offered.

6 to 11: You are probably moderately involved in your work and you may be reasonably satisfied with it. If you are happy with your work and feel that you lead a balanced life, that's fine. However, if your job satisfaction is low, consider doing something to improve it.

Take charge of your work and your life. Don't just react to your boss or other people around you. Instead, take the initiative and create your own ways to reach your department's goals. With your boss's help, see if you can shape your position so that you are doing more of what you like to do and are good at, while shifting or delegating other duties and responsibilities to coworkers with complementary talents.

Don't hold back, and don't be afraid of being thought of as too enthusiastic. Try to develop your own challenges. Visualize what would happen if another highly motivated person was promoted to your position. How would he or she tackle it? What challenges would another person find in your job? If it's not possible to develop challenges or change your current position—and sometimes it isn't—maybe you should consider another job or a transfer. Explore other options.

5 or lower: You are not involved in your job. Perhaps other aspects of your life are more interesting to you. Good! But low job involvement involves a lack of interest and enthusiasm that may spill over to other life components. It may even lead to poor health.

If your scores on both *The Job Satisfaction Questionnaire* and *The Job Involvement Questionnaire* indicate that you are dissatisfied with your position, you should probably do something about changing jobs or even occupational fields.

Don't wait for a crisis to clear your vision. Don't let job stress and illness dictate your future. Achieve the well-being that comes from living your desired life today.

Start by doing some self-analysis. Why do you dislike your position so much? What needs must your job satisfy to make you happy? For example, is your job satisfying your needs for self-respect, autonomy, authority, adventure, creativity and security? What kind of job would you rather be doing? What's stopping you from going after it? The information and questionnaires in Chapters 9 and 10 will help you answer these questions and clarify and attain your desired goals.

The Burnout Questionnaire

Do you experience chronic fatigue? Are your thought processes dulled? Are you irritable? Are you progressively withdrawing? Do you feel physically unwell? Is your work always with you? Do you wonder why? If you answered yes to more than two of these questions, you may be headed for burnout. Psychologists and physicians consider career burnout a chronic stress syndrome.

Work conditions that promote burnout include a lack of support, challenge, autonomy, variety, flexibility and security. Heavy work loads, ambiguous job descriptions, rude customers or clients, a lack of knowledge or information and impersonal work environments are other job stressors. Certain personal characteristics, attitudes and habits also facilitate the development of burnout. These include poor planning; an inability to manage change or to relax; and failure to care for one's physical, intellectual, emotional, spiritual and social needs.

Burnout affects the whole person. This syndrome is not limited to physical symptoms or poor job performance. It influences your intellect, feelings, relationships, and spirit as well. Burnout is a progressive and slow process, eating and wearing away at you a little at a time. Victims of burnout report reduced personal energy, diminished vitality and dampened enthusiasm for life. Burnout is similar to the disengagement stage of the career cycle; both syndromes are stress symptoms, which are influenced by lack of job satisfiers, particularly autonomy and a sense of accomplishment and confidence.

Psychologists and physicians consider career burnout a chronic stress syndrome.

Ironically, burnouts are often successful in their fields; that's what burns them out. Some bright women and men work terribly hard, make tremendous sacrifices, soar to the top of their occupations or professions, and then seem to run out of fuel.

To find out if you are on the path to burnout, complete *The Burnout Questionnaire*, then read over the explanation that follows. Circle *Yes* for the symptoms of burnout that apply to you, and *No* for those that don't.

The Burnout Questionnaire

1.	Are you increasingly irritable and impatient? Are you having more arguments with your spouse, friends and even strangers lately?	Yes	No
2.	Do you feel irreplaceable? Do you go to work even when you feel ill? Do you accept extra duties out of a sense of obligation?	Yes	No
3.	Are you always tired? Do you feel fatigued rather than energetic?	Yes	No
4.	Do you have very little to say to people? Are you seeing close friends and family less frequently, even if you live in the same city?	Yes	No

---

5.	Do you fail to establish an enriching and satisfying life, separate and distinct from your work?	Yes	No
6.	Do you take work home only to find you don't complete it? Do you find that even though you don't do it, the work dominates your environment, provoking guilt?	Yes	No
7.	Have you overtaxed yourself at work or at home? Do you feel persistent pressures—such as too much to do and too little time? Are you too busy to do even routine things like making phone calls and reading reports?	Yes	No
8.	Are you increasing your use of drugs (such as aspirin, sleeping pills, tranquilizers, alcohol or tobacco) to cope with job pressures or to unwind from work?	Yes	No
9.	Are you preoccupied with thoughts of self-blame, guilt, self-recrimination and anxiety? Do you feel powerless about certain aspects of your job? Do you lack feelings of success or challenge?	Yes	No
10.	Do you feel like nothing is going well? Do you find yourself talking mostly about work, and are your conversations mostly negative?	Yes	No
11.	Are you developing uncharacteristically rigid ways of thinking, or losing the ability to adapt to change? Are you adopting rigid, by-the-book approaches to challenges rather than developing individual solutions?	Yes	No
12.	Are you turning excessively to colleagues for help in coping with emotional or physical problems or with business and professional responsibilities?	Yes	No
13.	Do you use more board/workbook activities, audiovisual materials or support staff lately to remove you from direct contact with subordinates?	Yes	No

		Yes	No
14.	Are you forgetting appointments, deadlines and/or personal possessions?	Yes	No
15.	Are you suffering physical complaints such as aches, pains, headaches, and lingering colds? Have you had more severe physical or emotional illnesses such as ulcers, high blood pressure, colitis and nervous disorders lately? Have you taken a large number of sick days recently?	Yes	No
16.	Is joy elusive? Are you often overcome by a sadness you can't explain? Are you unable to laugh or joke about yourself?	Yes	No
17.	Do you hate going to work? Do you turn off as you enter your work-place? Do you feel as if you are operating like a robot that doesn't care enough to care? Do you get a knot in your stomach when you realize the next day is a workday?	Yes	No
18.	Do you constantly say about your job, "Is this all there is?"	Yes	No
19.	Do you fail to achieve desired professional goals such as financial gains, attainment of status,perception as an expert and respect and validation from others?	Yes	No
20.	Are you pessimistic about life? Do you always emphasize the bad, down or failure side of things?	Yes	No
Total Points		**Yes___**	**No___**

Scoring
Give yourself 1 point for each *Yes*. The maximum score is 20.

Interpreting Your Score
6 or less: You appear to be in good mental, emotional and physical health. You have leaned to mange stress and probably lead a balanced life. You seem to feel supported by others, and are attaining desired goals.

7 to 11: You may be a candidate for burn out. The higher your score, the greater your chances. Stop the syndrome before it becomes serious. Practice some of the following stress busters daily.

13 or higher: You seem to be burned out. Take quick action to change your work habits or job. While no one sign of burnout is serious on its own, when many are present, you may already be well on your way to burnout. Burnout is not only preventable, it can be temporary and treatable.

If you are prone to burnout, you probably have several of the following symptoms:

- Feelings of recrimination about work problems

- Cynicism

- Long workdays to compensate for diminished productivity

- Little social or love life, or a chaotic family life

- A one-track mind, which may lead to interpersonal problems

- Loss of energy and inability to relax; fitful sleep and frequent headaches, stomachaches, back pains.

- Drug use as an escape from stress

- Little or no time for play

- Anger and hostility toward others, including friends, colleagues, children and even pets

- A loner lifestyle

- A sedentary lifestyle

- A continuing restlessness that drives you to constant activity

On the other hand, if you thrive on long work hours, you may have the following characteristics:

- An ability to postpone thinking about problems

- Prompt reactions to signs of fatigue

- Avoidance of drug abuse

- Enjoyment of scheduled vacations

- A stable domestic situation

- The ability to organize and manage time

- The ability to make a distinction between your personal and professional life

- An ability to set realistic work goals

- An ability to maintain friendships

- A regular exercise program

- A belief that you have control over your life rather than feeling controlled

- A thirst for novelty and challenge rather than familiarity and security

- The ability to derive inspiration and energy from work

Preventing Burnout

Burnout is preventable and treatable; it can even be a catalyst for growth. Many executives stay healthy because they are committed and challenged, have control over their destinies, and feel supported by others. They thrive on adversity and have learned to use stress as a source of energy to help them get things done. They feel good about their accomplishments.

The pain of burnout may push you to higher levels of maturity as you choose new and more productive attitudes and behavior patterns. A life change, an altered direction, a new attitude, or a humorous twist can all help you acquire more energy.

Most Questers stay healthy because they are committed and challenged, have control over their destinies, and feel supported by family and friends. Surprisingly, Questers tend to be challenged most by adversity. Many have learned to use stress as a source of energy. Perceived this way, stress can be valuable. But it must be managed wisely. If you can adopt similar attitudes, you can reduce your chances of becoming ill.

To prevent burnout, choose productive attitudes and behaviors. Recognize the possibility of burnout, and stop the syndrome before it strikes or becomes worse. If you're facing high levels of stress, try some of the following stress busters.

Stress Busters

- *Find something stimulating in each day.* Make your life full and rich by seeking challenges at work or in leisure activities. Let each day bring new, manageable, and exciting opportunities for growth. Make your career a cherished, inspiring, living, and developing part of you.

- Respect yourself. Reward and reinforce yourself. Engage in positive self-talk. Tell yourself, "I am doing all I should right now. I'm okay just as I am. I'm human and I will make mistakes." Brag about yourself. Realize that you don't always have to prove something or excel, because you already know and like who you are.

- Develop a positive outlook. Look on the rosy side. See the glass as half-full instead of as half-empty. Reinforce the positive in yourself and in others. Most of all, develop your own sense of humor and learn to laugh at yourself.

- Readjust your attitude. The "Serenity Prayer" by Reinhold Niebuhr provides a good start: "God grant me the serenity to accept the things I cannot change, the courage to change the things I can, and the wisdom to know the difference."

- Keep problems in perspective. Mistakes, setbacks, and even outright failures can be valuable learning experiences. Accept responsibility for your actions.

- Get away from it all. Develop other interests outside of work. Learn to play. Make family, leisure and relaxation times fun.

- Learn to relax. Use techniques such as meditation and creative visualization to help you rejuvenate your mind and soul.
- *Get plenty of rest.* Leave your worries outside the bedroom and try to get at least seven hours of sleep every night.

- *Eat healthy.* Include lots of fresh fruits, vegetables and grains in your diet. Go easy on sugar, coffee, sweetened sodas and alcohol.

- *Stop and smell the roses.* Enjoy life's small pleasures, such as walking in the park, gazing at the stars, smelling flowers or watching small children explore their surroundings.

- *Exercise regularly.* Don't just be a passive observer. Get actively involved in some athletic or physical activities to play and relax.

- *Develop support systems.* Cultivate rich and meaningful relationships. Your interpersonal support systems can be built from a variety of people, including friends, work associates, family members, spiritual acquaintances, neighbors, clients, store clerks, service people and club members. Blow off steam to trusted friends. Don't keep all of your disappointments and frustrations to yourself.

- *Manage time wisely.* Make lists and prioritize your tasks. Plan each day to include the things that are important to you. Don't let your work overwhelm you. Don't try to control everything. After all, you are in control from within. Stay on top of your work and don't let it overwhelm you. This goes for housework as well as paid work. Consider paying for housecleaning help and using your extra time for relaxation or enjoyable activities.

- *Listen to your inner self.* Pay attention to your hopes, dreams, sorrows and beliefs. Listen to what your body, mind, spirit, and emotions are really saying, and then do what you feel is right. If you long for more time with your children, don't play golf with your colleagues. If workaholism is encouraged or demanded by your boss, decide whether your salary or status is more important than a healthy lifestyle. You may have to change jobs. Set aside time each day to listen to yourself, even if it's only for five minutes. Staying in touch with your spiritual core will help you to enhance your sense of commitment, enthusiasm and purpose.

- *Add spice to your life.* Try something different once in a while. Although unusual activities vary from person to person, you might try having a costume party, playing a game you enjoyed as a child, making a snow angel, going to an avant-garde movie or gallery, going skinny dipping or trying ocean kayaking.

• *Restructure your work time.* Make lists of all the factors that drain you and all those that energize you at work. As much as possible, spend your time on the positive aspects of your position, and intersperse the negative activities with short breaks and rewards. Avoid all unnecessary meetings and learn to delegate.

• Seek professional advice. You'll find many good books and articles on burnout and relaxation techniques at your local bookstore or library. If you can't cope on your own, most hospitals and mental health professionals can give you good advice on how to deal with burnout.

Chapter 8

The Courage to Risk: Psychological Aspects of Decision Making

Cultivating the will to risk requires strength. Questers tend to draw their strength from every dimension of their lives so that they can continue to grow and prevail.

Risk and accompanying change and growth require letting go of the familiar. You feel exposed and vulnerable. But that very stress gives Questers heightened awareness, hope and determination to proceed with change.

Questers' sense of inner control determines their success in new ventures. The link between a sense of inner control and the willingness to risk is strong. Having a sense of purpose and future plans strengthen Questers' assurance that they can have a positive influence on future events in their lives. Moreover, because most Questers believe in what they are doing and expect to succeed, they generally do. Most Questers believe their expectations are realistic even though they are reaching for their dreams.

Making a change requires letting go of the familiar.

Decision-Making Styles

How do Questers go about making risky decisions? What is their decision-making style? Most Questers take planned risks. They don't move on impulse, but carefully deliberate their decisions. Making decisions rarely comes easily. Questers often harbor doubts about themselves and their work options. Many struggle with doubts and uncertainties about their futures, their jobs and the consequences of their actions. They evaluate their purposes and their personal characteristics, as well as their occupational alternatives. But once they make a firm commitment to change, the rest of the process becomes easier.

Questers tend to be flexible risk takers. The risks they take are based on self knowledge and research. Questers do not discount security; instead, they take measures that carry them through a crisis.

Most Questers try to establish a balance between the intellectual and emotional, between the rational and the intuitive aspects of decision making. Although they consider a broad range of alternatives, they eventually select one. They are realistic enough to know that there really is no one right decision, only one that feels good for them at a particular time. They anticipate both good and bad outcomes. The process usually takes six months to two years. Even after they arrive at a probable decision, Questers remain open to new information and ideas. But once they have made a big decision, they usually stick with it. Most evaluate the results after they act. Questers tend to learn from their mistakes.

Melissa's Story

Small, dark-haired, attractive, energetic, intense and warm, Melissa belies her 44 years. Dressed in a dark gray suit and a becoming gold blouse, she projects a businesslike yet feminine, image. Melissa is impulsive and intuitive, but she plans her risk taking. Currently, she is director of training and development for a large retail outlet. After her first full-time job as an air line stewardess, Melissa returned to school to study education. She had grown tired of her nomadic existence. Her desire to challenge her mind led to college, then to a job as a high school English teacher. But six years was enough of that.

Melissa's desire for new challenges led her next into a management training program for a large retail outlet. She was a good manager. A promotion to manager of women's fashions in a large department store gave her a chance to exercise her flair for fashion and her well-developed people skills. But after six years, the familiar, uneasy feelings were back. Increasingly restless and tired, she looked around for other opportunities inside her company. Nothing seemed particularly attractive. Melissa knew she needed a change, but to what?

Melissa was anxious about her future. Her company's merger with another retail chain had resulted in reg ressive policies and procedures. Incensed at her lack of control over purchasing and personnel, and fr ustrated by both the lack of autonomy and yet total responsibility, she quit. Resigning may not have been wise, but Melissa chose to trust her instincts. Melissa's body and mind were giving her signals. "I felt like I was in a straitjacket. . . . I had frequent headaches and trouble sleeping," she says. Unemployed and scared, Melissa tur ned to friends and family for support. But she found none. "They thought I was crazy to give up this position, even after I told them why I had to leave." With no support from friends and family, sticking to her guns took real guts.

Actually, the decision to change jobs had ger minated some time before. Long before she quit, Melissa had begun putting back large chunks of her salar y. A full year before she left, she attended a seminar on career change that helped her identify her abilities and tr ansferable skills. Still, there is a difference between leaving one job for another and quitting with no prospects. Quitting was an impulsive (and perhaps irrational) act, something Melissa had never done before. Only the knowledge that she was at the breaking point propelled her forward.

What to do? First, Melissa assessed her net worth. By giving herself permission to live off her rainy-day resources, Melissa found she could manage for 10 months. The next move was a visit to a talented career counselor who could help sort out her feelings, identify her strengths and other personal characteristics, explore occupational options, and set some career goals.

Melissa's self-appraisal revealed she had knowledge, skills and experience in retailing, teaching, managing, coordinating, communicating and public relations. Testing told Melissa what she already knew: She had high abilities in English comprehension and expression, analytical reasoning and supervision. An interest inventory gave her top scores in leadership, business, supervision, human relations and teaching. Other inventories revealed her high needs for autonomy, variety, achievement, challenge, altruism and creative expression. With these characteristics, Melissa could do almost anything!

Further exploration helped Melissa gain insight into her purpose—helping others, primarily in a leadership or teaching capacity. Additional inquiry helped her identify her preferred lifestyle. Melissa decided she wanted a position with regular hours that would give her time to pursue her interests in scuba diving and art as well as allow her time for social activities.

The counselor helped Melissa realize that staying in a job she had outgrown would have been a mistake. Her next move was to set tentative career goals. Melissa decided to target her career search into three general areas: management, self-employment and training and development.

During the next five months, Melissa conducted a thorough job search. She reflects, "These were some of the best months of my life. It was very stimulating. I felt completely in control. I loved setting up my own schedule. I took 'me' on as a new project and worked like a dog!"

Melissa was determined to keep moving and to stay in touch with her network of friends and former associates. Good fortune stepped in when a former colleague called to offer her a chance to conduct some workshops in retail management. The $10,000 contract put a little more distance between Melissa and the poorhouse. She used some of that $10,000 as seed money for her job search, investing in a computer, an answering service, calling cards, attractive new letterhead and a handsome resume.

Systematically, Melissa explored her network of friends and associates, applying for job after job, until she had sent out more than 50 job inquiries. Some involved a simple letter and a resume. Twenty-one inquiries reached the interview stage. And one, for a job in the food processing industry, required seven interviews in a single day.

For each management interview, Melissa diligently researched her prospective employer and product. During an interview for the executive directorship of a community welfare agency, Melissa launched a series of tough queries to decide if she and the company were a good career match. Who really held the power in the organization? What kinds of skills did the director need? What was the director's scope of authority? The silence that met her questions was uncomfortable. Her interviewers decided they would have to postpone the search until they had determined what the job really entailed.

That wasn't Melissa's only fruitless job interview. But then another promising management opportunity slipped past, this time with a large flour milling company. So Melissa took a cue from a job search book and fired off a letter to the mill's vice-president of public affairs. Instead of the usual, "Thanks for your time," it said: "I'm sorry to hear that the position has been filled. I thought I'd be good for it. I also very much appreciate the time you spent talking to me. Because you know so much about the food processing industry, I would like to keep in touch with you from time to time as I continue my search. Would that be okay?" With an approach like that, who could turn her down?

Melissa's time-out period gave her the opportunity to seriously consider an idea that had long intrigued her: going into business for herself. The possibilities tempted her. Should she become a free-lance retail consultant? Establish a fashion boutique? Or maybe buy into a publishing position with a regional women's fashion magazine? The options were exciting. But Melissa decided her bottom line at this point was a regular paycheck. She also wanted a more balanced lifestyle than self-employment could offer. Although these options weren't right for her now, Melissa promised to reconsider them later.

Having ruled out self-employment, Melissa was ready to explore a third possible avenue: training and development. With a friend's help, she explored the options by reading relevant books and talking to people in the field. She identified a list of five firms that seemed compatible with her own personal characteristics. Then she began a serious, high-gear job search with letters to the vice-presidents of personnel and phone calls to top managers. When all five firms responded that they had no immediate openings, she shifted the nature of her campaign. She chose a young, growing, people-oriented, flexible organization that offered profit sharing and a competitive salary. Most important, the retail organization didn't yet have a fully developed training and development program.

Melissa armed herself for the attack. First, she made a series of phone calls to the company's top managers. Finally convincing them that she was serious, she landed an interview with the vice-president of personnel and the senior vice-president. The interview lasted four hours. The company brass were impressed, but the only job available was a junior position training salesclerks. Melissa persisted. What the company really needed, she asserted, was a more ambitious training and development program. A second interview was all it took to convince the company to hire her as the new director of training and development, at a higher salary and with six weeks' grace so she could finish her contract work and take a well-earned vacation.

How has her new position worked out? "Very well," she reflects one year later. Although the job hasn't grown quite as quickly as she had hoped and she doesn't yet have the size of staff she needs, Melissa is content. "I'm glad I didn't take the jobs that I thought would be dead ends. I'm glad I avoided traditional corporations. And I'm glad I took a chance with a growing, progressive organization, because now I can grow with it."

Does she have any regrets? "Absolutely none." In fact, Melissa says, quitting without having another job lined up was a good choice for her. "I might not have conducted such a thorough job search if I hadn't felt so pressured." A good job search, she now knows, is a long process. Melissa was lucky; she found her position in five months. "But, of course," she says wryly, "I had to work like a demon to do it."

Besides the obvious reward of a new position, Melissa's job search had other benefits. One was increased self-confidence. "I love my work," she says. "I feel good about myself, and at the end of the day, I have lots of energy left over." Melissa feels good because she is doing something worthwhile. Her new position gives her life meaning and purpose. While being 44 seemed like an added pressure at first, her age was no barrier in the end.

Being able to say with satisfaction that you risked for your dream is the biggest prize of all.

What Can You Learn from Melissa?

Melissa's experience demonstrates that while confidence and willingness to risk can be positive qualities, job searchers also need to protect themselves by reducing some of the risks involved in changing occupations.

Melissa's success was partly due to her willingness to invest in herself. By realizing that this was the rainy day for which she had been saving, Melissa could buy herself the time she needed.

Taking time out taught Melissa five important lessons.

First, she learned the importance of trusting her own instincts. Far from being disastrous, quitting one job before she had another lined up gave her more time to devote to her job search.

Second, she discovered that the most satisfying positions are often ones that allow you to tie together the threads of past experiences and interests.

Third, she found that mature age can be an advantage. Having reached the age and level of experience that demanded the opportunity to call her own shots, she discovered that the best job is the one you design for yourself. Creating your own job doesn't mean you have to be self-employed, only that your self be fully employed.

Fourth, she discovered she had many options. When people become tied to certain jobs and skills, they forget just how vast their actual choices are.

Finally, Melissa learned that the tremendous investment of energy a successful job search demands is exactly what allows people to look back and say, "Win, lose or draw, I gave it my all." Being able to say with satisfaction that you risked for a dream is the biggest prize of all.

Umberto's Story

Success doesn't always come easy. When it does, the experience can be astonishing, invigorating, and a little frightening. Those are the emotions Umberto, a former social worker, experienced when he turned into a restaurateur. At 40, this handsome, dark-haired entre-preneur with brooding eyes and a deep voice has mixed emotions about the success of his Italian restaurant and highly popular cookbook. A cautious risk taker, Umberto is in his fifth job, but his first "real occupational choice." Despite his cautious nature, experience has taught this West Coast entrepreneur that once the first risk is past, the rest follows naturally.

Umberto enjoys talking about career choices because he feels his own risk-taking pattern is fairly typical. "More and more," he explains, hands slicing the air around him, "I see people who, 10 or 15 years ago, would have been expecting to take a long, steady climb up the career ladder to the top of their fields. But they've tumbled off, and now they're beginning to rethink what they want, and it's not just to change jobs within their fields, but to change occupations and lifestyles completely."

Umberto has tried both. For the first 12 years of his professional life, he moved around in the social work system. Then he made a drastic move that changed not only his career, but his entire life. This is the story of that process.

Like many, Umberto greeted college graduation with uncertainty. With a B.A. in social sciences, he was not sure what he wanted to do. He took a job as a social worker for a small school division about 100 miles from his hometown. The job promised to combine his desire to do socially useful work with his interest in guiding adolescents. Weekly meetings with the school division's psychologist and evening courses and workshops led naturally to a B.S.W. degree. The job was especially gratifying because Umberto liked working with people. "Until then, as an only child, I had led a fairly protected life. The job exposed me to a lot of life that I hadn't seen before, and I was forced to do a lot of soul searching to clarify who I was and what I valued. You can't discuss values with kids without looking seriously at your own."

For the next few years Umberto worked tirelessly during the days; then, instead of spending time with his new wife, Brenda, he wrote reports endlessly during the evenings. Even in his sleep, Umberto was still writing reports and rehashing problems. Although the job was challenging, it was also frustrating. "You were supposed to help change the students' behavior, but you only saw them once every three weeks."

Five years of frustration was enough. Umberto looked for another job. He found one in the probation system, where, with a smaller workload, he could help delinquent youths. Now that Umberto had the opportunity to work intensely with his young charges, he felt he could make a real impact. His sense of progress was short-lived, however. No matter how effective he was, a rigid probation system thwarted his good intentions. Feeling disgruntled, he searched again for a position in the same field.

Umberto's third job involved investigating child neglect and abuse—a depressing and draining task. "What I saw literally made me sick." Now, Umberto had been a social worker for 12 years. "It felt like 30." His career growth had been agonizing, and what he had seen depressed and infuriated him. "I saw people who didn't rock the boat get promoted. Those who did and were their own persons didn't have a chance to advance. I was very good at my job, but there was no incentive to be creative."

Umberto had to maintain some balance in his life, so he took up painting and cooking to relieve his career pressures. But the tragedy of his life didn't fully strike

Umberto until he watched his father dying. He recalls, "It was a funny thing. Here you are, watching a beautiful man with white hair lying in his bed, dying of a hear t attack. You hear him ramble and wander and talk about his life and what he wished he had done . You watch death. Then you say, 'Wait a minute. What's going on with him is going to happen to me. What am I doing between now and my death?' You begin to assess yourself, and that's a shock. 'Am I going to do this for the rest of my life? Isn't there another way to earn a living?' That's what you wonder."

Suddenly, Umberto faced some serious self-evaluation. After a long discussion with his wife, she turned to one of his paintings and said, "Umberto, you're a very creative person, but this job is wiping you out. You're miserable, you have migraines. Please quit." The time had come. With his father's death and Brenda's permission to quit, Umberto's unspoken dreams could surface. Consumed with joy and relief, he burst into tears. "I didn't know what I wanted to do, but I just knew that I had to get out of social work. I saw that I had interests and talents , intelligence, creativity, and energy, and that, if I directed them to ward the goals I cherished, I could make it."

Umberto also realized he had never really made the choice to be a social worker in the first place . Chance and circumstance had led him into an occupation that made him miserable. Now, he wanted to choose an occupation that was right for him.

That took some time . While his wife encouraged him to quit right away, Umberto was reluctant to leave her carrying the burden of a hefty mortgage. With good management, he was able to accomplish his normal workload in eight hours and devote evenings and a few half-days to exploring his options. Gradually, he discovered what he didn't want. Umberto enjoyed making pastries, but he didn't think it would be profitable enough to pay the family's bills. And the artist's life was too solitary for his temperament. Then, at 38, Umberto realized that what he loved most was cooking and entertaining. As a child, he had cooked while his parents worked. Now a grown man, he was still cooking. Maybe he could turn this talent into a profitable venture.

There were other reasons Umberto wanted to succeed on his own. One was his hostility toward rigid authoritarian institutions. He also wanted to rise on his own merits. Excited now, Umberto realized that he didn't want to be a chef, confined to a hot kitchen all day. He wanted to be a manager. Too impatient to return to school for the business and management skills he needed, Umberto took the direct approach. He talked to the manager of a fast food outlet about entrepreneurship. The die was cast when he discovered the outlet's parent company had an excellent training program. Within a day of being accepted, Umberto quit his job.

Quitting was easier than he had anticipated. True, his salary would plummet to less than half of what it had been, but his family was prepared to skimp for a while. The next 18 months were among the hardest and the happiest of Umberto's life. He quickly advanced to become manager of one of the largest-grossing outlets in the chain.

Soon, Umberto began fantasizing about his own restaurant. During his months of training, he had discovered that he really loved the restaurant business, that his counseling skills could be put to good use dealing with employees and customers, and that he could get the immediate rewards he so desired. This time, quitting was even easier. "Having quit once before, I had finally managed to overcome my fears."

Within a month, Umberto had found the perfect location—a large old house overlooking a river. Raising the money was more difficult; the lowest interest rate he could find was 22 percent. Umberto thought it over carefully, then decided to remortgage his home and borrow the money from friends and family. With cash in hand, he decorated the house and designed the menu, using the motif of a typical northern Italian restaurant.

Il Palazzo opened with a staff of 20. In a city noted for sophisticated palates and numerous restaurants, Il Palazzo soon amassed a dedicated following. As demand for the secrets of his fine cuisine grew, Umberto followed his first success with a guide to Italian cooking. With astonishing presales of 40,000 copies, the book was a hit.

Achieving this elusive mix of culinary and financial success was no mean accomplishment. Long before he launched his new venture, Umberto had researched the market and the pros and cons of the restaurant business. He says, "This just felt right. I knew what I was getting into, so I felt ready to take the plunge." Even though, through preparation, he had reduced the risks of failing, this new entrepreneur still experienced anxiety. Today, he says, "I can hardly believe that this is the new me! I did have a difficult time leaving social work. But I remember my father's regrets. I didn't want to have similar ones."

What Can You Learn from Umberto?

Umberto learned to be a risk taker and a Quester by moving carefully at first, researching his options, and taking into account the needs and desires of those close to him. But as he grew more confident, risk taking became easier. Umberto's decision-making style also changed from that of a cautious, play-it-safer to that of an enterprising entrepreneur.

In addition to learning to risk, Umberto discovered four truths.

First, he discovered that selecting an occupation for expediency is not the best way to go. Had Umberto examined his career goals sooner, he may have fulfilled his dream much earlier. His unhappy work history was partly the result of entering an occupation out of propriety rather than conviction. Umberto's desire to make a difference could have been translated into a more suitable position much earlier in his career.

Second, he found that having his own business satisfied his growth and creativity needs. The right pieces to Umberto's puzzle eluded him for a long time. But he found that running a restaurant satisfied his needs for autonomy, creativity and working with people.

Third, Umberto learned that there are many ways to help people. He could provide a useful service to many people by offering them superb cuisine and pleasant surroundings. The number of individuals whose lives he enriched was far greater than those he tried to help as a social worker. Most important, he loved doing it!

Finally, he learned that it's never too late to change your occupation. Umberto's story punctures the fallacy that you can't change the direction of your career in mid-life. To be truly satisfying, your occupational choice should allow previously disregarded aspects of yourself to finally emerge.

The Process of Risking

In their planned risks, many Questers proceed through a series of stages as they move toward their goals. These stages are listed here:

Stage 1: Becoming *Aware* of Negative Feelings

Stage 2: *Defining* the Problem

Stage 3: Experiencing *Ambivalence*

Stage 4: *Preparing*

Stage 5: *Narrowing* Your Options

Stage 6: Taking *Action*

Stage 7: *Evaluating* the Decision

The stages do not always occur in the precise order outlined, and Questers may pass through some more than once. For instance, many experience ambivalence (Stage 3) even while they are preparing for risk (Stage 4) and narrowing their options (Stage 5). But if Questers omit one of the stages, they can face trouble. Moreover, in dealing with different problems, Questers may be at different stages. Because a decision in one life component (occupation, marriage or leisure) affects the processes in another, decisions need to be thought out carefully.

Your decisions are based on knowledge about yourself and your environment and are influenced by societal pressures and realities. Most involve an element of uncertainty, and all involve emotional and intellectual processes. In evaluating the information that goes into making a decision, consider intuitive cues such as body sensations, feelings and ideas that suddenly pop into your mind. Also take into account external information obtained by research and experiences. Realize that decisions are not irrevocable. They can be changed or modified as you learn more about yourself and your options. A proper balance of commitment and tentativeness is crucial in today's work world.

> *There are no firm right or wrong decisions because each decision is important for your learning.*

Making big decisions is challenging. There are no firm right or wrong decisions, because each decision is important for your learning. However, if you make a decision for the right reason, it will probably work out in your favor. No one can tell you if a decision to change jobs is the right move. But to grow and develop to your fullest potential, you have to be willing to

evaluate yourself and your current situation; if you are not
growing or satisfied, you should consider making changes.
And change involves risk a well as growth.

By learning how Questers plan for risk, you can alter the
direction of your life. Even now, you could be planning the
moves you would like to make, rather than waiting until the
situation becomes so awful that you feel forced to change or
are dismissed. Some of the ways you can reduce risk through
planning are described in the rest of this Chapter. You'll find
other factors to consider in making shifts in Chapters 9 and
10.

Stage 1: Becoming Aware of Negative Feelings

Gloria, petite and 55, is a clinical psychologist in pr ivate
practice who just completed her Ph.D. Her ambition and
ability are inspiring. Her obvious intelligence is balanced
by magnetic beauty. Stunning green eyes glitter with
excitement and the worldliness of experience.

For all of her success, Gloria hasn't had an easy life. Her
father died when she was eight years old. By her early
teens, she was burdened with an alcoholic mother.
Working part-time, she was able to put herself through an
honors program in mathematics. After graduation, she
worked in the actuarial department of an insurance
company until she and her new husband, an up-and-
coming lawyer, decided to have a family. Because she had
missed out on a happy home life, having one now was
important to Gloria. But once more, she was disappointed.
At 39, with four teenagers, she was on her own again.
Although her ex-husband did pay some child support, the
money wasn't enough to maintain the family's standard of
living, so Gloria returned to school for a year to train as a
math teacher.

Being a teacher seemed like a good career choice. She
would have contact with people, the salary was good, and
the hours and holidays would give her time to be at home

with her children. By all external standards, Gloria was successful. After teaching elementary school for four years, she was promoted to principal, where she stayed for five more years. But when the school administration offered her a promotion to a larger school, Gloria turned it down. She reflects, "I was feeling tired and irritable." Her frequent outbursts of tears and anger seemed to have no apparent cause. The laughter seemed to have gone from her life.

Feeling bored and trapped, Gloria knew she was no longer growing in her job. "I had no intellectual stimulation. I had mastered the job. Even if I had moved on to the other school, it would have been more of the same." That fall, Gloria fell ill. Bones aching, she huddled in bed. Friends told her to go to the hospital, but Gloria knew it was only the flu. She also knew that what was making her ill was the fact that she didn't know what to do with the rest of her life. She stayed in bed for 10 days. Finally, she asked for a sabbatical. "I needed time to rethink the direction my career was taking."

Gloria's body was sending her messages in the form of the flu with accompanying tiredness and aching bones, but labeling her feelings proved hard. Most life changes are heralded by just such physical cues. At first, you ignore them. Eventually, you cannot. You may feel lousy a lot, or you may feel that something is wrong with your relationship or that you never laugh anymore. Everyone's body has some physical equivalent for fear, despair, or euphoria—a dull ache in the gut, a feeling of heaviness inside, tears that well up like a flood, a sense of soaring. Sometimes, these feelings are hard to label and distinguish.

Stage 2: Defining the Problem
Once Gloria admitted she had a problem, she was able to move into Stage 2: defining the problem. "In thinking about my career, I realized that I went into teaching for the wrong reasons. I made a cold-blooded decision because I

needed the money and liked the hours. But I was never really happy teaching. My subconscious was telling me that I could change and try something that I had wanted to try for a long time." Because Gloria was no longer financially responsible for her children, taking a risk felt better now.

Gloria had entered the second stage of decision making. This stage is usually a subtle modulation from Stage 1, like a change of key in music. Feelings of discontent are translated into vague impulses that you'd like to chuck your job and start something entirely new. Gloria was aware she couldn't stay in teaching, so she thought of trying her longtime dream, psychology.

Gloria recognized the need to change. Her second stage began with the realization that she wanted to get out of teaching. By listening to and accepting what her body, mind, and soul were telling her, Gloria identified the feelings behind her dissatisfaction. Her decision to do something about the problem (try psychology) resulted in her leaving a familiar way of life and taking her first step into the unknown. Defining the problem and deciding to make changes in your life are important preliminary steps in the decision-making process.

Stage 3: Experiencing Ambivalence

Gloria's "I will!" was followed by the third stage of the decision-making process, "But can I?" As anxiety asserts itself, many people experience such conflicting emotions before taking a risk.

Gloria was afraid because she was leaving the security of a monthly paycheck and a pension. As she stepped into an unknown future, she was acutely conscious of her 49 years. How would she do? She had no job in sight. But she was also excited about testing herself, about trying something new and challenging, and about experiencing adventure and change. Being anxious about risk taking is normal. Most people feel apprehensive about losing their known worlds. In Gloria's case, she was trading the horrors of the known for those she couldn't yet imagine. She was giving up a lot.

Stage 4: Preparing

Gloria explored psychology by taking three night school courses while she worked. During this time, she also analyzed her personal characteristics and her suitability to psychology. Then she took a sabbatical to study full-time. This allowed her to further assess her suitability to psychology and to initiate some preliminary steps toward achieving her tentative goal. Her contingency plan was to return to teaching, at least for a while.

> *To invite change takes courage and hope; to see it through takes skill.*

Preparing for risk also takes resourcefulness and work. Most Questers try to be in charge of change by setting tentative goals; understanding themselves; gathering realistic, up-to-date information about occupational options and related training routes; and preparing contingency plans. To invite change takes courage and hope; to see it through takes skill. To make good decisions, you must control the elements of the risk that are controllable.

Setting Tentative Goals

Questers usually think carefully about what they want to do. They separate their needs and desires from what society dictates or what friends and family consider best. Most establish tentative short- and medium-term goals. Rather than viewing these goals as a huge, all-encompassing mass (such as changing jobs), they break them down into manageable sub-goals (such as learning more about their needs, interests, and strengths, or reading about the kinds of jobs that fit their personal characteristics). Examined task by task, each step is much more manageable. Breaking down your goal into manageable units makes the formidable seem possible. When setting their goals, Questers pay careful attention to their inner voices and dreams. These help identify what's really important to them. Many have learned that disregarding these messages inevitably leads to more dissatisfaction.

As they gather information about themselves and their career options, it is natural for Questers to review and revise their goals. Questers' goals give them a sense of direction, b ut they are not ironclad. Gloria's tentative goal was to leave teaching. Her ideal goal was to be a psychologist. She enrolled in a psychology program, but just in case her dream didn't w ork out, she retained the option of retur ning to teaching. Taking courses in psychology gave her time to explore herself and the field to deter mine if she was suited to her new career choice. Her commitment to leave teaching and enter psychology was flexible enough to allow her to make changes if her plans didn't jell.

Exploring Options
Seeking relevant, up-to-date information is the first step in illuminating the dark, unknown world one enters when making a major career change. Many Questers use this information as a guide for at least par t of the jour ney. Two kinds of information are essential to any occupational shift: knowledge about yourself and knowledge about your career options in the current economy. You also need to know where you can get this information, what Internet sites and pr inted materials to consult, what personal contacts y ou need, and what professional assistance workshops or counseling options are available.

Gloria found out more about herself and her career options from a vocational psychology course. She learned, for example, that she has social, in vestigative, and artistic interests, and that she has strong needs f or achievement, altruism, autonomy, creativity, and challenge. Her purpose is to help others, and her skills and strengths include inter viewing and diagnosing, advising and teaching, counseling and testing, designing and implementing programs, collaborating and problem solving, and writing and speaking. All of these traits—coupled with her compassion, ability to inspire and emotional stability—are compatible with practicing psychology.

Gloria also explored the types of jobs available in the field, the probability of finding a compatible position, and the feasibility of establishing a private practice. She surfed the Internet and consulted directories such as the *Occupational Outlook Handbook* and *National Occupational Classification System* as well as specific books about psychology careers. She interviewed and shadowed psychologists employed in various settings. The information she acquired helped reduce some of her anxiety.

Networking

Another way Questers keep abreast of information in various fields is through networking. By attending professional meetings, workshops and conferences, they develop and maintain contacts with people in their chosen fields. Gloria joined the American Psychological Association and attended local chapter meetings. This helped her keep up with recent developments and opportunities in the field as well as meet and maintain contact with future colleagues.

Managing Money

You can reduce the risks of changing jobs if you prepare yourself financially. Melissa's nest egg enabled her to conduct a full-time job search. Gloria prepared herself financially by taking a sabbatical. Both women and Umberto learned to live on a considerably lower income so that their savings and money would stretch further. Some Questers' spouses go back to work full-time to supplement or even bring in all the family's income. One Quester who went into business for himself reduced his lifestyle dramatically. He says, "It got to the point where I had to reduce my lifestyle substantially. ... I was living on rice and watered-down tomato soup."

If you want to return to school, you should check out the

financial aid packages available from both public and private sectors. To help finance studies and business ventures, many Questers borrow from friends and relatives. Others approach liberal bank managers with well-researched proposals.

Don't use lack of money as an excuse for not making a career change.

Don't use lack of money as an excuse for not making a desired career shift. Like the Questers, as you work toward your career goal, you will find ways of surviving. But, for a while, you will have to work hard, think creatively, and be willing to forgo some material comforts. Few Questers regret these sacrifices.

Establishing Support

Dispelling misinformation, reducing ignorance, and having financial resources tend to make Questers feel more secure in their decisions. But they don't live by facts and material needs alone. Questers' make their job shifts easier and reduce their anxieties by soliciting the support and guidance of others. Whenever you begin a large, new venture, you need to feel that the people close to you care. Many Questers receive help from partners, family members, friends and colleagues. Others seek help from spiritual advisers or professional counselors. Not only can caring individuals provide encouragement and empathy, they can also help you to see your decision more objectively and to analyze it critically.

Gloria received lots of support and encouragement from her friend, Brad. A professor and the director of psychological services for her school division also gave her encouragement to earn her Ph.D. Positive feedback from clients and professors gave her a tremendous sense of accomplishment. Even though Gloria's children were not living at home, they often showed support for their busy mother by helping with chores such as grocery shopping and mowing the lawn. Hard work, a sense of humor, and prayer also helped Gloria cope with major changes.

Laying Down a Safety Net

One reason why career changes evoke so much anxiety is that they seem irreversible. But this is not necessarily so, particularly if you think hard and creatively. Many Questers build in fail-safe and retreat positions, contingency plans for an alternative course of action if the present one turns out to be a disaster. Just knowing that other possibilities exist reduces the risk. Identify the worst possible disaster that could occur, then decide what you could do about it. Doing so will not only relieve some of your anxiety, it will also prepare you for that possible outcome. Gloria's "worst possible disaster" would have been to return to teaching. Having that contingency plan reduced her anxieties and negative fantasies.

In times of acute pressure, Questers have learned not to panic. Deadlines can always be moved. Gloria didn't make her decision to leave teaching immediately. She took a year's sabbatical to give herself time to think. A time limit, particularly one imposed by someone else, need not be cast in stone. A prospective employer will wait another day or two while you mull over a job decision. In any major life decision, you can learn to allow yourself breathing or incubating time.

A word of caution, however: Don't continually extend a self-imposed time frame. There's a difference between giving yourself a buffer to reflect on a decision and procrastinating. Once you commit yourself to realistic goals and set deadlines, put your plan into action.

Stage 5: Narrowing Options

Once Questers have assessed their personal characteristics and needs, identified and explored career options, and reduced the risks as much as

In any major life decision, you can learn to allow yourself breathing or incubating time.

possible, they begin narrowing their alternatives. Doing so isn't always easy.

Gloria used both her intellect and her intuition to e valuate her options. Although she evaluated the pros and cons of each of her choices mathematically, she learned that this important technique has its limitations . Incomplete and inaccurate information, human impatience, and the difficulty of calculating the emotional components of hope and fear (as well as various unconscious projections) complicate the process.

So, in addition to pr ioritizing her options, Gloria took a week off from her b usy schedule to relax in the mountains. During this time she did no conscious thinking about her decision. However, her unconscious was working continuously. While she was taking a walk on the sixth day of her vacation, the answer to her question came to her. She was now convinced that the practice of psychology was right for her.

By turning away from the muddle of decision making, Questers listen to their subconscious minds . They let go of the intellectual component of the process b y letting their decisions incubate. Intuitive insights usually ar ise when we are in a relaxed state. Of course, it is impor tant to first tackle problems consciously by compiling as much information as possible and analyzing the data. The intuitive hunch may then come as a flash of insight when y our mind is not f ocusing on the dilemma. "Sleeping on it" allows the intuitive or incubative process to take over. Many creative people repor t finding solutions to problems either upon a wakening or during a moment of reverie. Almost everyone has had the e xperience of groping for a name, only to ha ve it swim obligingly to the surface soon after they stop pursuing it.

The incubation period gives the decision time to ger minate. Typically, intuitive insights both precede and f ollow the exhaustive use of analysis and logic. Sometimes, the failure to resolve problems is due to the inability to put them in perspective. Being overly concerned with certain facets of a problem may cause you to miss others, so you overlook better solutions. Intuition permits you to delve into the conscious and subconscious storehouse of everything you have ever learned. Tapping into this rich reservoir allows you to perceive the many possible solutions inherent in complex problems. It also helps you clarify what you really care about.

Turning away or letting go may seem like procrastination, but you can distinguish it in two ways. First, rather than feeling guilty about it, you consent to it. Second, rather than a shutdown, it represents an attentive waiting, a poised readiness. Sometimes, you move ahead best by sitting still. It takes time for seeds to germinate. At some points, particularly before moving into action, it is not only permissible but desirable to let go so that your deepest convictions can emerge.

Stage 6: Taking Action

Questers don't move into action until they have prepared themselves both cognitively and emotionally. But once they decide to take action, they commit themselves to a goal, make plans, and follow through.

Making Plans

After making a choice by committing to a goal, Questers develop tentative plans. They realize they must be flexible in their planning because of the rapid changes occurring around them. They try to make their career choices reversible, so they can change direction in midstream if the need arises. Some have learned the hard way that rigid adherence to long-range goals and plans doesn't work in times of change. Questers also ask themselves a number of questions about their personal characteristics and desired goals: for example, "Do I feel good about where I'm heading?" And, "Are my plans getting me where I want to go?"

Gloria's planning process involved investigating the psychology programs of local schools to deter mine their suitability for her, as well as their reputation in the professional community; applying to the schools of her choice; and preparing a budget.

Taking action also requires acquiring job search and business planning skills. It may also mean returning to school on a full- or part-time basis for upgrading or retraining.

Going for It
Making a final commitment ends the action stage . Regardless of how well you prepare, acting on any decision means taking some steps into the unknown. There is always something new to learn about yourself and the situation. But once you've made a commitment to change, the rest of the process is easier. For most Questers, this step, though risky, brings a heady sense of relief. Finally, you've done all the dreaming, researching, thinking, worrying, and phoning, and you are ready to act by quitting a job, accepting a position, establishing a business, getting married, or embarking on some other adventure.

Gloria's action stage began when, after her sab batical, she was interviewed by the school board about a new principalship. Would she accept it? Gloria decided not to. That first step to act began with an e xit. This propelled her to continue with her plans to earn her Ph.D. so that she could attain her goal of having a psychology practice. Gloria followed through on her plans by completing the Ph.D. coursework and internship. Opening her office was the next step in her commitment to the pr actice of psychology.

Stage 7: Evaluating the Decision
Gloria was asked to evaluate the gains and losses she experienced from her career move. "There is no way I could go back," she replied. "It would be like dying. I think it's far better to keep trying new things, because you're not going to grow if you sit still."

As Gloria says, for every risk she took there has been a positive payoff. "And each time I risked, I learned to do it more effectively. I really feel that there isn't much that I can't do at this point in my life. I feel I've walked a million miles, mostly on my own." Like all of us, Gloria has fallen on her face, but she has learned something from every negative experience.

Would she do anything differently? "Not very much," she replies. She has made errors in her practice and has been something of a workaholic. But Gloria's only true regret is that she stayed so long stagnating in her previous job.

Fortunately, Gloria had few doubts about succeeding. "You have to believe that, even though all of the odds are against you, you'll make it." Visualizing herself in the situation she wanted to be in helped Gloria to move forward. And, while she doesn't always feel confident, she has learned to put her doubts on the back burner.

Having succeeded at this risk, Gloria has definite plans for the future. She wants to keep working, learning and growing, though not at the pace she maintained to attain her Ph.D. and start a practice. Now, she wants to reap the benefits of her hard work, to have more time for herself, her partner and her family. Gloria feels her age was a definite benefit. She says her accumulated personal and work experiences gave her the confidence and knowledge to make her dream a reality.

Gloria's evaluation of her gains echoes that of most Questers who change jobs. The majority acquire a considerable amount of personal satisfaction and a sense of inner harmony. They attain greater self-awareness and control over their personal and professional destinies. Among other rewards, they list enhanced job satisfaction and involvement, improved relationships with partners and family members, more leisure time, healthier and more rewarding lifestyles and more meaningful lives.

If you have tackled a life challenge carefully and still experienced a poor outcome, you will probably be discouraged. Don't
be. It's unrealistic to have perfect results all the time. Learn
from your mistakes. You will have many other opportunities. If
you are not happy with the consequences of your risk, ask
yourself if you were motivated by internal
aspirations or by the desire to please
others, and what you should have done
differently. Next time, you will improve your
performance.

*Money can be
a trap that
creates the
illusion of
security.*

The fear, excitement, pleasure and joy of
changing jobs rejuvenate most Questers.
They also learn some pretty important lessons from their
career moves. As one says, "Money is far from being the most
important thing in life. On the contrary, it can be a trap that
becomes a false goal and creates the illusion of security."

Growth is a major gain, says another: "If you are just living for
the next coffee break or the next vacation or raise or retirement or death, you are not really living. You are existing."

Most Questers feel like those you have met. They haven't
really tallied up any major deficits from their career moves.
Some experienced material losses, such as loss of a steady
income, retirement benefits, security, seniority, investments or
health or insurance benefits. But, for most of them, these
losses are minor. Though a number of Questers, particularly
those who became self-employed, took substantial pay cuts
to become established, they retrieved those losses. Most say
that planned risk taking paid off and will practice the same
steps again when they take their next risk. Only about 25
percent said they would do something differently. Among this
group, most said they would leave a stagnant job sooner,
pursue a work problem with a senior company executive, take
more time to explore additional options, leave more gracefully,
or seek help from a career counselor.

Making changes is a necessary part of growing. But the

306

responsibility for making changes rests with you. Sometimes this means taking a step into the unknown and parting with a familiar way of life. If that's the case, muster all the courage you can and think of yourself as a Quester, and you will become one. Remember, next time it will be easier.

Making changes is a necessary part of growing.

What's Your Decision-Making Style?

Are you happy with the occupation you selected, or do you wish you had done things differently? How do you go about making major decisions? Do you plan your decisions, balancing intellect and intuition? Are you anxious and slow, or intuitive and impulsive? Can you detect some regularity in your decision-making style?

To understand your decision-making behavior, think of decisions you've made about career shifts in the past. In each statement below, choose the one that best describes how you usually decide.

1. Planning

____ A. I'm thoughtful, organized and plan ahead.
____ B. I can't make up my mind. Frequently, I put things off.
____ C. I do what feels right, and make up my mind quickly.

2. Evaluating alternatives

____ A. I think of a number of options, but stop after a reasonable search.
____ B. I keep going over possibilities.
____ C. I make a quick, overall survey of the possibilities, hoping something will hit me.

3. Deciding among alternatives

____ A. I take intellect and feelings into account.
____ B. I use my intellect or rational mind.
____ C. I listen to my feelings.

4. Assessing the consequences

____ A. I think of both the good and bad outcomes .
____ B. I focus on the bad things.
____ C. I expect things to work out.

5. Describing my emotions

____ A. I'm anxious and excited.
____ B. I'm anxious.
____ C. I'm excited.

6. Examining the time frame

____ A. I take a fairly long time.
____ B. I take a very long time.
____ C. I take little time.

7. Deliberating

____ A. I think it out carefully, then decide with few regrets.
____ B. I agonize over the alternatives.
____ C. I make up my mind quickly and stick to it.

8. Ambivalence

____ A. I rally behind my choice after checking it out.
____ B. I experience serious doubts and may change my mind.
____ C. I don't think about it after launching into action.

9. Reviewing

___ A. I think about what I've learned from it.
___ B. I worry and regret not doing something.
___ C. I put it out of my mind.

Total Number of Responses:

___ A responses
___ B responses
___ C responses

Scoring and Interpretation

6 or more A responses: You tend to base your decisions on both intuition and intellect. You make decisions slowly and are more concerned with good outcomes than with fear of failure or the need to be perfect. You usually plan and review without worrying a lot.

6 or more B responses: You seem to be anxious and bide your time. You make big decisions with great effort, hesitancy and apprehension. You take considerable time thinking about the decision or asking others for feedback. You also tend to put things off.

6 or more C responses: You are probably an intuitive, casual, impulsive risk taker. You tend to decide quickly. You may feel optimistic and spend little time in introspection. Once you've made the decision, you put it out of your mind.
Few people are entirely A, B, or C risk takers. Because most people are mixed, there are several risk-taking styles. The person who is slow to take a career risk may be more impetuous when buying a home. A person who operates largely on hunch may, through exploration and discipline, be able to identify the consequences before acting. Some inconsistencies are both inevitable and healthy. No one is a perfect risk taker, but you can learn to be a more effective risk taker.

There is no such thing as a wrong decision if y ou make it for the right reason. You can learn to be a more effective and efficient decision maker by following some basic guidelines.

- Know what you want and why you want it.

- Research your options and use y our intellect and intuition to clarify your goals.

- Develop an action plan and go for it, but realize that goals are not written in stone and plans should be fle xible.

- Ask for help when you need it.

- Believe you will achieve your goal.

- Work hard and persist.

- Don't be afraid to try. Even if you have setbacks, you will win.

Chapter 9
Prepare to Change

The Questers' stories have shown that you can take the initiative in your own career development during changing times and prevail. Now it's your turn to do something about a dissatisfying career—and life.

As you have seen, change is a normal aspect of personal and professional development. If you make voluntary moves, your transitions will be more pleasant than ones forced on you by layoffs or termination. And you will be more prepared. But even involuntary changes can have happy endings.

In this Chapter, we will review the decision-making process described in Chapter 8 and look at other important factors you should consider when making career decisions and pursuing desired goals. If you are contemplating a career change, coping with a job loss, reentering the workforce, returning to school, starting your own business or looking for a job, you'll find help in this Chapter. The decision making steps form the acronym, ADAPNAE.

A career change can take months or even years of exhaustive soul searching. Long before you make the shift, you need to know the steps involved in a successful move, how to master the troublesome feelings that accompany change, where the possible challenges lie and how to maximize your gains while minimizing your losses. You need to understand yourself and your career options. You must set career goals and know where to find advice and help on job search and marketing techniques. And, if you plan to be self-employed, you must learn how to explore business opportunities and plan for success. Creating a life worth living and finding the courage to pursue your dreams are not easy. But, like thousands of others have shown, you can do it.

As we saw in Chapter 8, there are seven stages in the decision-making process.

Stage 1: Becoming *Aware* of Negative Feelings

Stage 2: *Defining* the Problem

Stage 3: Experiencing *Ambivalence*

Stage 4: *Preparing* for Risk

Stage 5: *Narrowing* Options

Stage 6: Taking *Action*

Stage 7: *Evaluating* the Decision

Keep in mind you will probably backtrack several times as you gather information about yourself and your options. Some people refer to this as a "waffling" process, which may involve redefining goals, looking at alternative ways of attaining them, distancing, reexamining, revising and reevaluating. Throughout the process, remember to take time to listen to and trust your intuition; then follow its direction.

In this Chapter, we will cover the first five steps in the process. The final two steps—acting and evaluating—are covered in Chapter 10.

1. Becoming Aware of Negative Feelings

Your body and mind may be sending you messages about the state of your job satisfaction. These messages can be physical—such as lingering colds, flu or headaches—or they may translate themselves into verbal messages you can no longer ignore. "I can hardly wait until Friday!" is one message. Counting the minutes until your next holiday is another. In this state, you feel disequilibrium or a loss of balance. It's important now to listen to and accept your feelings. This will help you move beyond your uneasiness. Admitting you are unhappy is the first step in making a change. Remember, the change process isn't nearly as painful as your current state.

It's easy to project the blame for your feelings onto other people or situations. You may shout with frustration, "No one understands me," or "My partner is impossible to live with!" But, regardless of your source of discontent, you must come to terms with the fact that you don't like what you are doing and who you are becoming. The ultimate target of these negative feelings, whether conscious or unconscious, is yourself. How did you become this trapped, stagnant, unhappy person?

Perhaps you've been working five or more years in your job and it appears to be going well. You've had steady promotions, salary increases, praises from superiors and admiration from subordinates. Even your parents are proud of you. Then, one day, you get a queasy feeling that something is … missing. But what? Like the victim of an accident, you anxiously grope around to feel if your arms and legs are still attached. You run the film of your life in reverse, but you can't figure out what's wrong.

Often, no one single event is responsible. Instead, it's been a gradual process. You may have been seriously ill, your marriage may be falling apart, or you may lack energy and be irritable with your friends. Many of these reactions can be traced to your feelings about your job. The uneasy feelings many Questers experience are related to some negative aspects of their work. In many instances, the discontent is intensified by some other traumatic events in their lives, and self-evaluation begins.

You must verbalize your dissatisfaction by admitting you have a problem.

These feelings may persist for months or even years, depending on your ability to tolerate them. Sooner or later, however, you must verbalize your dissatisfaction by admitting you have a problem. Listen to and accept your feelings. While it's still too early to speak of "plans," you will sense that something needs to be done. Seeking a solution to a problem before it becomes too serious makes good sense. It allows you to use your skills to better advantage and enables you to be prepared if trouble strikes.

2. Defining the Problem

You need a good written definition of your problem. You must look at the psychological and spiritual issues behind your dissatisfaction and clarify what you would like but are afraid to undertake.

At this point in the decision-making process, your goals will be fuzzy. They may be wistful, full of yearning without much expectation of gratification, and yet, they may also contain a kernel of hope. That kernel can blossom into a clearer idea of how you would like things to become. The danger now is that you will abort your fantasies as too distracting or unrealistic. Dismissing these dreams prematurely means ruling out sound possibilities. Be charitable to your brainchild. Your ideas and fantasies need care and nourishment. Listen carefully to your hopes and dreams; you may discover they reflect your deepest needs and give you insight into your raison d'être.

Describing the Symptoms

First, you must describe your symptoms. Ask yourself, "What's making me feel this way? What is it about my situation that is unpleasant? What is my desired goal?" The discrepancy between your current situation and your goal needs to be overcome. Unfortunately, while you may not like where you are, sometimes it's hard to decide where you want to go or who you want to become.

The Job Satisfaction Questionnaire and *The Job Involvement Questionnaire* may have helped you identify the sources of your dissatisfaction. Here are some additional questions to consider:

- What do I like about my job? What do I dislike? Would I do this kind of work even if I didn't need the money? Is the work congruent with my purpose, needs and values?

- Do I have much in common with my colleagues, customers, clients and others with whom I deal?

- Why did I choose this job? Did I select it for prestige? To be of service? For security, power, money, independence, challenge, personal satisfaction or other reasons? Do I still have these rewards?

- Am I doing my best work? Do I see work results? Is my work damaging my self-confidence or my health?

- Am I committed to my company? Do I have growth opportunities? Does my company really need me? Am I proud to tell others where I work? Where do I want to be next year? In five years? Will staying with my company help me get there? Why or why not? What will I lose if I leave?

- Is there a possibility that my employer will downsize or merge in the near future?

- Are other factors that are not job-related in my life having a detrimental effect on my performance and attitude? Do I have a satisfying and intimate relationship with my partner or spouse? Do I have a partner? If not, would I like one? Do I have satisfying leisure activities? Do I have enough money and time to pursue these activities? Is my health good? If not, is it affecting my attitudes toward work?

- Am I a candidate for burnout? (Check your score on *The Burnout Questionnaire.*) Is job stress adversely affecting my confidence and health? Am I irritable and impatient? Do I have enough time for leisure or family activities? Do I have difficulty sleeping? Do I have low energy or other physical problems? Am I drinking or taking drugs to feel better?

- Am I enjoying success in my career? What is my career dream? Have I attained it? Can I achieve my dream where I am? Why or why not?

- Can the bad points about my job be resolved without making a move? Can I restructure my job? Why or why not?

- Can I change jobs and remain in the same company? If so, what can I do?

- Do I want to change employers or occupational fields? Do I want to become self-employed? Can I take time out? How easy or difficult would be for me to get another job in the same field? In a different field? Do I want to return to school for upgrading or retraining?

If your responses to these questions suggest you are not happy with your job, you may be ready for a job change. What did your responses to the questionnaires in Chapter 7 tell you?

If the negative points you listed about your company can be

resolved and you are committed to it, work at improving the weak spots and look for advancement within. If, however, you are dissatisfied with your position, the negative points can't be resolved, and you are not committed to the organization, consider moving on.

Describing the Barriers

The next step is describing any barriers that may be blocking you from making a move. Examples could be fear or uncertainty about change; fear of losing a secure income, pension or other benefits; *Every risk* fear that the change will interfere with your *involves fear.* relationships because of disapproval from your partner or children; fear that you will lose power, prestige or status; fear of having to live up to an image, making a mistake or being embarrassed; fear of returning to school for retraining or upgrading; and uncertainty about what to do next. Other blocks include guilt that a change might create family hardships and uncertainly over where to go for help with your career search.

These fears can be barriers to your progress. Growing, which is really just a matter of abandoning a comfortable position, usually involves pain. Trying to avoid pain by constructing rigid roles, defenses, viewpoints or excuses only makes the process more difficult. The first and most important risk you can take is to be honest with yourself. Acknowledge your fears. Like all emotions, fear has a purpose; it alerts you to take action to protect yourself from loss. Every risk involves fear. Lack of fear signals either that you don't care whether you lose what is at stake or that you don't believe you are in danger.

It is vital to work through any negative feelings or fears you have about the decision. Often, people hesitate to follow their hearts because they are afraid to fail. Fear will not go away as long as you continue to grow. The only way to conquer fear is to learn to manage it and continue pursuing your goals.

Underlying most fear is a lack of trust in your ability to perform or to handle situations. You fear because you are not feeling good about yourself. Of course, some fear is good. It keeps you alert to danger. But continuous fear is destructive, a barrier to growth and success.

Fear is the result of conditioning. You probably learned very early to be cautious. Parents warn young children, "Be careful … " This conveys messages that the world is dangerous and you won't be able to cope. As long as you continue to grow, you will have fear. However, because fear is learned, it can be unlearned. You can reprogram your old attitudes and beliefs

---

Tips for Managing Fear

- *Live in the present.* Fear is the acronym for False Expectations Appear Real. Because most fear centers around the future, don't spend time worrying about what might happen. Instead, deal with the present. Do what you can to research your goal, then develop an action plan to minimize setbacks.

- *Let go of "attachments."* Fear usually accompanies the process of letting go. The more attached you are to something, the greater your fear of losing it. If you are attached to a good-paying job, you may be afraid to leave for work that promises more fulfillment. Fear is a reassuring signal that you are about to stretch yourself to move forward. But growth requires letting go of the past, material possessions and people. Ask yourself, "What do I need to let go of? What scares me most about letting go? What is the worst thing that can happen if I let go? What can I do to minimize this risk? What people, resources, support and information would make my goal less risky?"

- *Watch your self-talk.* Keep a log to track the negatives you repeat to yourself. Each time you catch yourself saying something that fuels your fear or is negative, say, "Cancel," and replace it with a more positive affirmation or statement.

- *Know and accept yourself.* Know your heart and your passion. Fear begins when there is a discrepancy between your actions and your real desires and purpose. When you live in a manner consistent with your calling, you experience harmony and stability. On the other

---

hand, you experience disharmony, indecision and doubt when you ignore your spiritual self. You are a unique person with a special mission that only you can perform. Follow this passion and work at achieving the goals and activities that are compatible with it. Believe in yourself and know that you will attain your goals.

- *Note your priorities.* What do you really want? What do others think you should have? Replace the "shoulds" with your own values. Make the shift from a "having mode" to a "being mode." Having is possessing, it can disappear as easily as it came. The being mode is not as transient. In this state, you are centered. Your personal power will help you achieve your goals. You feel comfortable with the steps you need to take to achieve your goal. As you turn your priorities around and follow your heart, you'll achieve more. Money and possessions will often be the byproducts.

- *Take time out for yourself.* Let go of your "busyness." Constant activity alienates you from your real self. Develop your spiritual side. Learn to go within by seeking solitude and quiet times; enjoy nature, meditate, listen to relaxing music or write in a journal.

- *Understand and befriend your fear.* Step back and look at it. Notice that fear usually takes the form of thoughts and feelings in your mind. Don't get sucked into the fear; instead, watch it calmly. Where do you feel the fear (for example, as butterflies in your stomach, palpitations of your heart or knocking knees)? How does the fear look (for example, what color and shape is it)? What is the fear saying to you? Once you learn what the fear is saying to you, you can talk back to it—for example, by writing in a journal or while relaxing. You will probably be surprised to discover that your fear is not as awful as you thought it was. But even if you learn that it is a monster, you will be more able to deal with it effectively. The unknown is always more frightening than the known.

- *Form a support group.* Associate with people who make you feel wonderful about yourself and who encourage and support you in achieving your goals. Pick individuals who are ahead of you in personal growth. See each other regularly to give one another feedback and encouragement.

- *Develop the will to risk.* Like any skill, you'll get better with practice. Start with small risks in your daily activities. For example, say hello to someone on the street or do something silly. Each day, write down at least five ways that you can stretch your risk taking. Before you go to bed at night, plan the risk you intend to take the following day. Close your eyes and practice it in your mind's eye. Make your visualization as clear as possible. For additional suggestions, refer to "Tips for Enhancing the Courage to Risk" in Chapter 3.

- *Perceive yourself as a powerful person.* You are in control and you always have a choice. Not taking action in any situation is exercising a choice. Identify your reasons for staying in a job you dislike. Ask yourself, "What comfort do I get? What image am I holding on to?" When you can identify the factors that are holding you back, you will be able to move forward.

- *See yourself as someone who has choices, takes action, and operates from a position of inner strength.* As your power builds, so will your confidence and your ability to risk. Shift your vocabulary from that of a victim to that of someone with power and strength. For example, "I can" instead of "I can't"; "It's a challenging opportunity" instead of "It's a problem"; "I'm responsible" instead of "It's not my fault"; and "It's a learning experience" instead of "It's terrible."

- *Think positively.* If you want to change your life for the better, start thinking more positively about yourself and the opportunities available to you. Listen to inspirational tapes, read inspirational books, post positive quotes around your home, state and write affirmations and begin the day with a positive thought.

- *Make a winning decision.* Before making a decision, affirm that you will win regardless of the outcome. Look forward to the opportunity for learning and growing even if the results turn out differently than you planned. Believe there is no such thing as the wrong decision if you do it for the right reason. Learn to trust and follow your intuition, the messages you get from your body as well as external cues. Lighten up. Think of yourself as a lifelong student. Each experience is a valuable lesson. After making a decision, accept total responsibility for it and correct any errors.

- *Learn patience.* Patience means knowing it will happen and giving it time to happen. It requires trusting that you will achieve your goal if you follow your heart, maintain your optimism and work hard.

- *Live a balanced life.* Become involved in a variety of activities. If you create an identity in only one life component (such as work), you will feel empty, helpless and lost if you lose your job. You will also be afraid to take chances, thus diminishing your creativity. On the other hand, if you are involved in a variety of activities (for example, a relationship, family, friends, hobbies, spiritual pursuits and community activities), your life will be more complete. You may even find new enjoyment in a job that was previously unsatisfying. Moreover, a job loss will not be as devastating, because these outside activities will help satisfy your needs.

with new ones to manage your fears.

The first step in managing your fear is identifying it. Write down all the fears you think are stopping you from attaining your career goals. Be honest with yourself. Other suggestions for managing fear are discussed below.

Doing Something About the Problem

If you don't recognize the need to change, then maybe you're not ready to make the move. In this sense, a major life change such as a job shift is similar to the decision made by alcoholics when they want to quit drinking. Before they can embark on a cure, they must admit to their problem. Then they must commit themselves to doing something about the problem by attending Alcoholics Anonymous or seeking other assistance.

Similarly, if you really dislike your work and have identified and dealt with the barriers that are stopping you from making a move, then you must do something about moving on or improving your current situation. After you have worked through these blocks, you are ready to commit yourself to change (or decide not to change). You cannot start a new chapter before you have finished the old one.

To nurture a career, you must take charge of it. Once you are convinced that a job change is in order, go for it. Turn a deaf ear to the cynics who tell you it is immature to expect your job to be interesting and satisfying. Patience may be a virtue, but resignation is not. If you are thinking there must be more to

Guidelines for Taking Action

- *Avoid guilt.* The sense that you are letting everyone down can be the most difficult aspect of quitting a job. Don't worry about what your mentor or colleagues may think.

- *Avoid idealizing your former position.* Why mourn a job you have outgrown or one that no longer meets your needs? Traditional and emerging fields offer many exciting options.

- *Don't remain with a job you dislike because of security.* Security during these times of globalization, rolling recessions, mergers and political change is wishful thinking. Having a positive attitude, believing in yourself, working hard and being willing to risk will help you steer your career through stormy times.

- *Realize that change involves tradeoffs.* Change may involve some temporary personal or financial sacrifices. But most Questers agree that in the long term, the gains far outweigh the losses. They feel they've gained greater job and life satisfaction, independence, flexibility and control over their personal and professional lives.

- *Listen to yourself.* When you make a career switch, you will have to overcome the obstacles of others' expectations. Don't base your self-respect on what your coworkers, parents or friends think. Listen to your own feelings. They will help you identify what you really want. If you make the move that feels right for you, you will feel better about yourself. This may also bring you closer to your family and friends. Moreover, no one else can define what you consider dangerous. What is a matter of course to one person may be agony to another. The intensity of a personal risk is largely in the eyes of the beholder.

- *Don't make excuses.* Be honest. As Mark Twain said, "There are a thousand good excuses, but no good reasons." If your career has been stagnating, deciding to stay can be just as traumatic as making a move. Too often, the refusal to make a decision turns out to be the wrong decision. While circumstances often force people to take lesser jobs, choosing to remain in a position with no hope of advancement or satisfaction is not only self-defeating, it can be enormously risky. True, there must be some balance between reflection and action. But if you are just putting in time, the losses of enthusiasm, self-confidence and enjoyment may be greater than you realize.

- *Don't be afraid to fail.* Look at failure as a learning experience. Questers eliminate much failure by planning and persisting. But when they do fail (and they do) they say, "I've done my best. I'm only human. I forgive myself." Then they take time to figure out what went wrong, modify their plans and try again.

- *Don't be afraid to change.* It might be comfortable to live as you always have, but if you persevere, the new behavior will soon become the comfortable way, and you will have eliminated the dissatisfaction.

life, start making some of your dreams come true now. A useful word of caution, however: Don't change jobs while you are in the midst of other turmoils. Making a career move when you are experiencing the pressures of family or marital problems can be disastrous. Wait until you can concentrate fully on your new position.

3. Experiencing Ambivalence

The decision to change can provoke mixed feelings. You might feel anxious, depressed and guilty, yet excited at the prospect of trying something new. A certain amount of ambivalence is natural. Inner emotional preparation—weighing losses as well as gains, fears as well as hopes—is a necessary prerequisite for successful risk taking. As you let go of old structures, perhaps you will discover that you miss the friendly, familiar babble of the gang at the water cooler. Friends may say you're crazy to change jobs. The fear of failing may seize and shake your convictions. At the same time, you may be exhilarated at the opportunity to test yourself, to enjoy some excitement and adventure.

Ambivalence is the push and pull between the desire to approach and the desire to avoid. One day you may think, "Of course, I can change fields! Lots of people do it. It can't be so difficult." The next day, or even the next minute, you might despair, "There are too many unknowns. I'm better off staying put."

Both feelings are valid. Careless risk takers need to think through the difficulties ahead before they take action. Anxious risk takers, on the other hand, need to look for the pluses. Rather than focusing on just one set of possible outcomes, try to keep risk taking in balance by considering all of the pluses and minuses. Fear balanced by excitement and purpose offers the emotional balance that planned risk taking requires. Don't be overly alarmed by the first few stages of decision making. They usually are the most intimidating. Once in action, you will find the situation less fearful.

Feeling Too Much Anxiety
If the prospect of undertaking a change is so great that your stomach is churning, you can't sleep, you have constant headaches or you have a rash, your body, in its great wisdom, is telling you to forgo the risk. Don't persist in the face of pervasive anxiety.

Milton, a highly skilled rehabilitation counselor, was approached by a prospective partner to start an executive recruitment agency. For weeks before making the move, he went straight to bed immediately after dinner and pulled the sheets over his head. He tried to make light of it by brushing off his exhaustion as the terror anyone might feel at starting a new venture. But, in his personal and professional life, Milton had undertaken many risks before and had never felt this way. Clearly, his physical response was evoked by something else.

Milton later discovered that the hard-sell, aggressive style required for executive recruiting was not for him. His underlying fears turned out to be prophetic. The difference in basic values and counseling styles between the two partners proved to be such a handicap that, within five months, they had agreed to part ways.

Yvonne had a similar experience. She applied to a school of social work. Soon after being accepted, she developed a chronic headache. It disappeared the day she called the school's director to say she wouldn't be attending. Yvonne's body was correctly telling her that she didn't have the temperament for social work. She realized she would need more autonomy and would get too involved in her clients' problems. Today, Yvonne is a happy and successful freelance journalist.

The moral is clear: If your body tells you to stop, consider rejecting the risk. Doing so may also be a risk—the risk of trusting your deep feelings more than some abstract notion of what ought to be best for you. Lists or inventories may be useful in making risky decisions, but ultimately they won't work unless you also consider your feelings. Constant headaches counterbalance a bigger paycheck any day of the week.

4. Preparing

Obviously, it's important to prepare for a career change. You will want to set tentative goals, assess personal characteristics, explore occupational options, figure out how to manage your money, establish support systems and lay down safety nets.

Setting Tentative Goals

The key to avoiding potential potholes is to set tentative career goals before you explore new roads. Goals force you to focus on what you really want. So what do you want to do? Where do you want to go professionally? What kind of person do you want to become? As you think over your responses, remember to be open and creative. Years from now, as you review your life, what regrets do you imagine you might have?

Considering what you might do is an important step in increasing your job satisfaction. Explore the whole range of possibilities before you. Fantasize about the ultimate goal, your shining star. If you could do anything in the world, what would it be? When you were a child, what did you dream of becoming? Dare to admit your fondest fantasy. Identifying this dream will help you set goals that are in tune with your inner self, goals that will help you identify what is really important to you.

Try this guided fantasy exercise to help you clarify your career goals:

> Close your eyes and imagine yourself working at your
> ideal occupation and living your ideal lifestyle. Describe
> your whole day in detail, including getting to work, your

work tasks and surroundings and your evening activities. Pay particular attention to the details of your home and work environments, work duties, leisure activities, feelings about your various activities and people you encounter. Then ask yourself a few questions: What made you excited and happy about your work and other activities? What made you frustrated, resentful, unhappy or bored? Your positive and negative feelings will help you identify the kind of work and lifestyle you want.

What kind of occupations would enable you to pursue your life purpose? For example, if your purpose is to promote family harmony, you could express your mission by being a social worker, a family living teacher, a writer, a counselor, a psychologist, a religious leader, a mediation lawyer or a full-time parent. If you are not sure what your purpose is, review your response to the activities described under "Tips for Developing Purpose" in Chapter 3 or identify a long-time dream or longing. This will be compatible with your purpose.

Once you know what you want, you will be more willing to take the risks necessary to achieve your goals. So don't underestimate yourself or what you can attain. And don't let money, or the lack of it, influence your career goals at this stage.

Write all of your ideas or fantasies down in a notebook. Include everything you want to do, be and have. The sky is the limit. Don't be inhibited by seemingly unrealistic goals. Select three to five dreams that are most important to you, that you are committed to accomplishing within the next year and that you are most excited about. State why you want to achieve these goals, when you expect to realize them and the benefits of reaching each one.

As you assess your personal characteristics and occupational options, you may want to revise these goals. Career planning is an ongoing process that is constantly subject to review and revision as you learn more about yourself and the world around you. So, consider these goals as guideposts you can rebuild throughout the planning stage. Like the Questers, you must be able to balance tentativeness with commitment.

Getting to Know Yourself

Choosing a satisfying career and lifestyle requires a very good understanding of yourself. Begin by completing the exercises that follow. They will help you assemble an accurate picture of yourself—your interests, needs, accomplishments and other personal characteristics. Uncovering a you that you didn't even know existed can be fun and exciting. Because there are no right and wrong answers, this is your chance to be honest about who you really are.

Stating Your Purpose
Identify and acknowledge your deepest dreams. Review the exercises discussed under "Tips for Developing Purpose" in Chapter 3. Write down your major life themes or patterns, and translate these into a "working" mission statement. Ask a partner or close friend for feedback.

Identifying Your Interests
Your interests are simply your likes and dislikes, your preferences and distastes. You can identify your interests by taking an interest inventory or by analyzing the activities you enjoy.

For some people, psychological tests, administered and interpreted by a competent psychologist or counselor, can be useful. They can help illuminate potential new directions, reveal valuable insights and add a sense of certainty about your plans. But most people can identify their own interests by completing exercises like those described below.

Exercise 1

First, think about your leisure activities, school and continuing education courses. Remember those that you liked and excelled at. Review the job accomplishments of which you are particularly proud and review why.

Now make two lists. In the left column, list at least ten activities you enjoy. In the right column, list activities you detest.

Next to each item, note why the activity is appealing or unappealing to you.

Finally, classify your interests into patterns. Exercises 2 and 3 will help you do this.

Exercise 1—Enjoyable Activities

Activities I enjoy	Activities I do not enjoy
1. _____	1. _____
2. _____	2. _____
3. _____	3. _____
4. _____	4. _____
5. _____	5. _____
6. _____	6. _____
7. _____	7. _____
8. _____	8. _____
9. _____	9. _____
10._____	10._____

Exercise 2

An easy way to classify your interests is to arrange them on the basis of work tasks you enjoy. Most occupational tasks involve working with data, people, things or ideas. Read over the descriptions of the four work tasks below and rank them in order of preference, 1 representing your highest preference and 4 your lowest.

Exercise 2—Data, Ideas, People and Things

____ *Data tasks:* These are impersonal tasks that involve working with people indirectly (for example, with files, accounts and business communications) or formulating and/or following schedules, directions and business operating procedures.

____ *Ideas tasks:* These are intrapersonal tasks involving insights, theories and new ways of expressing something, perhaps with words, paint, equations or music.

____ *People tasks:* These are interpersonal tasks such as caring for, educating, entertaining, serving, persuading or directing others.

____ *Things tasks:* These are non-personal tasks involving machines, tools, living things and materials such as food, wood or metal. The four kinds of tasks usually blend together to varying degrees. Moreover, although any occupation involves some work with data, ideas, people and things, typically only one or two of the work tasks predominate.

Exercise 3

According to the research of career psychologist John Holland, people can be categorized into one of six personality types: Realistic, Conventional, Enterprising, Social, Artistic and Investigative. People in these categories seek out corresponding occupational environments based on their interests. Because most people don't fall solely into one of the major personality types, Holland devised a coding system to indicate an individual's primary, secondary and tertiary types. These codes are reflected in three-letter combinations—each letter corresponding to the first letter of one of the six types. For example, an ESA code indicates a person is most like the Enterprising type, next most like the Social type and third most like the Artistic type.

Read over the descriptions of the personality types below and rank them according to which types you think you are. Then translate your three highest types into a three-letter code.

Exercise 3—Holland's Categories

_____ *Realistic (R):* You enjoy activities that involve the precise, ordered use of objects, tools, machines and animals. Examples include agricultural, electrical, manual, physical, and mechanical activities. Characteristic occupations include auto engineer, surveyor, carpenter, typesetter and fish and game warden.

_____ *Conventional (C):* You enjoy activities that involve the precise, ordered use of data, such as keeping records, filing materials and organizing numerical and statistical data. Characteristic occupations typically are in the clerical, computational and business fields and include accountant, credit manager, office worker, library assistant and data processing clerk.

_____ *Enterprising (E):* You enjoy activities that involve interacting with other people to reach organizational goals or for economic gain. Leadership, interpersonal and persuasive activities dominate your interests. Characteristic occupations include market analyst, lawyer, personnel recruiter and retail or restaurant manager.

_____ *Social (S):* You enjoy activities that involve interacting with others for enjoyment or to inform, train, develop, care or educate. Characteristic occupations include claims adjuster, social worker, teacher, minister, interviewer, therapist and community recreation administrator.

_____ *Artistic (A):* You enjoy activities that involve using various materials to create art forms and products. Activities and objects related to language, art, music, drama and writing fascinate you. Characteristic occupations include drama coach, dance teacher, musician, writer, interior decorator, photographer and artist.

_____ *Investigative (I):* You enjoy activities that involve exploring and examining physical, biological and cultural objects to understand and control them. Scientific and mathematical activities are found here. Characteristic occupations include economist, internist, chemist, psychologist, actuary, dentist, computer operator and engineer.

Write your three-letter code here: _____

Summarizing Your Interests

To summarize your interests, go back over the preceding
exercises and look for patterns. What interests keep appearing?
Identify your interests in the categories described in Exercises
2 and 3 (data, people, things or ideas and Holland's types).
Have you found any surprises in your interest profile, or is it
pretty much what you expected? Relate your interests to
occupations you would like to explore. For example, if you like
activities that involve people tasks (Exercise 2) and you
characterize yourself as a Social type (Exercise 3), you might
be satisfied as a social worker, therapist or teacher.

The Work Wheel

The Work Wheel can help you view your interests with
occupational options in mind. The body of the Work Wheel
shows the locations of 23 job fields (which are g roups of
similar occupations) that encompass all occupations listed b y
the U.S. Department of Labor in the *Dictionary of Occupational
Titles* (DOT). Job field names and locations (A to W on the
wheel) suggest differences in the work that is done and the
people who do it. Although the jobs in a field diff er in their
locations on the wheel, most are near the points sho wn. A job
field's location is based on its pr imary work tasks—that is,
working with data, ideas, people or things. Arrows show that
work tasks often heavily involve both people and things ↕ or
data and ideas ◄•►. Related Holland symbols are indicated
on the map.

You can see the relationship betw een the four work tasks
(data, ideas, people, things) and Holland's types, shown on
the periphery of the wheel. For example, Enterprising
(Business Contact) occupations are located at the upper left.
Data work tasks and (to some e xtent) people work tasks
predominate. Investigative (Science) occupations are located
at the lower right. Ideas work tasks and (to some e xtent)
things work tasks dominate.

Your interests can be tr anslated into spokes on the wheel.
Identify your interests on the wheel, then in vestigate
occupations in the related job fields . For example, if your code

is ESC (spokes 1, 2, 3, 4, 5, 12), you might want to look into job fields in spokes 1, 2, 3, 4, 5 and 12.

This is a simple diagram, but it is a start—a way of beginning to look at occupational alternatives.

Think about your interests as you go through the rest of the activities in this Chapter. Add your likes and dislikes to your list. Then modify your interest profile as necessary.

Probing Your Needs

Since needs form the basis of behavior, unfulfilled needs and conflict among needs inevitably result in job dissatisfaction.

Your job needs reflect your reactions to your current work situation and to your personal needs. As you gain competence,

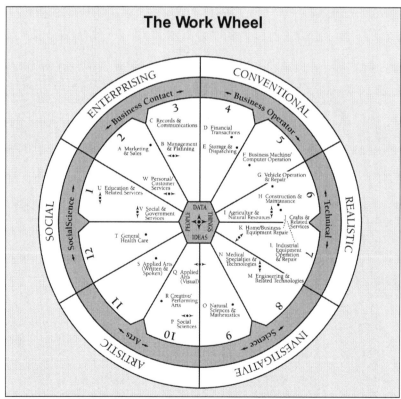

© 1986 by the American College Testing Program, Iowa City, Iowa.
Adapted and reprinted with permission.

a job that once seemed challenging ma y become boring. A young person with a job that in volves extensive travel may be quite satisfied. But for a married person with children, tr avel may be displeasing.

Prioritize Your Needs

The range of human needs is limited only b y the imagination, but some needs contr ibute more to job satisfaction than others. To identify needs that are impor tant for your job satisfaction, look over the list in Ex ercise 4. Then rank your top six needs and y our six least impor tant needs. Finally, complete the questions at the end of the e xercise. This will help you clarify your sources of job satisf action and dissatisfaction.

Summarizing Your Needs

What are your highest and lowest needs? What needs does your current job satisfy? What needs does y our current job not meet?

Exercise 4—Prioritize Your Needs

_____ 1. *Achievement:* Mastering challenging or difficult tasks .

_____ 2. *Adventure:* Seeking change, a fast pace and excitement.

_____ 3. *Altruism:* Helping others and contr ibuting to society.

_____ 4. *Associates:* Having contact with fellow workers.

_____ 5. *Autonomy:* Having control over your work and freedom from constraints imposed by others.

_____ 6. *Challenge:* Achieving mastery and acceptable levels of difficulty, responsibility and complexity.

_____ 7. *Competition:* Pursuing a rivalry with others.

_____ 8. *Creativity:* Inventing new things, designing products and developing ideas.

_____ 9. *Financial returns:* Having a good salary and benefits.

_____ 10. *Aesthetics*: Making beautiful things; contributing to the beauty of the world.

_____ 11. *Growth:* Developing talents and potential, learning new skills and innovating.

_____ 12. *Intellectual stimulation:* Practicing independent thinking; understanding how and why things work.

_____ 13. *Involvement:* Being involved in and identifying closely with your job.

_____ 14. *Management:* Planning your work and managing others.

_____ 15. *Power:* Having decision-making responsibility over finances, people and other resources.

_____ 16. *Prestige:* Attaining recognition and respect from others.

_____ 17. *Spirituality:* Adhering to a set of religious, spiritual or moral principles.

_____ 18. *Security:* Having a secure job.

_____ 19. *Supervisory relations:* Having a supervisor who is fair and with whom you get along.

_____ 20. *Surroundings:* Enjoying pleasant working conditions.

_____ 21. *Variety:* Having the opportunity to do different kinds of tasks.

_____ 22. *Way of life:* Being free to be the person you want to be and live the life you want to live.

_____ 23. *Purpose:* Expressing your real self and deriving meaning and satisfaction from that.

_____ 24. *Teamwork:* Holding the trust and support of your colleagues and contributing to group goals.

_____ 25. *Locale:* Working in a desirable location.

_____ 26. *Leisure:* Having time and money for leisure.

_____ 27. *Self-confidence:* Feeling good about yourself.

_____ 28. *Resources:* Having the resources to do an adequate job.

_____ 29. *Skills:* Using your education, experience, knowledge and abilities.

_____ 30. *Work hours:* Enjoying the freedom to work a desired length of time; doing work that doesn't interfere with your desired lifestyle or with overtime or unusual hours.

_____ 31. *Advancement:* Having opportunities for promotion.

_____ 32. *Professional development:* Receiving paid study leave or time off for courses.

_____ 33. *Using own ideas:* Having the ability to generate and use your own ideas.

_____ 34. *Other:*

Now review your scores from *The Job Satisfaction Questionnaire* and rank the six job facets that are most important to you. Then rank the six facets that are least important. Did you rate the needs that are most important to you as very satisfied on your current job? If not, these facets represent unfulfilled needs that may be contributing to your job dissatisfaction.

Were the needs you ranked important on *The Job Satisfaction Questionnaire* similar to those you ranked highest in the exercise above? If not, you need to review your needs again to identify the six you would most like from a job.

Also identify the specific life experiences that have helped you satisfy these needs. For example, if you have a need for autonomy, list the activities in your life that give you a sense of autonomy, such as being in charge of the car pool, supervising employees, scheduling softball games or managing a bank. In addition, describe the feelings you experience when you are in control.

Pay attention to your needs; they represent job facets that are important to you.

Assessing Your Accomplishments, Skills and Other Strengths

People often confuse interests with abilities. While you may enjoy doing the things you do well, the relationship between interests and abilities is only moderately high. People with high literary interests, for example, aren't necessarily capable of producing a novel, poem or play. They may simply enjoy reading. Prospective employers are interested mainly in what you have accomplished through a lifetime of paid and unpaid experiences—in other words, your track record. Evaluating your experiences as objectively as possible adds new dimensions to the complex and emerging picture you are developing of you.

First, look at what you have accomplished in job-related or indirectly job-related endeavors. For example, if you worked as a controller in your most recent job, your job-related accomplishments might include the following items:

• Designed a computerized reporting system used by three subsidiary companies.

• Worked closely with outside consultants to rationalize the use of microcomputers within the company.

• Regulated inventory to reduce short-term interest charges incurred by the company.

• Taught a financial class to graduate students at a local university.

Do you remember how much you enjoyed these activities in your job? Use action words to describe them, such as designed, researched, trained, supervised, directed, wrote, managed, created, negotiate and prepared. Now make the list as long as possible. Ask your partner, close friends and colleagues to help you identify these accomplishments. Don't forget the successes of subordinates who were under your direction or supervision. These, too, belong in your list of accomplishments. Carefully think back over your career. What was accomplished because of your input? What would not have been done without you? What do you consider your most important or most satisfying job-related accomplishments? List them here.

My Job-Related Accomplishments

1. _____

2. _____

3. _____

4. _____

5. _____

6. _____

7. _____

8. _____

9. _____

_____

_____

_____

10. _____

_____

_____

Next, include the educational accomplishments of which y ou are most proud. Unless you have just recently g raduated, do not include your high school accomplishments. Instead, list your college courses and activities, graduate work, and continuing education experiences. Include both direct and indirect educational accomplishments—those that related directly to your studies and extracurricular activities performed (e.g., jobs, athletic activities) while attending school.

My Educational Accomplishments

1. _____

_____

_____

2. _____

_____

_____

3. _____

_____

_____

4. _____

_____

5.
_____
_____
_____
_____

Now list your civic accomplishments. These include achievements directly related to your hobbies and your civic, charitable and religious activities. They should relate to, or demonstrate your competence in, some aspect of your work. For example, a major contribution to a fundraising effort can demonstrate organizational or sales ability.

My Civic Accomplishments

1.
_____
_____

2.
_____
_____

3.
_____
_____

4.
_____
_____

5.
_____
_____

You may also have untapped talents that can be turned into a new occupation. Ask your friends what dormant talents they think you may possess. You may even want to take a battery of tests from a psychologists or career counselor which can reveal a wide range of possibilities.

My Untapped Talents
1. _____
_____
_____
2. _____
_____
_____
3. _____
_____
_____
4. _____
_____
_____
5. _____
_____
_____

Your next step is to analyze each of the accomplishments you listed above. Consider them one by one, paying special attention to the skills, knowledge or personal attributes that enabled you to achieve them. Think about your personality and the specific skills and abilities you have acquired. These accomplishments might include the ability to program a computer, use insurance actuarial tables, or interpret psychological tests. Personality traits might include patience, willingness to work hard, ability to handle people or logical thinking.

Finally, list your weaknesses. These often turn out to involve tasks you dislike. For example, you may feel so uncomfortable at meetings that you become inarticulate. Or you may hate the paperwork that goes with your job so much that you put it off and get backlogged.

My Weaknesses
1.
2.
3.
4.
5.

Now figure out some workable strategies to reduce your weaknesses. For instance, to improve your performance at meetings you might take a speech course or join Toastmasters. Or to straighten out your paper work, you might resolve to set aside 30 minutes each day as catch-up time.

Appraising Other Personal Strengths

Taking stock of your other personal characteristics is another essential step in the search for self-knowledge. Certain characteristics are essential in almost all kinds of work: For example, being responsible, efficient, resourceful, flexible, cooperative, objective and sensible are basic to a professional attitude in any job. On the other hand, some personal characteristics are important only in specific occupations; in fact, they may be undesirable in others. For example, while being a loner is fine for a scientist, who must spend long hours in research, it is not suitable for a construction worker, who has to perform as part of a team.

To discover your other personal characteristics, make a list below of about 10 characteristics that best describe you. Use adjectives such as active, assertive, attractive, calm, careful, competent, confident, curious, discreet, democratic, eager, energetic, enthusiastic, helpful, humorous, loyal, mature, obliging, open-minded, precise, sociable, stable, strong-minded, tolerant and warm.

Ten Characteristics that Best Describe Me

1. _____	6. _____
2. _____	7. _____
3. _____	8. _____
4. _____	9. _____
5. _____	10. _____

Identifying Your Strengths

The exercise that follows will help you pinpoint your many strengths. First, analyze your successes. Next, identify at least three successes that gave you a great deal of satisfaction in the past five years. These can be drawn from any area of your life (for example, substituted for son's soccer coach and team won or earned 15 credits at community college). Now (a) identify what gave you positive feelings and (b) list the skills and abilities you used to accomplish these.

Example

Success	What Gave Me the Positive Feeling?	What Skills/Abilities Did I Use?
Substituted for son's soccer coach	Working with eager boys, helping coach, contributing to team's first win of the season	Organizing, fast thinking, encouraging others, being enthusiastic, working with parents
1. _____	1. _____	1. _____
2. _____	2. _____	2. _____
3. _____	3. _____	3. _____

A. Personal skills.

These are personality traits that can be beneficial for some kinds of jobs, but not for others. They are part of your nature, but they can be developed. For example, flexibility is beneficial when working with a community recreational program, but detrimental in jobs requiring strict accounting practices. You can learn to become more flexible. Circle the personal skills that apply to you, and add any other skills you possess that are not listed.

Adventurous	Ambitious	Analytical
Assertive	Businesslike	Competitive
Confident	Conservative	Cooperative
Courageous	Creative	Curious
Discreet	Efficient	Energetic
Enthusiastic	Formal	Frank
Friendly	Helpful	Honest

Independent	Industrious	Intelligent
Inventive	Kind	Likable
Loyal	Motivated	Patient
Persevering	Poised	Positive
Precise	Quick	Relaxed
Reliable	Sensitive	Sociable
Stable	Tactful	Thorough
Tolerant	Trustworthy	Unassuming
Understanding	Versatile	Warm

_____ _____ _____

_____ _____ _____

Now list five best personal skills.

1. _____

2. _____

3. _____

4. _____

5. _____

B. Transferable skills.

These are generic and can be used in a variety of jobs. Once you have learned a transferable skill, you can apply it in different job settings. These skills fall into three areas: (i) communication skills, (ii) organizational skills and (iii) technical/physical skills.

i. Communication skills can be categorized into writing, helping and creating categories.

Writing skills: Circle the following writing skills that apply to you, and add any additional skills that are not listed.

Analyzing	Clerical	Creative Writing
Editing	Foreign Languages	Formatting
Letter Writing	Note Taking	Persuading
Reading	Record Keeping	Report Writing
Researching	Summarizing	Technical Writing
Translating	Typing	

_____ _____ _____

_____ _____ _____

_____ _____ _____

Analyzing	Clerical	Creative Writing
Editing	Foreign Languages	Formatting
Letter Writing	Note Taking	Persuading
Reading	Record Keeping	Report Writing
Researching	Summarizing	Technical Writing
Translating	Typing	_____

_____ _____ _____

_____ _____ _____

Helping skills: Circle the following helping skills that apply to you, and add any other skills that are not listed.

Advising	Arbitrating	Articulation
Coaching	Convincing	Counseling
Empathizing	Interpreting	Mentoring
Motivating	Negotiating	Parenting
Researching	Summarizing	Reading
Persuading	Public Speaking	Supporting
Teaching	Training	_____
understanding		

_____ _____ _____

Creating Skills: Circle the following creating skills that apply to you, and add any other skills that are not listed.

Acting	Aesthetic Sense	Composing
Cooking	Designing	Drawing
Illustrating	Interpreting	Interior Decorating
Inventing	Landscaping	Observing
Painting	Photography	Playing Musical Instruments
Sculpting	Singing	Writing

_____   _____   _____

_____   _____   _____

_____   _____   _____

ii. Organizational skills can be categorized as managing or analyzing skills.

Managing Skills: Circle the following managing skills that apply to you, and add any other skills that are not listed

Accomplishing	Assertiveness	Classifying
Controlling	Decision Making	Delegating
Detail-Oriented	Effectiveness	Filing
Follow-Though	Organizing	Precision-Oriented
Problem Solving	Scheduling	Supervising
Systemizing		

_____   _____   _____

_____   _____   _____

Analyzing Skills: Circle the following analyzing skills that apply to you, and add any skills that are not listed.

Analyzing	Budgeting	Calculating
Comparing	Counting	Critiquing
Evaluating	Financial Saving	Integrating
Interpreting Statistics	Investigating	Investment Planning
Remembering Numbers	Reviewing	Thinking

_____   _____   _____

_____   _____   _____

iii. Technical/Physical Skills can be categorized into technical and physical areas.

Technical Skills: Circle the technical skills that apply to you, and add any other skills that are not listed.

Auto Repair	Blueprint Reading	Building
Drafting	Computers	Construction
Laboratory	Graphics	Keypunching
Medical Laboratory	Mechanical	Tool-Oriented
Working with Machinery	Electronics Drawing	
	Programming	

_____   _____   _____

_____   _____   _____

Physical Skills: Circle the following physical skills that apply to you, and add any other skills that are not listed.

20/20 Vision	Active	Acute Hearing
Athletic	Assembling	Coordination
Exploration	Eye-Hand	Finger or Manual Dexterity
Physical Strength	Coordination	
Taste	Sensitivity to Touch	Smell

_____   _____   _____

_____   _____   _____

Now list your 10 best *transferable skills.*

1. _____   6. _____

2. _____   7. _____

3. _____   8. _____

4. _____   9. _____

5. _____   10. _____

C. Professional/Job skills

Professional skills relate to a specific occupation and are usually generalized (for example, knowing the steps to take when inspecting a building, knowing how to operate a printing press, knowing the names of good customers on a sales route or developing a grade-six science program). You may use generic skills in developing professional skills (for example, a good memory helps you remember customers' names on a sales route).

Now list five professional skills you possess.

1. _____

2. _____

3. _____

4. _____

5. _____

Skills Summary

Now, summarize your skills. List 15 skills you listed above that you possess and would like to use in a job. Consider those that would give you positive feelings.

1. _____	6. _____	11. _____
2. _____	7. _____	12. _____
3. _____	8. _____	13. _____
4. _____	9. _____	14. _____
5. _____	10. _____	15. _____

Next, identify the skills you possess in three categories: personal skills, transferable skills and professional/job skills. Next, analyze your prospective jobs for the actual skills they require. You will be pleasantly surprised to see that you possess many of these skills. You may also indicate which skills you would like to develop further and the plans you have to accomplish this.

Completing the Picture

Little by little, you have put together a wonderful picture of yourself. Nobody has precisely the same combination of qualities you have. Look back at how you have evaluated various aspects of yourself. Decide how your purpose, interests, needs, accomplishments and other personal strengths add up. What pattern do they form? Which qualities do you want to use in your next job? What would you like to change?

To synthesize this information, complete the diagram in the next section.

My Ideal Job
On the diagram below, indicate the following:

1. Your purpose or dream

2. Skills and knowledge you want to use on your job

3. Needs and values you want your job to satisfy

4. Interests you want your job to reflect

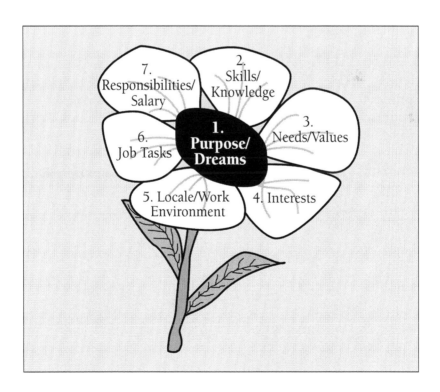

5.   Your desired work environment and locale

6.   Job tasks and duties you want to perform

7.   The amount of responsibility you want to exercise and your desired salary

Your next step is to explore your career options. You might be surprised to discover just how many options you have!

Investigating Career Options

As you read and worked through the exercises above, you engaged in focused self-exploration and soul searching. Until now, you have given most of your attention to your private world—what you dream of, need, want, are and could become. Now it's time to look at reality.

Before deciding to change jobs or make other modifications in your life, investigate all your options.
Determine if other, unrelated aspects of your life are having a detrimental effect on your job performance and your attitude. Are you missing an enjoyable and intimate relationship with a partner or spouse? Do you enjoy satisfying leisure activities? If not, you may find that one of the reasons for your dissatisfaction is a gap in other areas of your life. For example, feeling lonely or having an unhappy marriage can cause your attitude and job performance to drop. Maybe this is the time to get involved in a community activity or a hobby. Doing so can add new, rewarding dimensions to your life that can indirectly make your job more satisfying.

For example, you may have decided that you can get what you want by remaining in the same company, at least for a while. If so, you might want to make some adjustments to your current position or transfer to another type of job. Let's take a look at each of these options.

Living with Your Present Job

A key way to make a job change is to gain the recognition and support of the political powers who affect your job. To do so, you must understand your job's political environment and how to handle it effectively. Office politics need not be vicious or self-serving. By playing along, you are being sensitive to how key people—people in roles that affect your work—react to your work. How much power you have is determined by both the formal organization (the organizational chart) and the informal organization (the actual relationships among individuals) of your company.

Understanding the formal relationships is easy, but figuring out the informal relationships requires you to be more observant. What roles do people really play in your firm? Who is involved in outside activities with whom? The combination of key individuals' information sources, pipelines, seniority, personalities and relationships all decide how much power they really have.

Do you know what your superiors really think of you? What kind of performance evaluations have you received within the past two years? What suggestions for enhancing your performance did your immediate supervisor offer as a result of your evaluations? Did your supervisor advise you about future promotions, salary increases or other rewards? Did you ask?

Ask yourself the following questions to understand more about your superiors and the politics of your work environment: What kinds of people are my superiors? What are their backgrounds? What are their goals? How do they live? What are their beliefs? Remember that religious, social, and ethnic backgrounds can be important. After you have identified who holds the power and what kind of people they are, you will have to determine whether you can reasonably expect their support.

In addition to your formal performance evaluations, you can

learn more about how you think superiors would rate your performance on the following criteria. Score yourself from *5 to 1 (5 representing very high and 1 representing very low)*:

Rate Your Job Performance

____ Performance of overall job

____ Knowing what superiors want

____ Helping superiors achieve their performance goals

____ Helping superiors do their jobs effectively

____ Sensitivity to superiors' biases

____ Ability to communicate with superiors

____ Loyalty

____ Team player

____ Ability to set priorities and work toward them

____ Ability to anticipate supervisors' needs

____ Level of motivation

____ Ability to meet deadlines and work under pressure

____ Ability to communicate effectively

____ Effectiveness in leading and participating at meetings

*Total Score:*_____ (Highest possible score is 15)

Your score and responses should help you identify your strengths and weaknesses, discover ways to do better work and present a more favorable image. Here are some other suggestions.

• Develop a program to overcome deficiencies you noted in your performance ratings.

- Make sure you are devoting enough time to the highest-priority projects. If not, plan a work schedule that will get those high-priority items off your desk quickly and efficiently.

- Improve your conduct in meetings. Be prepared, contribute ideas and, without compromising your values, try not to take controversial stands that will antagonize the most powerful committee members.

- Motivate yourself. Maybe you have become complacent. You have nothing to lose by making an intensive effort to improve your performance, but you could have a lot to gain.

- Improve your management skills such as organizing, problem solving and supervising. These enhanced skills will come in handy if you decide to move on.

Having top management on your side makes you more promotable and increases the challenges that come your way. If the physical structure of your company makes this impossible, explore ways to creatively redesign or restructure your job. Then propose some changes to your superiors. Faced with similar situations, some Questers have virtually rewritten their job responsibilities.

Try to develop your own challenges. Visualize what would happen if another highly motivated person was promoted to your job. How would he or she tackle it? What challenges would another person find in your job? If someone else in your position could contribute more to the company, your lack of challenge may lie in your attitude or performance. Try to be indispensable. If it's not possible to develop challenges on your current job—and sometimes it isn't—then consider another job or transfer. For more suggestions on how to enhance your current position, read Chapter 4, "Growing in Your Current Job."

Changing Jobs Within Your Company

Sometimes it's less risky to change positions within your company than moving to another organization. Know what's going on in the company. Read memos, listen to rumors and attend meetings. Anticipate changes. As companies pare down their workforces, it's important to be alert to your organization's plans.

Determine the kind of position that will satisfy your needs and use your skills and other attributes. Get to know the key people in the right department and make your interests known at the appropriate time. Show how your skills and accomplishments will contribute to the department. Also pay attention to job listings posted on bulletin boards or company newsletters. You may have to be patient, but if you've made a favorable impression, you could be in luck.

Changing Occupational Fields

A change in occupational fields usually requires a lot of exploration. Initially, at least, it will probably also offer a lower salary. But even though your success will involve many more unknowns, starting anew needn't mean starting at the bottom. If you have investigated your job options, you can usually find new challenges that equal or better the ones you previously enjoyed. Even if you change occupational fields, your past experiences and knowledge will hardly be wasted.

If changing fields is your choice, and it has been successful for a number of Questers, research your options thoroughly. Bear in mind that people in the prospective field may try to dissuade you, warning that you don't have the appropriate background. Before giving up, determine if their warnings are valid. Find out how many of your personal, professional and transferable skills will fit the occupations in this field.

Going into Business for Yourself

Maybe you have already considered going into business for yourself. The number of self-employed people in the North America is increasing steadily. Part of this trend toward self-employment is caused by recessionary dips. As people find themselves unemployed, laid off or unable to find desirable work elsewhere, many carve out their own niches. Business people who plan well, cut corners and know how to work hard can do very well indeed. Opportunities abound.

When you create a business, you become the employer, controlling your work and lifestyle and choosing where you live and work. Research on job satisfaction indicates that self-employed people are among the happiest workers. Most self-employed Questers are living proof. Questers who are in business for themselves tend to score very high on *The Job Satisfaction Questionnaire* and *The Job Involvement Questionnaire.*

Like many Questers, people who go into business for themselves usually have a strong need for autonomy, possess a broad range of talents, desire variety and flexibility and are not afraid to take chances. They are able to get along well with others and have the perseverance, self-discipline, energy and stamina to work the long hours needed to carry them over the rough spots. Money is not their primary motive, although, in the long run, many do well financially. If you have dreamed of being your own boss, don't let the fear of losing a steady paycheck stop you. Economic security is a personal possession. Relegating it to others is a mistake. Consider the hundreds of thousands of people who sweated out years of stagnation in boring jobs only to have inflation make a nightmare out of retirement.

Broadening Your Career Horizons

Regardless of whether you decide to change jobs or stay put, expand your thinking about your career. Researching career options takes time, but the benefits are numerous. It reduces uncertainty, tempers fantasies, and saves time, energy and money. In addition to knowing yourself, researching options is key to making a good choice.

Before you embark on your new venture, explore more than

three career options and check such things as the number of positions listed in the want ads, salary, benefits, employment outlook, advancement opportunities, duties, work environment, education and licensing requirements. Find out what personal qualities are best suited to the job, how to get your foot in the door, what kind of lifestyle workers in that job typically have and what occupations are related to the field.

Finally, take a good look at yourself, considering the minimum wage you can live on, what education you need to fill the gap between the skills you possess and job requirements, how you'll support yourself during your training, what you consider as the job's advantages and disadvantages, and how well the job fits your attributes and desired lifestyle.

Listed below are some sources of valuable information to help you in your evaluation.

The Internet
The Internet offers excellent sites for exploring general occupational fields, job descriptions and educational institutions. Most professional and business associations and post-high institutions have web pages that provide information and links to additional resources. Many printed directories listed below are also available online. For updated sites, use one of the popular search engines to obtain desired information.

Printed Materials
Directories, pamphlets and books contain invaluable information on occupations. Some popular directories available on the Internet and in the reference section of your local library are the *Occupational Outlook Handbook*, *National Occupational Classification System*, *Dictionary of Occupational Titles*, *Encyclopedia of Careers and Vocational Guidance*, *Encyclopedia of Careers and Work Issue* and Careerdirectionsonline.com. Libraries also have hundreds of books and vertical files with updated information on specific occupations and educational institutions.

Rehearsing

How about trying out an occupation to determine how well you fit? Take an evening or weekend job or work as a volunteer or intern during your vacation. Consider investigating other areas while you enjoy a sabbatical, or enroll in a course offered by an educational institution, professional association or industry.

Shadowing

Spend a few days following a professional or business person. This will give you a feel for the day-to-day job realities and work environment. Shadowing can also develop into mentoring relationships and networking contacts. Some large companies have job shadowing programs, but many smaller one's don't. Speak with the human resources department or, in a very small company, the manager.

Informational Interviews

Informational interviews are excellent sources of data and can be fun, too. People generally like talking about themselves and their jobs. Interviews are great networking tools, as well. They can also uncover a prospective employer's needs and even lead to a position. Conduct as many as possible with professionals in your desired field. Contact friends, relatives, colleagues and personnel in human resources departments or people representing professional trade, labor or business associations to locate knowledgeable professionals. Check *Gale's Encyclopedia of Associations* which provides a comprehensive listing of Canadian, United States and international associations. Also review other guides on the Internet and local library.

Before the interview, prepare carefully. Include the following questions:

- How did you get started in the work?

- What's a typical day or week like?

- What do you like most about your position?

- What do you like least?

- What kind of challenges do you deal with?

- What skills do you need to get a job in this field or with your organization?

- What is the future for this field?

- What are the opportunities for advancement?

- What is the average salary range or hourly pay?

- How did you get employed by your organization?

- How does your company compare to others in the field?

- What are your company's mission, goals and growth potential?

- Who else should I speak to about this kind of work?

- What professional associations should I contact?

- Would you enter the field if you could do it over?

- Do you have any additional advice?

Follow up each meeting with a thank-you note.

Additional Resources

You can get a lot of good information by attending career fairs, touring businesses, enrolling in career courses, working through a computer guidance system and viewing Internet sites of companies in desired industries and educational institutions.

After you've investigated each option, write down your thoughts. Do you have the skills or can you acquire those needed? Does the occupation fit your personality, interests, needs, passion and desired lifestyle? Do your family and friends believe you're suited to this work?

Getting the Education You Need

Every occupation, including self-employment, requires some education or training, formal or informal. Investigate the length and type of program required, alternative education and training routes and their suitability. College broadens the mind and teaches much-needed skills, but you can also gain knowledge from workshops, seminars, night school courses, independent study, correspondence schools, on-the-job training or apprenticeship. Before deciding to enter a new field, consult with professionals and company executives to learn what kind of skills you need to become employable, where you can get your training, how long it will take, what it will cost and if financial or other assistance is available.

Don't despair if college is the preferred route. Thousands of adults return to school every year to discover that they are excellent students. Because they often have clearer goals and more experience than they did when they were young, mature adults often earn higher grade point averages than younger students. If you believe you can't afford a college education, remember that financial aid is often available for adults. Corporations will often pay for part or all of your schooling. Colleges and universities usually try to accommodate adults and often offer some of the following options, as well.

• *Part-time study.* In addition to evening and summer programs, some schools now offer weekend college programs. Courses are often conducted from Friday afternoon through Sunday evening several times a month.

• *Experiential learning.* A few colleges and universities offer some type of credit for work or volunteer experience. Proper documentation (usually in portfolio form, with samples) is required to determine the number of credits acceptable. Although it is next to impossible to earn such credit at the graduate level, this can put you several steps ahead in an undergraduate program.

• *Exams for credit.* Ask if you can be tested on your

knowledge and skills in areas for which you already have experience. Although most institutions limit the credit you can earn this way, it is possible to earn up to a year's worth of credit.

- *Credit through contract.* By devising your own curriculum, you may be able to earn a degree outside the classroom. The usual procedure is to draw up a mutually agreeable learning contract, specifying what will be learned and required to obtain credit.

- *Online learning.* Online education is a form of distance education. Some online certificate or degree programs enable students to earn their GED, Associates, Bachelors, Master's and in some cases, PhD in many disciplines. Others offer varied continuing professional development. courses. A few, combine online and in-class delivery. Peterson's, long-time publishers of educational guides (www.petersons.com), provides a searchable list of programs offered by national and international colleges and universities, along with other useful information. Also check other online catalogs such www.pbs.org/learn/als. Internet search engines such as Google and Yahoo! offer links providing easy access to the myriad programs offered globally.

For online learning programs not under the auspices of an accredited institution, check the Distance Education and Training Council site (www.detc.org) to find out if a particular program is recognized by an authority relevant to your field. Remember, however, that because Web sites change hourly, some of these sites may have changed by the time you read this.

People of all ages and backgrounds are attracted to online learning. Online training offers limitless possibilities to those who have computers, high speed Internet connections and the desire to better themselves and their careers. Online learning offers greater flexibility than traditional education. "You can work at your own pace and set your own study schedule," offers a student. If English is your second language, you can review material several times to ensure understanding. Course work is usually available 24 hours every day.

Although online learning offers many advantages, it's not for everyone. Since students interact with each other and the instructor via the Internet, you must feel comfortable using these tools. Working by yourself may be a disadvantage. You must be able to organize time and complete course work on your own. Face-to-face contact is limited. If you enjoy personal attention, listening to teachers and other students, and need eye contact to focus, a traditional classroom may be a better choice. Some companies may think academic standards of online institutions are not as rigorous as the more traditional programs.

Managing Your Money

How you manage your money will be vital to your success. Before changing or quitting jobs or returning to school, consider the following suggestions.

• *Prepare.* Planning and the willingness to live on less for a while will stretch the time you can go without a full-time job. You'll not only have more time to find that ideal position, you'll also eliminate a financially controlled deadline. Before making a career shift, determine how long you can live without an income. How much can you live on, and where will you get needed cash? A careful review of expenses and potential income may show that you can manage for several months without a salary.

• *Create a budget.* Identify your monthly income. List all current income sources, including salary, unemployment benefits or severance pay, interest and dividends, savings and your partner's income. Also itemize assets that can be converted into cash, including pension funds, insurance policies and stocks. Finally, identify future income sources, such as student loans and assistance from relatives.

Next, identify your expenses. Include housing, education, furniture, clothing, dry-cleaning, medical and other insurance, entertainment, transportation, utilities, food and restaurants, taxes, job hunting and miscellaneous costs. Add 15 percent as a cushion.

Can you lower your standards temporarily? Look for ways to cut. Involve family members in your financial discussions. What expenses can they cut? List a lower number for each expense.

• *Live frugally.* Saving early in the process will allow you to have enough for essentials later. Will your old car do? Do you need to eat out? Stay disciplined. Use coupons. Look at your needs, rather than your wants. (But do treat yourself sometimes!)

• *Look for additional income sources.* Can you get a part-time survival job working as a sales clerk, waiter or delivery person? Maybe you could register with a temp agency. Can a family member help? Any income helps. Contact your creditors. Work out interest-only or reduced payments early. Most will cooperate. Reduce your credit card purchases. Pay cash to save interest charges and prevent overspending. If you must use credit, pay the full balance each month. Cash in "luxury" assets. Comparison shop for insurance and other expenses. Trade down to a less costly home or share a residence.

• *Deduct job hunting expenses from your income tax.* This is allowed if you're moving to similar work. These "miscellaneous deductions" require receipts. Allowable expenses include employment or career counseling, resume costs (word processing, printing and mailing), phone and transportation.

If you're relocating to another city, you can deduct some moving expenses. Education costs are also deductible if you're upgrading your skills to maintain or enhance your present job or salary. However, if you're changing fields, establishing a business or have been unemployed for more than a year, you can't deduct these. Contact an accountant for more information.

• *Review your health coverage.* Under the COBRA law, if you've worked for an employer that provided medical coverage and had 20 or more employees, you can continue your coverage. Check U.S. Department of Labor's Web site at http://www.dol.gov/ebsa/faqs/faq_consumer_ cobra.html. If you're not insured, you can investigate other options at the same site. Many local clinics provide services on a sliding scale fee. Don't ignore problems because you're uninsured. Stay healthy!

• *Borrow.* Some debt is okay, provided it excludes mortgage payments and doesn't exceed 10 to 15 percent of your income. The easiest loan option to negotiate typically is one from your parents. To maintain family harmony, agree on an interest rate and repayment schedule. Consult an accountant to determine if it's taxable.

Credit unions are often cheaper and easier to approach than banks. If you deal with a bank, shop around. Consider borrowing from your 401k, your company profit sharing plan, your life insurance policy, or your stock investments. Check the feasibility of a home equity loan or reverse mortgage to tap your home equity.

• *Get assistance.* Numerous government departments and non-profit agencies offer advice on financial assistance and debt management. They include Service Canada (www.servicecanada.gc.ca/en/common/contactus/index.shtml) and SPRINGBOARD Non-Profit Consumer Credit Management (www.ncfe.org). Software products such as Quicken Basic and Microsoft Money can also help you keep track of various accounts.

Establishing Support Systems
Once you have decided to change jobs, don't try to be a hero

and make the change entirely on your own. Be open to support. You'll feel better emotionally, intellectually and even financially if you have help from close and supportive family or friends.

A reputable professional career counselor or industrial psychologist can also provide support and feedback; help you identify your needs and interests; and provide accurate, up-to-date job and labor information. A poor one, on the other hand, will cost you time and money and may even weaken your self-confidence—so stick with an accredited professional. Set up a preliminary meeting to determine what services are provided and at what cost. Ask for references. Free or inexpensive counseling is readily available at many colleges, continuing education centers, churches and some organizations. You may also consider participating in workshops offered by these institutions or government agencies.

But wherever you seek help, be careful not to be constrained by phrases like "you should" or "you ought to." While you may tolerate such comments from a partner or relative, you should be wary if a counselor or therapist uses them. In the final analysis, go with your feelings. Even the most talented counselor can't make decisions for you or guarantee that you will find your dream job.

Laying Down Safety Nets
Few decisions are ironclad, but to protect yourself from surprises, build in a fail-safe or retreat position. Constructing a safety net will help reduce your anxiety. Review your responses to the questions in the "Describing the Barriers" section earlier in this Chapter and consider the following:

• What is frightening about the change?

• What do you stand to lose?

• What barriers are preventing you from reaching your goals?

- What can you do to overcome them?

- Which people might help you reach them?

- What are your chances of success? Why?

- What are some possible positive and negative outcomes?

- What are the chances that the negative outcomes will occur?

- How can the odds be reduced?

- Do the positive outcomes outweigh the negative consequences?

- Do you still want to achieve your goal?

By preparing for the negative as well as the positive, you are developing a backup plan. Realizing that there are no right or wrong moves can also be helpful. Viewing a career mistake as a detour or growth opportunity may allay your uneasiness. After all, experience really is the best teacher.

Developing Positive Attitudes and Behaviors
Success is 15 percent aptitude and 85 percent attitude. It will be your attitude, not your aptitude, that determines your success in your new venture. You are the actor and the director of your life. You create your own script by the thoughts you think. Your love and respect for yourself as well as your fears are perceived by those you meet. Those people then mirror or reflect these thoughts back to you. If you want to change your career and life for the better, it is essential to be optimistic. Review some of the following:

• *Use positive statements about such things as being in control or being blessed.* Practice self-talk every day. "I like myself because … " "I can … " "I will … " Don't criticize, condemn or complain. Instead, think about ways to improve the situation. Avoid phrases such as, "I can't," "I'm too old," and "I will never … "

- *State and write affirmations that promote positive thinking.* For example, "I can change ... " "I am w orthwhile," "I can perform ... easily and effortlessly."

- *Think, act, and look happy and successful.* You will begin to think, feel and actually become happ y and successful.

- *Concentrate on your successes.* Create a "success collage" with pictures that illustrate who you want to be and what y ou want to accomplish. Include the goal you want to attain, how you want to look and the prof essional and personal image y ou want to project. Look at it every day.

- *Eliminate negative thoughts and feelings.* If you have negative feelings about a situation or another person, wr ite them down on a sheet of paper, then burn the paper or tear it up and thro w it away. Replace negative thoughts with positive ones. Each time you catch yourself using a negative phrase, say, "Cancel," and replace the negative thought or statement with a positiv e one.

- *Take your mind off your problems.* Get involved in pleasurable activities. Rent a movie, attend a concer t, meditate, listen to music or engage in physical activities.

- Greet others with positive, cheerful statements. Associate with positive, happy people. Stay clear of complainers.

- *Look for and expect good things to happen.* Count your blessings. Fill your mind with positive and constructive thoughts, desired outcomes and helpful ideas. You are special and have unique talents.

The following analogy, presented by Executive Development Systems, Inc., illustrates how positive thinking works: All the water in the world cannot sink a ship unless it gets inside of it. Similarly, all the sorrow, fear, anxiety, frustration, jealousy and worry in the world cannot sink you unless they get inside your mind! To keep them out, fill y our mind so full of happiness, positive and constructive thoughts, desired outcomes and helpful ideas that there's no room for the negative to seep in.

5. Narrowing Your Options

The key to successful career management is finding a position that is compatible with your personal qualities and goals. To determine this, establish priorities and evaluate alternatives. Complete the following checklist for each occupation you are considering. Circle Yes or No for each statement.

If you have **10 or more** *Yes* responses, you're probably on the right track. If you have **10 or more** *No* responses, reconsider your options.

1.	I have the necessary intelligence and skills to do the work.	Yes	No
2.	The option is compatible with my needs, values, interests, and other personal characteristics.	Yes	No
3.	I can acquire the necessary knowledge and skills to do a good job.	Yes	No
4.	The occupation will give me a sense of meaning and purpose.	Yes	No
5.	I know how people in this occupation (or who are self-employed in this field) live on and off the job, and I find this an acceptable lifestyle.	Yes	No
6.	I can afford the training required for the job, or I can obtain the necessary finances to go into business for myself.	Yes	No
7.	I can imagine staying in this occupation for at least four years.	Yes	No
8.	My spouse (or close friend) believes I can succeed at this kind of work.	Yes	No
9.	My shortcomings will not be a problem (for example, health, vision, hearing, size, strength or personality traits).	Yes	No

10. I know where to get the necessary training or experience to enter this occupation or to become self-employed.   Yes   No

11. I have identified all the potential difficulties in preparing for and working in this field.   Yes   No

12. I know safeguards I can build in to protect myself from the challenges identified above.   Yes   No

Total Yes responses: _____

Total No responses: _____

Using Your Intellect and Intuition

To narrow your options even further, complete the following activities, which use both intellect and intuition.

Prioritize your options mathematically. Make a chart by drawing a series of vertical and horizontal lines so that the paper is composed of squares. At the top of the page, list all the criteria (one in each square) that you consider important in your job. Include purpose, needs (such as income, responsibility, public image, creativity, challenge, achievement and variety), interests, skills, and the degree of perceived risk. Relocation possibilities, required study, lifestyle and approval or disapproval of your spouse or partner are other criteria you could include. Down the left side of the page, list each occupational option.

Next, for each alternative consider your important criteria (identified at the top of the page). If an option doesn't satisfy a criterion, place a minus one (-1) in the appropriate column. If the criterion exists, but not as much as you'd like, record a zero (0). Finally, if the criterion exists to a desired state, record a plus one (+1). Add the points for each option and place them in the total column at the far right. The occupation with the most pluses should meet the greatest number of criteria important to you. Study your assessment to determine why this option got the highest score. If one option is not an obvious choice, review your criteria and make necessary adjustments. But don't stop here.

Tap into your intuition. What does your intuition tell you about these options? Listen carefully to your inner voice. Trust it. It instinctively knows what is best for you. If necessary, take time out to reflect on your priorities or try some of the exercises below to help you tap into your intuition.

• *Write in your journal.* Jot down your daily thoughts, feelings, and hunches. Pay attention to what you write and how it feels at the time. Note the thoughts and feelings that emerge when you finish.

• *Draw or doodle.* Write out a question that clearly and simply states what you want to know or answer. Underneath your question, draw whatever comes to your mind or flows through your hands. Continue to draw until you have nothing to add. Look at the meaning behind the drawing and the symbols within it. Note the sequence of steps. Pay particular attention to your thoughts and feelings as you look at the picture, such as joy and excitement or sadness and confusion.

• *Ask your dreams for the answer.* Tell yourself, "I want to have a dream that will give me the answer to my question," or, " I will have such a dream, remember it and understand it." Dreams usually come to us in language or symbols we can understand. Examine the sequence of events, how you felt upon awakening, and how the dream ended. Note the internal and external cues you receive the next day.

• *Listen to your intuition.* Take at least five minutes every day to listen to your intuition. Ask for help, direction or anything else you want an answer to. Have faith it will come.

Modifying Career Goals and Making a Choice

Now that you've gained additional insights into yourself and your career options, review the career goals you set earlier. Are they realistic and sufficiently ambitious? Are they consistent with the options you rated highest after investigating your personal characteristics and career alternatives? If not, you need to make some changes.

By now you should be ready to make an occupational choice. Determine your first, second and third occupational preferences. These may change as you gather additional information or as various circumstances in your environment change.

6. Acting on the Decision

Once you have made up your mind about your general occupational goal, take steps to realize it. Action requires developing a step-by-step method of attack. Devise a well-planned campaign to market yourself for the job, establish your own business or return to school. It is helpful to create an action plan that answers the following four questions:

- Where do I begin?

- Who can help me?

- When do I begin?

- How do I begin?

Because you and your environment are constantly changing, your plans should be flexible. An exercise that can help you keep your plans open-ended is the Personal Map of the Future. Select three occupational goals or job objectives and describe, on the map, the steps you can take this week, this month, this year, and thereafter to attain your goals. Consider possible barriers and what you can do to overcome them.

Keeping these possible barriers and safeguards in mind, write down your first-choice plans, indicating date or time limits, people involved and resources required. Written plans are efficient; the act of recording each step gives you a handy timetable against which to assess your progress. Planning also gives you a greater sense of security and a better chance to control your life. Few people proceed immediately from starting point to end goal. Most take many intermediate steps along the way. Be as specific as possible about what each step involves before acting. You might, for example, decide to go back to school before taking a job. In that case, find out about programs that give credit for experience or by

Attaining Your Goal

- *State your goal and deadline in specific terms.* Dare to dream. Make sure your goal is consistent with your purpose.

- *Verify that your goal is sound and desirable.* Project the consequences. It should benefit you and other people.

- *Write down your goal and reasons for wanting it.* Give it your full attention. State your outcome in positive terms. Make sure your outcomes reflect things you can affect.

- *Identify and overcome barriers.* Specify obstacles that could keep you from reaching your goal. If the worst thing happened, what could you do? How can you break through these barriers? What information do you need to pursue your goal? Where could you go for this? From whom could you get support? What can you do to make this less risky? What kind of measures could you build in to make it less urgent? Less irreversible? Less overwhelming?

  List all the groups, people, resources, character traits, education, personal strengths and tools you have at your disposal to help you overcome your barriers.

- *Set a schedule for completing your goal, but be flexible so that you can incorporate new ideas.* Use a daily organizer to plan activities that will help you reach your goal.

  Break the goal into small steps. Each day do at least one activity related to achieving it. Determine the resources (for example, people, organizations, associations and printed materials) that can help you get where you want to go. Make the first step something you can do today. Ask yourself, "Is what I'm doing or about to do moving me closer to my goal?"

- *Ask a friend or relative for support.* Meet with him or her often to review your progress. Call on this person when you need a boost. Remember to associate with positive people who support your goal.

- *Remove all negative mental obstacles, such as fear, worry or anger. Avoid phrases such as "I can't."*

- *State and write affirmations and intentions daily.* Affirmations are potent statements of truths that sink deep into yoursubconscious and help you become the person you want to be. Use positive statements such as "I can be what I want to be." And, "I am proud of myself."

- *Continually visualize the outcome you desire.* See yourself attaining your goal. If you find this difficult, try making a collage or taking a photograph depicting your goal. Then experience achieving your goal: hear, smell, touch and imagine yourself living your goal today.

- *Act as if you have already achieved your goal.*

- *Embrace failure or rejection.* View setbacks as learning experiences or detours as you move toward your goal.

- *Keep your mind, body and spirit in top working order.* Eat healthy foods, exercise regularly and don't forget to nourish your soul.

- *Review your goal periodically.* Modify it as you learn more about yourself and career options.

examination. Whatever you finally decide, take time to write down each step. This will keep you motivated and moving.

You've come a long way in your career quest. You know yourself better and you've explored options, set goals, and made plans. *Now it's time to act.* Action requires commitment.

Write your action steps on your daily calendar, and regularly reappraise your goals and plans. Modify these as you learn more about yourself and your career options.

Stay focused on your goals. Believe you will achieve them. Base all your decisions on the overall direction you want your life to go. This will help you stay on track. Momentum will build. You will become unstoppable.

Achieving your goals will give you feelings of accomplishment, confidence and exhilaration. You will also gain a sense of purpose, inner peace and greater control over your personal and professional life.

If you have decided to change jobs, why not get started on your job search this week? Chapter 10 shows you how.

Chapter 10

Dare to Change

This Chapter continues with the ADAPNAE decision making process (described in Chapter 9) by providing an overview of basic knowledge and tools needed to perform a successful job search. If you are interested in acquiring business planning skills, refer to resources on the Internet, books in your local library or speak to small business resource consultants in your community.

6. Acting on the Decision
Clarifying Your Goal

Are you clear about the job you really want? Do you know in what industry you want to work? Do you know what skills you have and want to use in your job? Do you know what "value added" you can offer potential employers? Are you familiar with the current buzz or key words people in your industry use to describe your skills? Are your goals compatible with your passion, needs, values, interests and other personal traits?

To conduct a successful job search in today's market, you need to stand out and show potential employers why they should hire you. One way to do this is to incorporate a "value added" proposition into your campaign. In the corporate world, companies use value propositions to answer their target market's question, "Why should we buy your product?" In the same way, your value proposition should effectively answer your potential employer's question, "Why should we hire you?" Your value proposition should consist of three components: The employer's needs, your supporting qualifications and your added value. By addressing each of these components, you are showing the targeted employer what you have to offer.

To address the target market's needs, you must research companies of interest. To pinpoint your supporting qualifications, include specific skills, education, experience, credentials and accomplishments. The key is to match your qualifications to the employer's needs. Select only the most important, relevant qualifications for use in your value proposition. This is the unique benefit you bring to the table which should be the "clincher" in your sales pitch.

The more clearly you can specify what you can offer the employer, the more likely you will be to attain your goal. A well-defined goal focuses and directs your job search. Your overall goal should include your desired job title and industry, your special skills and accomplishments, what you can offer the employer (your value added proposition) and desired location. Read the following to see how Questers do this.

Overall Goal Which Includes Desired Job Title and Value Added Proposition
Your overall goal with a value added proposition should describe your ideal job. If you know the basics about your ideal position and what you can offer your potential employer, you will find it easy to write your overall goal statement. These basics include:

- Field or industry (e.g., financial, education, pharmaceutical or computer)

- Job title, functional area and organizational level (e.g., bookkeeper, mechanical engineer, or sales and marketing manager)

- Area of specialty, if applicable (e.g., special training or skills)

- Your value added proposition—what you can do for the employer

- Type of company (e.g., size, organizational philosophy and advancement opportunities)

- Location (e.g., near home or in another city, region or country).

An overall goal statement such as, "I have skills and experience in the Insurance Industry which I can offer a nice company on the East Coast," won't help focus and direct your job search as much as this one: "I would like to use my seven years of experience in management and accounting to obtain a job as *Financial Manager* with an *Insurance Company* on the East Coast where I can create a work environment that has team cohesiveness, satisfaction and productivity."

The following sample goal statements incorporate the basics.

- I would like to contribute to the success of a medium-sized *Construction* company in the Midwest where I can use my leadership, labor relations and health and safety knowledge and skills, as a *Personnel and Labor Relations Manager*, to help the company enhance employee morale and productivity, and control costs by not having to deal with problem employees or regulators.

- I would like to work as a *Business Analyst* for a *Bank* on the East Coast where my strong technical and communication skills, sound understanding of business processes, and 10 years of hands on experience in project management will help the bank increase profits and improve customer/client services, and enable me to meet my needs.

- I have 20 years of college teaching expertise, sensitivity to people of different cultures, knowledge of social agencies and traveling experience which I can use as an *English as a Second Language Instructor* to offer cross cultural sensitivity to a *Junior College in the North West* which will provide me with the possibility of tenure.

Now write your own overall goal statement. Include your desired job title and industry, skills and accomplishments you want to use, what you can offer the employer (value added proposition) and desired location. Use the following as a guide.

- I have _____ skills and accomplishments which I can use in the position of _____ (specific job title) to offer _____ (value added proposition) to a company _____ (field or industry) located in _____ (desired area). The company will enable me to _____ (what you need to meet your own needs, values and other characteristics).

Your overall goal, which has a specific job title in a desired industry, should be a concise description of what you can offer the company by using relevant skills. In the foregoing goal statements, the specific job titles are *Personnel and Labor Relations Manager* in the *Construction Industry*, *Business Analyst* in the *Financial/Banking Industry* and *English as a Second Language Instructor* in the *Education Industry*, respectively. Does your overall goal include the forgoing?

If you have substantial experience in a particular field, and want to remain in the field, focus your job search there. You can also define second and third job targets b y considering different types of industries or a new geographic locale.

Once you've clarified your overall goal, job title, industry and value added proposition, you're ready to focus on your job search. Begin by targeting the companies that can off er the position you want. Review your progress periodically. Modify your goal and targeted position as y ou learn more about yourself and your desired industry.

Establishing Information Sources

Research is crucial before job search. Throughout the search, you will need substantial information about prospective employers.

The Internet is a must in learning about industries and companies. Google and other search engines are e xcellent ways to obtain desired information. "Cruising the Information Superhighway," later in this Chapter, discusses how to use the Internet for job search.

Many general directories that contain listings and descr iptions of companies and industries are available online, in electronic format and in print. These include *Rich's Business Directory*, Dun and Bradstreet's Million Dollar Data Base on the Inter net and *Ward's Business Directory of U.S. Private and Pubic Cor porations*.

> *Throughout the job search you will need substantial information about prospective employers.*

Numerous magazines and newspapers that can help keep you updated on the changing business scene are also available online and in pr int. These include *The Wall Street Journal, Fortune, U.S. News and World Report, Business Week, Canadian Key Business Directory, The Globe and Mail, National Post* and local newspapers.

Most local libraries have elibrary resources where users can research regional industries and companies. Librarians can help you with your research if you call or visit the library. Also check trade periodicals and professional association publications, your local Chamber of Commerce's directory of industrial and business firms, industrial directories published by government departments and the Yellow Pages of your telephone directory.

Network as well. Keep abreast of new developments and add to your list of colleagues and acquaintances by joining professional, trade or civic groups and attending professional meetings. Consider volunteering for a community agency. Networking reaches into all parts of the business world. Remember, people like to do business with individuals they know. For more on networking, read the "Networking" section later in this Chapter.

Marketing Yourself

Now it's time to move into action. Don't just passively answer help-wanted advertisements, listed on web-based resources such as www.monster.com, www.careerbuilder.com or local newspapers, by sending resumes. Take charge of your job search. Be creative, show initiative and radiate optimism.

To get your ideal job, you must promote yourself. If you don't tell others what you can offer, how will they know what you can do? Where to start? Begin by viewing yourself as an entrepreneur with a value added proposition, as discussed earlier. Think of yourself as a product to be sold, rather than a job seeker. Just as companies push products, you need to sell yourself to a prospective employer. Rely, not only on your resume and contacts, but on your total presentation, including your communication and persuasion skills and your visual image. Selling yourself takes time, effort and practice. Most of us have a false sense of humility, modesty or shyness when it comes to selling ourselves. If these attitudes are holding you back, consider the following suggestions.

Prepare. Identify organizations with which you'd like to work before they advertise openings. Know their philosophies, needs and goals. Your ability to get the job depends on how your accomplishments and skills can benefit potential employers, and how well you communicate these benefits. Design resumes and other marketing materials to show how you can address their needs. Show how your experience, skills and accomplishments match their job requirements, and how you'll benefit the organization. Demonstrate how you can make or save money, help people feel good or expand markets.

Look and act professional. The impressions you make in the first few minutes will make or break your sale. Develop a positive image—a neat, professional appearance and a self-assured demeanor. Your written and verbal communications should be positive, direct and to the point. Appear comfortable with your accomplishments and confident about your future.

Appear savvy and contemporary. Know your market. Research the norm for the area, industry and company. Dress one notch above customers to communicate professionalism without intimidation. If casual dress is the norm in the organization, wear the team uniform. If formal business attire is the norm for both genders, wear a tailored suit and shirt. Coordinate pieces. Wear flattering colors and styles, well-maintained shoes. Have your hair styled professionally and manicure your nails. Avoid strong fragrances. Radiate energy, enthusiasm, friendliness, confidence and competence.

Develop a positive mindset. Focus on what you can offer. Believe in yourself, your product. Expect good things. To enhance your confidence and optimism, review, "Tips for Building Self-Confidence," in Chapter 3. Start by saying aloud, "I am an intelligent, confident person with many skills to offer." Say it regularly and with conviction. Confidence shows in your eyes, your words, your gestures, your very being; you transmit it directly to the people with whom you come in contact. Remember, you are constantly reflecting your thoughts. So, if you don't like who you are, change your belief about yourself.

Prepare an elevator speech. The name reflects the fact that the pitch can be delivered in the span of an elevator ride of about 30 to 60 seconds or approximately150 to 225 words. This mini speech should introduce yourself, describe your experience, accomplishments and skills, and demonstrate what you can do for the person or company (your value added proposition). Elevator speeches can be given over the phone or in person — at professional conferences or sports events, when you meet strangers or make cold phone calls.

An elevator speech is as essential as a business card. Before writing any part of your speech, research your audience. Know yourself, as well. Define precisely what you are offering, what problems you can solve and what benefits you can bring to a prospective contact or employer. Outline your talk by using the following questions; "Who am I?" "What do I offer?" "What problem is solved?" "What are the main contributions I can make?" "What should the listener do as a result of hearing this?"

Prepare your script ahead of time. Write what you want to say in conversational English. Keep it succinct, easy to deliver, and an accurate reflection of your personality, skills and product or service. Start with a "hook," a statement or question that piques the person's interest to want to hear more. Introduce yourself, stating your name, what you do, and how your skills, product or service can benefit the person or organization. Employers are interested in things that make or save time and money, help people feel good or expand markets. Also state what you like about the organization.

The speech should reflect your personality. If you're fun and upbeat, show this; if you're serious, illustrate this. Deliver your speech conversationally. Be friendly, genuine. Intend to establish a relationship or open doors. Observe listeners' reactions such as confusion or interest. Practice delivering your speech to trusted friends and request feedback. Make necessary modifications. It's OK to deliver speeches differently each time. It will sound more natural, but always keep it short and include the main points.

Target decision-makers to determine job openings. Request introductions, cold call or email. To capture attention, offer creative comments about the organization, and devise innovative solutions to identified challenges. Be genuine. When you're excited about a job that reflects your passion, possibilities arise. Similarly, when you're natural and honest, marketing is easy, successful. Toot your own horn. Keep people informed about recent accomplishments. Use "I" statements to demonstrate achievements. Express feelings and opinions directly, honestly, assuredly. Maintain eye contact. Hold your head high, shoulders back.

Use the phone and email. Call busy people before 8:30 AM, after 5:30 PM, and during the lunch break. Leave messages. If they're not returned, call back. Don't leave more than three messages over a ten-day period. Call again in a month. If you don't get responses to phone messages, send emails. Consider using voice mail and email as advertising tools. Compose "commercials" revealing interesting facts about what you can offer.

Network continuously. Networking should be mutually beneficial. Offer contacts assistance and ask for help. Word of mouth is the best marketing strategy. Ask people, who have contacts in desired organizations, to help you secure meetings with decision makers. Thank contacts. Timely, consistent follow-up is essential. Call or meet contacts periodically. Record contact activities. Read Networking later in this Chapter.

Be visible. Get involved in community events such as Chamber of Commerce activities and professional meetings.

You'll get most value from a group if you become a member, and go to the same group's events rather than attend new groups all the time. Volunteer.

Enhance communication skills. Practice giving presentations, conducting meetings and listening. Join your local Toastmasters. Know how to work a room. Arrive relatively early. When meeting people, offer a firm handshake, give a modified elevator speech, and pass out your business card with contact information. Discuss common subjects such as industry gossip or interesting things people have done. Move around. Before leaving, indicate your desire to meet again.

Prepare a portfolio illustrating sample accomplishments. A portfolio can help set you apart from the competition. Buy a black portfolio case and plastic protective sheets that will fit inside. Make a scrapbook documenting your work projects and successes to share with prospective employers during interviews. Many sales people carry and present portfolios or scrapbooks about their products and services to prospective clients.

Include the following items in your portfolio: letters of recognition from customers; letters of commendation from immediate managers and upper management; company awards; community service awards; product brochures you developed; task force documents that demonstrate your participation; published articles; an outline of all projects you worked on for previous employers; photographs that document your work-related successes; and certificates illustrating completion of professional seminars.

Update your portfolio frequently to reflect new accomplishments and achievements. Consider creating a web page or putting your portfolio on a DVD. You can even use your portfolio to present your case for an internal promotion or pay increase. This tool can give you a cutting edge advantage over your competition. Above all, it will help you remember all the things you do that make you valuable—things that you and others may take for granted or even have forgotten.

Balance patience with persistence. Know the difference between what's really happening and what you think is happening. When decision makers don't call at assigned times, it's probably because they don't have time. If people say they haven't had an opportunity to look at your resume, they probably mean more pressing projects have come up rather than they're not interested. Ask when to call back. Keep in touch. If you miss one job opportunity, believe that a better one will come along and you are going to get it. Continue to maintain confidence, persist and have faith.

Preparing Your Resume

When it's time to prepare your resume, you'll find many guides to help you on the Internet, at libraries and bookstores. Consider your resume as a sales tool. Entice the reader to give it more than the 20 seconds an initial resume reading gets. Write it in positive language emphasizing your accomplishments. Most of all, phrase it carefully to satisfy the needs of each job target. Opinions differ regarding the length of the resume. Professionals and executives generally have resumes of three pages or more. Human resources personnel prefer resumes of one or two pages. Again, know your market.

The three distinct resume formats are: reverse chronological, functional, and a combination of the two. *Reverse chronological* seems to be the most popular with hiring managers. They prefer employment data be provided with the most recent job listed first, followed by the next most recent, and so on. In that way, it's easy to see career progression from an entry-level position to a more senior status. It's also easy to detect gaps in dates of employment. These gaps lead some candidates to use a *functional format* instead. Functional formats stress skills you have, rather than where and when you used them. These formats are best for those who have been out of the workforce for long periods because they were raising children, job seekers who are transitioning from one occupation or industry to another, and students who have just graduated from college and have little "real-world" experience. However, sometimes combining a *functional format* with a *reverse chronological format* makes the most sense. These are called combination resumes.

With the *combination format*, skills that are relevant to the current job search are placed in a special section b y function, while the professional history or work experience is presented in a standard, reverse-chronological format. This format offers the best of both worlds, and is highly popular with moder n job seekers and hiring managers.

Write a different resume and cover letter for each job target. Tailor your resume to each potential job. Employers want to see how your skills match job requirements, and how you'll benefit the organization. Ensure your resume reflects a clear objective and summary statement which focuses on how your accomplishments can benefit or add value to the job. Review current employment ads and job descriptions to identify key words that describe skills, personal characteristics and experience required.

Use key words and active verbs. Describe significant accomplishments in previous positions, using key words requested in ads. Use active verbs (for example, advised, coordinated, designed, investigated, wrote) to describe your accomplishments, with quantification such as n umbers, percentages, evidence of quality and results, whenever possible. For example, "Completed a $3.5 million project three months ahead of schedule and four percent under budget." Avoid vague statements. For example, say, "managed a team of eight software engineers" rather than "responsible for supervising software engineers."

Include relevant information and a cover letter. Whether you choose a chronological, functional or combination f ormat, include:

- Job code and title of the position f or which you're applying (At the top of y our resume and cover letter)

- Name, address, phone and fax numbers, email address (Each on separate lines)

- A clear summary statement (A brief summary of your skills, experience and value added proposition)

- Professional experience. (Include employment history, and relevant accomplishments and skills)

- Education and training (Specify degrees, areas of concentration. Include related workshops, courses)

- Related special skills (Foreign languages, computer software programs).

- Other (Professional affiliations and offices held, related volunteer work, publications, honors/awards, licenses or certificates)

Prepare a scannable resume. A scannable resume maximizes your chances of matching your skills and other strengths to job requirements. Since many large organizations scan resumes for key words stipulated in job descriptions, the more key words you provide, the more opportunities you'll have to acquire suitable, available positions. Increase your list of key words by including specifics; for example, list software programs you can operate and software languages you know. If you are fluent in a foreign language, mention it. Use the jargon specific to your industry, but spell out acronyms.

Avoid fancy treatments such as italics, underlines, bold tabs, indents and shadows. Don't use vertical or horizontal lines, graphics or boxes. Don't condense spacing between letters. Avoid two-column formats. Use capital letters for section headings. Balance the amount of white space with type . Use crisp, dark type such as those produced by laser printers so that every letter can be recognized. Ensure that the letters don't touch one another.

Although email is the preferred method of sending resumes today, have a hard copy available to send by fax, regular mail or to bring to the interview. Use white or light-colored 8 1/2 by 11 inch paper, printed on one side only. Match your cover letter and envelope stationery to your resume paper. Don't fold or staple your resume. Use only standard typefaces, such as Arial, Helvetica, Times, Palatino, Geneva or New York, and font sizes of 11 to 12 points. Use all capital letters for section headings. Provide each company with a laser printer original of your resume. Use "fine mode" to fax your resume.

Be concise, truthful, accurate and confident. Many companies hire resume verification services to check statements. Include only what's essential. Too much information will obscure your outstanding qualifications. Ask people who know you well to read the resume to determine whether it is capturing everything you can offer. Rewrite your resume as you learn more about yourself and the market. Spell-check your resume and ask someone to proofread it for errors and typos.

Get your resume to hiring managers, whenever possible. Create ways to identify and meet hiring managers. Network. Ask for introductions. Make cold calls. If you are asked to send your resume, follow-up each mailing with a phone call or email within three weeks. If you don't hear from anyone, call again. Send short cover letters with each resume. Consider including a portfolio with sample accomplishments. Since many employers dislike downloading email from unknown people, consider sending your resume and cover letter as part of the email message. You can also attach a hard copy version of your resume in the same email.

If you are applying to a want ad, type the job code and title of the job for which you are applying. If you send your resume by email, repeat this information on the subject line, at the top of your resume and cover letter. This should be followed by your name, address, phone, fax and email—each on a separate line.

Select and cultivate references with care. Maintain close contact with these people throughout your job search. Choose business or professional people who have supervised you in one or more of your most recent positions, and who will talk positively about your abilities. If possible, choose individuals in positions of equal or superior levels of responsibility to those of hiring managers, and whose positions relate closely to the kind of job you are seeking.

Identifying Job Opportunities and Contacting Employers

Once you have researched the market and prepared your resume, you are ready to begin making initial contacts with potential employers. Throughout your campaign, the objective is to secure as many interviews as possible with potentially interested employers.

Networking

Networking is the best way to get a job. By increasing your contacts, you learn about job openings before they are advertised. Networking gives you useful information, such as what positions are available or when companies are in a hiring mode. But networking is more. Real networking involves giving and sharing without expecting anything in return. By helping each other, everyone benefits. How can you interact with others to both give and get? What have you got to offer someone you just met?

Networking is the best way to get a job.

To start the networking process, list all the people you know who might help you gain access to an employer. These can be friends, colleagues, relatives, acquaintances, your banker, insurance agent, doctor, spiritual leader and lawyer. Call former employers, suppliers, customers or clients and club members. Tell everyone you know that you're looking for opportunities to use your skills and would like their help. Talk to people everywhere—religious meetings, trade shows, hallways, coffee shops and airplanes. Attend seminars, parties and business meetings. Take an active role in community affairs, politics and service clubs. Speak at professional and trade associations and other groups. Create ways to meet decision-makers. Ask for introductions. Make cold calls. Exchange business cards.

Join professional and alumni groups. Many act as intermediaries between job hunters and employers. They also publish journals, newsletters, membership lists, trade show catalogs and other materials. Contact directors of local Chambers of Commerce and service organizations such as the Rotary and Kiwanis Clubs. *The Encyclopedia of Associations* and your local Yellow Pages list good information. Contact the placement office of your alma mater, and register with executive recruiters and placement firms.

Build new contacts by conducting *informational interviews* in person or by phone. Modify your elevator speech. Explain your interest in the field or industry and ask for 10 to 20 minutes of the contact's time. Clarify that you're asking for information, not a job. Be brief, direct and professional. Give enough personal information to demonstrate your sincerity and qualifications. Ask questions about the job market, the field and job-hunting tips. Appropriate questions include these: "Describe a typical work day." "What do you like most and least about your position?" "What skills and experience are required for job entry?" "Where can you get these skills?" "Are there any special licensing requirements for the field?" "How long is the training/education?" "What personal characteristics do you need to perform this job well and enjoy it?" "What are some industry trends?" "What do companies look for?" "What is the typical salary range?" What are the opportunities for advancement?" "What other sources (people, associations, journals, etc.) should I investigate?"

Network on line. Like every other aspect of job search, networking has moved to cyberspace, and a wide variety of web sites have been develped that are dedicated to bringing people together via the Internet. From social networks like www.facebook.com to business sites like www.linkedin.com or others run by professional or trade associations, online meeting places are linking professionals across the globe.

Online networking provides unmatched freedom enabling participants to post inquiries at any time and from any place. In addition, it puts you in touch with thousands of people you would not have the opportunity to meet otherwise.

Before joining the world of networking in cyberspace, do your research. There are networking groups for nearly every industry and interest, and the sophistication of these online ventures ranges from simple chat rooms and message boards to those dedicated to job leads. Look for groups that match your interests and goals. Find out how long they have been in existence and how credible they are. Don't limit yourself to one group. Join three or four, ensuring the groups provide variety. For example, join a group for your particular industry, as well as a broader group, like a general business discussion board.

Think about *privacy*. Find out how much personal information you're required to provide and what the site plans to do with the information. Take the plunge. Introduce yourself like you would in any other social situation. Create a simple online posting that tells others in the group who you are and what you can offer.

Don't forget the importance of face-to-face contacts. As productive as online networking can be, keep your involvement in other in-person networking opportunities, as well. In fact, most online organizations provide these opportunities as well.

Get out to events or be active on online. Have your elevator speech ready. When you meet people, focus on them. Give them your full attention first and listen to them. Don't say too much yourself unless somebody asks you for information.

People will trust you more when they notice you care more about others than yourself.

Networking Tips

- *Prepare.* Decide what strengths or achievements you want to stress. Rehearse your elevator speech outlining your experience, accomplishments and skills.

- *Believe networking is the job of looking for a job.* Talk with people wherever you go—religious meetings, professional conferences and casual get-togethers. Let them know what you can offer. Each original contact can substantially increase your network.

- *Focus on the person.* Offer assistance. People don't care how much you know until they know how much you care.

- *Create ways to meet people who are in hiring positions.* List the people you might want to see and find a way to get someone to help you meet them. Ask for introductions. Make "cold calls."

- *Keep your interviews brief.* Ask for 10-minute appointments.

- *Leave every meeting with several new names.* Ask for leads. Make friends with administrative assistants. Remember their names.

- *Send a thank-you note to each person who helps you.* Follow-up every telephone or face-to-face meeting with a short note. Politely state that you appreciate the person's assistance and consideration. This will encourage him or her to remember you.

- *Use the Internet to increase the number of people who know about you and your occupational credentials.*

- *Exchange business cards with everyone you meet.* Make notes on the back of each card you receive indicating where you met the person and any important points. Organize these in a file.

- *Continue to network after you've landed the job.*

Answering Help-Wanted Ads

Help-wanted advertisements on the Internet, in newspapers or industry newsletters are a good sources of potential job opportunities; but, because of the volume of replies they generate, you must respond to many advertisements to receive any responses. Answer all enticing prospects, even those that are a month old or more, until you accept a new position. Always include a cover letter.

Your cover letter should be accomplishment-oriented, responding directly to the qualifications listed in the ad. Referring to the advertisement, outline your reason for writing, your accomplishments and what you can offer the company in the first paragraph. In the second paragraph, elaborate on what you can offer, giving specific examples. Show how you could help to solve a departmental problem. List four or five accomplishments that best relate to the company's stated needs. In the third paragraph, outline biographical information. Use the final paragraph to request a face-to-face interview, and indicate whether you expect to be contacted by the company or you plan to phone. It's best to take the initiative.

Calling will demonstrate your interest and assertiveness. Begin by introducing yourself and explaining that you want to ensure the correspondence was received. Ask how many candidates will be interviewed and how and when they will be chosen. Again, request an interview.

Identifying Specific Companies

The best way to make direct contact is to call the hiring managers of the organizations of interest. This direct contact with executives in a large number of firms may uncover opportunities that are not, and never will be, advertised. The resulting interviews may convince a company to create a new position just to get you into the organization. When a well-qualified candidate appears at the right time, most companies would prefer hiring him or her to the expense and time involved in searching for and interviewing applicants.

But before you make contact, research each organization of interest. Know the organization's history and organizational chart including divisions, departments and subsidiaries. Be informed about its philosophy, mission statement, management style, values, policies and procedures. Know whether the organization embraces employee psychological health and well-being. Corporate cultures that fully embrace employee well-being, encourage active employee participation, promote employee growth and development, and place priority on employee health and safety. They are also concerned about quality, service and ethical behavior.

Also be familiar with the executive who has direct responsibility for the functions you want to perform. Learn about the hiring manager's professional background, personality traits, departmental priorities and strategies and schedule.

Identify why you want to work for each organization. Know whether your mission, needs and values are compatible with those of the organization. If so, develop a convincing case for your employment. Concentrate on the contribution you can make. Demonstrate how hiring you will contribute to the company's performance or success. Emphasize your past accomplishments to show why you can fulfill this need.

After completing the forgoing, try to connect with the decision maker directly. Introduce yourself to the person who has authority to hire you. The purpose of this initial contact is to stimulate the decision maker's curiosity and exchange information. Show how you can meet the organization's needs. Call before or after general office hours, and during lunch when executives may answer the phone. When leaving repeated voice or email messages, list a different benefit you can provide for each message. This will both qualify and distinguish you. Keep messages succinct.

Sometimes you need to get through the gatekeeper to reach the executive. Gatekeepers are their supervisor's designated agents charged with limiting unnecessary, potentially wasteful and unexpected interruptions that may negatively affect the executive's productivity. Most are, however, anxious to help superiors identify cost saving opportunities, new products and services, or creative employees that could add value to their organizations.

If you want a telephone or face-to-face appointment with the decision maker, succinctly describe who you are, what you do and how you can add value to the company. Make the gatekeeper a partner in your quest for success. He can become your advocate, squeezing an appointment into a booked calendar, talking you up or giving suggestions. Be considerate of his time. If the decision maker is not available, determine the best time and method (e.g., email or phone) to make contact.

When you connect with the decision maker, ask if he has a few minutes. (Most will give you a few minutes or ask you to call back at a convenient time.) Introduce yourself and explain the purpose of your call. (Clarify whether this is a job search or an informational interview.) Indicate why you like the company, and give your elevator speech. Be sure to match your job target to the organization as closely as possible, and indicate how you can add value. Be alert and sensitive to the other person's responses. Ask the contact if he would be interested in seeing your resume. Thank your contact for his or her interest and time. If he indicates interest, follow-up with an email or regular mail cover letter and resume.

Make direct contact with large, medium-sized and smaller organizations that fit your requirements. Don't be discouraged by rejections. They are normal.

Cruising the Information Superhighway
Cruising the Internet is a popular way for candidates to find jobs. It's popular with employers, too, because it reduces the time required to fill positions. Candidates can send many resumes to different employers, and interested employers can

respond quickly to candidates that can add value to their company.

Online positions can be accessed by anyone with a computer and modem. The Internet offers several ways to help you find a job. The World Wide Web offers millions of pages of job listings, resume banks and company-sponsored job databases. Some of these services are free; others charge a fee. Job postings—the online equivalent of classified ads—are a good place to start.

A focused and functional way of using the Internet is to check the updated web sites in your industry and functions. There are literally sites for everyone. You may also find surprising sites that make your head spin—from jobs in Asia to sites for men and women in the military. And, as you read this section, they are continually being modified or created.

Web sites range from www.monster.com and www.careerbuilder.com which are big career hubs, to industry niches like www.jobsinthemoney.com, for financial professionals. You'll find job listings in the nonprofit sector at www.philanthropy-journal.org. There is also a public relations site for marketing, advertising, training and information technology at www.roundtable.org.

You may want to target specific companies by Internet, as well. Jobs disappear, but companies usually don't. Check your desired company's web site to identify what they do and with whom you should speak, and to read their annual report and recent press releases. Keep track of their online job postings. This will help you evaluate the company with a critical eye. Look for cues on their home page. If you look carefully, you can discover more than job openings. You can learn about the corporate culture.

If you want to relocate, the Internet is a perfect place to begin your search. Try www.careerpath.com. This site lists domestic newspapers, and many have their own web sites. Reading a paper from the geographic region you are targeting can help you get a sense of the jobs, industries, and lifestyles in the area. You can discover a lot by reading articles and real estate ads in different areas.

You can also get considerable information by visiting chat rooms and forums. You may also want to build an email address book to connect with like professionals.

While using the Internet can be fun, helpful and productive for savvy job searchers, it's important to avoid some common pitfalls. Don't get hooked into spending hours cruising the Internet just for fun. Stay focused on your search. Know who you're posting with. If you post your resume to a large site, make sure you know what their policies are. Ask questions to protect yourself. Know the site's disclosure policies. Does the site send your resume out, or will it stay at that site? Do you have a say about its release? Will the site send you information, or do you have to go and get it? You need to maintain control of your own career, including where your resume goes and who sees it.

Stay focused on your search.

Be choosy when posting resumes. Know how often data is updated. Identify contact information of site operators. Determine whether there's a fee for service, know promises made and refund policy. Get feedback from people who have used the service. Manage time. Check sites approximately twice a week. Every time you connect, start someplace new. Move from general to specific. Visit large recruiting sites first, such as www.careerbuilder.com, www.working.com and www.hotjobs.com. Move on to smaller, exclusive resources, including sites dedicated to your field (e.g., www.dice.com for the Information Technology field). Take one day off a week to relax.

Don't use resume forms provided by most databases unless this is required by the employer. Many employers are now requesting potential candidates to cut and paste information using their formats. Most of these forms don't allow you to spell check, revise or save work. Most insist on chronological resumes. These are not as appropriate for career changers as functional resumes with their emphasis on skills and accomplishments.

To get your email considered, follow given instructions. Address your email to the person or organization indicated. Use the job title or code cited in the adv ertisement so that it can be routed to the appropr iate person. If you are "cold emailing" an employer, briefly state your objective in the subject line. Ensure the cover letter introduces you, specifies how you meet the employer's needs, and entices the recipient to read your resume.

Stay cyber-safe. Limit postings. Post your resume in databases of one or two large job sites as w ell as a few smaller sites targeted to y our employment goal. This gives you "maximum exposure" (many employers representing varied industries and regions) and "targeted e xposure" (employers looking for qualified candidates for specific positions). Read privacy policies. Note what personal information will be collected, ho w it may be handled, and whether the site reserves the right to sell it.

If you want confidentiality, delete resume contact information such as name and phone n umbers, and replace these with an email address set up specifically f or your search. Services such as Yahoo! email are helpful. Use appropriate names such as architect@yahoo.com. Don't link your resume to personal information. Modify your employment history, as well. Remove all dates and employers from your resume, and replace them with accurate but generic descriptions. For example, change "IBM" to "a m ultinational information technology company."

Don't let your resume sit in cyberspace. If you don't get responses within 45 days of posting, remo ve it. Employers may not be looking for your skills in this database, or there may be excessive competition between candidates with similar skills. When your search is over, delete resumes.

Extending Your Network

What other job search avenues should you explore? Register with executive recruiting and placement firms, university and college placement offices, trade and professional associations and your local Chamber of Commerce. Executive recruiters, who conduct employee searches at a company's expense, are usually glad to hear from you. Although most are looking for specialized talent, all have high-level contacts with many organizations. Cruise the Internet, and refer to your phone book. Investigate all sources.

Being Effective in Interviews

Now that a wide audience of potential employers is aware of you, expect interested ones to begin phoning. The calls will be of three types: a simple request for an interview, a request for additional information, or a phone interview that can range from several questions to a complete session. Whatever the purpose, get the caller's complete and correct name and title. Be prepared to discuss your background and experience, state the contribution you expect to make, and explain why you are making a change.

Focus on the most important aspects of the job and relate your accomplishments to the problems requiring immediate attention. This will stimulate the caller's interest. If, by the end of the conversation, the caller has not suggested an interview, you should do so. If the caller does not want to set up an interview until a later date, indicate that you will follow up the conversation with another call to arrange an interview time. If you don't receive a call from correspondence you sent, follow up with a phone call. Ask whether your resume was received. The interview usually determines if you receive a job offer. Whether you are interviewed by one person or a selection board, this may be your only opportunity to sell yourself to a prospective employer. It also is your best opportunity to gather sufficient information to properly evaluate an offer.

The interview usually determines if you receive a job offer. Your first objective in any interview is to convince an employer you can make a contribution and are the best candidate for the position. And, because both you and the organization are selling and evaluating, you will want to use the interview to gather enough information about the company and its staff to evaluate the job in relation to your own personal characteristics and goals. In the next section you'll find some ways to maximize your preparation efforts—and your face-to-face effectiveness.

Advance Strategies

- *The key to a successful interview is preparation.* Research the company. Prepare questions to ask and review those that may be asked of you. Then plan how to manage and structure the interview to your advantage. Analyze the job and the company. Call any contacts you have to get an insider's perspective. Use the Internet to download information. Know the company's products and services and be conversant with recent developments in the industry. Know the complete names and correct titles of all interviewers.

- *Be prepared to discuss your background and experience and to state the contribution you can make.* Outline your five top selling points for the job. Rework your elevator speech for the specific job, and practice it several times. Prepare examples of what you can offer the employer. Displaying a great spreadsheet of a project plan is much more persuasive than just talking about one.

- *Know how to respond to behavioral interview questions.* In the behavioral or situational interview, the interviewer uses a probing style to ask questions seeking very specific

400

examples. They often start out with, "Tell me about a time . . ." or, "Describe . . ." or "Give me and example . . . "The interviewer is looking for details of your past abilities and specific work performance. He or she rates each response to determine how well you reacted in the past and to predict your future performance in their company. These situational questions are thought-provoking. Consider your answers carefully. Samples of behavioral interview questions are provided in "Typical Interview Questions" in this Chapter. They have B at the end of the question.

- *Program your mind for success.* Review your strengths. Listen to motivational tapes. Have a friend give you a pep talk. Repeat positive affirmations such as, "I will succeed." Visualize yourself performing the job.

- *Practice your delivery.* Use a tape recorder or video, role-play with a friend or get feedback from a career counselor.

- *Prepare responses to potential questions.* Most questions will concern the relationship between your personal characteristics and accomplishments and the prospective position. Write out succinct answers to all questions such as: "Tell me about yourself." "What are your most significant accomplishments?" "What is your typical way of dealing with conflict?" See the questions outlined in "Typical Interview Questions" below.

- *Be prepared to offer references at the end of the interview.*

During the Interview
- *Dress professionally.* Know whether the company dress code is formal or casual and dress accordingly. Take along a note pad, copies of your updated resume targeted to the job, a written list of questions, information about the organization and a list of references. Make sure all correspondence is neat and error-free.

- *Arrive a few minutes early.* Treat the receptionist with respect. Assume that anything you say will be reported to the interviewer.

- *Smile and use the interviewer's name when you first meet him or her.*

- *Make small talk.* The first few minutes of an interview are often informal. This is when the interviewer can judge your ability to socialize. Comment positively on something you notice in the interviewer's office, such as a painting or photo. Before arriving, scan the newspaper for one of the day's headlines. If it seems appropriate, you can then offer some light comment on a news items as an icebreaker.

- *Radiate interest and enthusiasm about the job and sincere interest in the company and its goals.* Confidently offer past-performance examples to show how you'll contribute to the company's bottom line. Be genuine and smile when appropriate.

- *Practice good posture.* Use a firm handshake, and maintain eye contact.

- *Listen carefully and answer questions directly.* If you are unclear on anything, ask for clarification before you respond. Answer questions promptly and briefly, but don't give one-word answers. If you consider a question too personal, say so. Otherwise, be as open and honest as possible. Offer plenty of examples illustrating what you've done in the past. This will show what you can accomplish. Demonstrate specific areas of expertise, answering when, where and how.

- *Intersperse your own questions among the interviewer's.* Relate them to the company, your accomplishments and future contributions. The questions you ask can be even more important than your answers to the ones asked of you. By asking the right questions, you demonstrate your knowledge and contributions you can make. Your questions can also guide the discussion into areas that highlight y our accomplishments. Finally, by asking questions, you will get the information you need to evaluate the company and the job. Some questions you might ask include: "What is the first problem that needs my attention if you hire me?" "How has this position been performed in the past?" "Why is it vacant now?" "What is the scope of the author ity I would have?" "How would you define your ideal candidate?" "How would you define your leadership style?" "When are you going to make the hiring decision?"

• *Know how to respond to illegal or unethical questions .* Most discriminatory questions are asked by untrained interviewers. These include those related to r ace, marital and family status, disabilities and criminal convictions. If asked an illegal or discriminatory question, examine the intent of the question and respond with an answer that applies to the job. For example, in response to, "Who will look after your children when you're on a business trip?" say "I can meet the travel schedule this job requires."

• *Be alert and sensitive to the interviewer's reactions and feelings.*

• *Don't share negative comments about former bosses or other companies.*

• *Watch your body language.* Don't constantly move your foot, sway in a swivel chair, chew gum or use jargon.

• *Never negotiate your salary until you've been offered the job.* Early in the screening process, employers want to know how much money you want, so they can eliminate you from consideration. If you want too much, you may not be happy with the job and won't stay. If you ask for too little, they may think you have little experience. If salary is brought up during the interview, ask what salary range the company has in mind. Be prepared for this line of questioning by researching your market value. Know what similar types of organizations are offering, and what colleagues in the field are ear ning.

• *Never, never, turn down a job offer during an interview.* Thank the interviewer and ask if you could consider the offer overnight or for a few days. Remember, you don't really have an offer until you get it in wr iting. A written offer will avoid misunderstandings. Don't play games. If you don't want the job, say why and ask to be k ept in mind for future opportunities.

• *Close the interview effectively.* Review your relevant accomplishments and your value added. Emphasize what contributions you can make. Ask for the job if you want it. Employers like to hire people who are enthusiastic about their work. Follow-up the interview with a phone call, email or letter at a specified time. If you ask when the company will be making the decision dur ing the interview, you will know the appropriate time, date and method to mak e contact to lear n of your status.

According to employers, some common errors candidates make during interviews include the following:

• Not asking what qualities the ideal candidate should possess

• Failing to give specific examples of relevant skills and experience

• Moving a foot constantly or fidgeting in the chair

• Asking questions that have already been answered

• Dressing inappropriately

• Using jargon or unrelated acron yms

• Not having a clear career f ocus

• Complaining about prior employers

- Failing to make eye contact

- Lacking excitement when discussing the future

Typical Interview Questions

- Tell me about yourself.

- What are some of your most significant accomplishments?

- Give an example of a time when you used good judgment and logic in solving a problem.

- Were there any unusual difficulties you had to overcome?

- Why are you leaving your position? What did you like most and least about your last job?

- What would your former superiors, colleagues and subordinates say about you?

- Why do you think you are an effective supervisor?

- Describe a situation in which you were able to use persuasion to successfully convince someone to see things your way.

- How do you go about making important decisions?

- What types of decisions are easiest for you to make? What kinds of decisions are most difficult?

- Describe one or two innovations of which you are particularly proud.

- What are your greatest strengths and weaknesses?

- Give a specific example of a time when you had to conform to a policy with which you did not agree.

- Do you think you are overqualified for this position?

- How do you feel about reporting to a younger person?

- Describe a time when you were faced with a stressful situation that demonstrated your coping skills.

- What are your future hopes? Where do you see yourself five years from now? Ten years?

- Why do you want to work for this company? Why should we hire you?

- What changes would you make if you came on board? How would you tackle ... task?

- What is your typical way of dealing with conflict?

- Describe a recent situation in which you had to deal with a very upset customer or co-worker.

- Describe a time when you anticipated potential problems and developed preventive measures.

- Why have you had so many jobs?

- How do you stay current in the profession?

After the Interview

- *Send a neatly written email or typed or hand written thank-you note to your interviewer within 24 hours after the interview.* Take this opportunity to list three points that demonstrate what you can contribute to the job. You can also include points you forgot to mention during the interview.

- *Make a follow-up phone call if you haven't heard from the company by the date they specified during the interview.* Ask for feedback on your qualifications and interview performance if you're not offered the position. Don't take rejection personally. Consider this meeting a practice session.

- *When you're offered a position, note your gut reaction to the people and the work environment.* People chemistry is a crucial element of job satisfaction.

- *Once you and the employer have reached agreement on all aspects of the position, get the offer confirmed in writing.*

Staying Motivated

It's a challenge to maintain a positive, self-confident attitude when your letters and phone calls are not being returned and your interviews bring rejection letters. But perk up. Here are some ways to stay enthusiastic and optimistic.

- *Know what you want.* It's important to have clear career goals that represent your passion, not what others think you should be doing. It's difficult to maintain enthusiasm when you're applying for positions you don't really want.

- *Review your goals periodically.* If necessary, modify them to represent what you've learned about yourself and the market place during the search.

- *Investigate growth industries to determine how your skills fit.* Creatively investigate ways you can transfer your skills to a new industry. For example, your accounting skills are needed in the meat-packing industry as much as in the computer industry.

- *Explore all job search avenues.* Visit Internet sites. Try executive recruiting firms, temp agencies, college placement offices, trade and professional associations, management consulting firms and your Chamber of Commerce.

- *Take charge.* Don't just passively answer help-wanted ads or send out resumes to personnel departments. Get the names of hiring managers in the departments at companies where you'd like to work. Call and ask about jobs available and skills required. Then, if appropriate, revise your resume to fit their requirements, demonstrating your value added.

- *Develop a different resume for each job target.* Make sure your resume lists a clear job objective, summarizes relevant accomplishments and demonstrates your value added proposition.

- *Enhance your network.* Keep abreast of new developments in your field and add to your list of colleagues and acquaintances by joining professional, trade or civic groups. Join on-line networking sites such as www.linkedin.com and www.ryze.com, and volunteer in the community.

- *Develop a routine and stick with it.* Even if you're unemployed, get dressed as if you're going to work every day. Make a weekly and daily list of goals and activities, and work on them daily. Ask yourself, "What can I do today to move my job search campaign forward?" Or, "What follow-up steps can I take today?" Can you email more targeted resumes, cold call the project manager at a company to determine job leads, or follow-up on resumes you sent out last month? Tangible, daily accomplishments provide stimulation and help you maintain enthusiasm, energy and motivation.

- *Secure as many interviews as possible with potentially interested employers.* Make as many contacts as your information and time will allow. Follow up every telephone interview or meeting with a thank-you note. A polite, pleasant note thanking the person for his or her time and help will encourage the recipient to remember you.

- *Write and state affirmations.* Say, "I'm an excellent programmer (or whatever) with many special skills to offer." Say it out loud regularly and with conviction.

- *Develop a support system.* Stay in contact with positive, supportive people to keep your spirits up. Many people withdraw during a job search because they don't like to answer questions such as, "How's the search going?" If this happens to you, respond with a brief, "Everything's great," then shift the focus to something else.

  Sometimes, though, it's good to have a friend to commiserate with, someone who understands and can function as a sounding board for your frustrations. Although partners are helpful, they may lack the intimate understanding of just how painful a job search can be. Professional career counselors can be helpful here. Be sure, however, to check the experience and credentials of a counselor, including his or her education, philosophy, tools and techniques used, and years of experience.

- *Take a break from the process periodically.* Reward yourself for accomplishing a certain number of goal-directed activities.

- *Maintain a healthy lifestyle.* Eat well, get at least seven hours of sleep a night and exercise regularly.

- *Develop your spiritual self.* Allow yourself quiet time to meditate or pray. Enjoy nature. Take walks in the park or by the water.

Getting Additional Information

Before you accept any position, get all the facts. Going blindly into a job can prove disastrous. Ask tough questions. This will strengthen your position as a knowledgeable and thoughtful employee. Find out what happened to the last person in the job. Know why he or she left, and why the company has not found a candidate from within. The interviewer's reactions are as important as the answers he or she gives. A defensive, hostile, or evasive response may signal a real problem. Also be aware of your gut reaction to the people and the work environment.

Follow up by meeting prospective peers and top brass. Ask them about their jobs, the company and its problems. Find out how they spend their time. Feel out possible problems you might have working with the immediate supervisor or subordinates. Chemistry between coworkers is a crucial element in any job. If you don't like the people you work with, the job duties are irrelevant. Try to determine the nuances of the decision-making process, the pecking order and the philosophy of the top brass. Ask if night or weekend work is expected. If you don't understand how an organization works, you'll soon be frustrated. For example, do your superiors go by the book, or are they entrepreneurs who believe rules are made to be broken? You'll need to ask many questions before the big picture falls into place.

Most important, know yourself. Many factors contribute to your job happiness. If the job requires a move across the country or from the suburbs to the city, to a new industry, or even to a different-sized company, make sure you can adapt. Ask about salary increases, stock options, company benefits, pension plans, vacations, sabbaticals, club memberships, opportunities for promotion and relocation expenses. Once you and the employer have reached agreement on all aspects of the job offer, get it confirmed in writing.

Depending on how far along you are in your job search, the time you're allowed to consider an offer will vary from a few days to a week. Your objective is to gain enough time to expedite and evaluate additional offers. You can do this by immediately advising prospective employers of your deadline. Do this only if you are definitely interested in the first offer. If the other organization is not ready to make a decision, you may be turned down prematurely.

Making the Decision

How can you decide whether a decision is right for you? You must thoroughly evaluate each job offer, both individually and in comparison to others. Never accept an offer on the spot. Making a commitment is the single most challenging act in risking. It is the moment when you declare your intentions. Even if you have received only one offer, evaluate it carefully. You have three options: to accept, to delay and reconnect with other prospective employers, or to reject it and continue your job search with renewed enthusiasm and effort. The best way to reach a decision is to use both intellect and intuition. Review the subsection, "Using Your Intellect and Intuition," in Chapter 9.

If a decision doesn't feel right, don't force it. The appropriate decision will come forward at the right time. Remember, you have the required knowledge stored in your subconscious; give it time to surface. This filtering process can help you decide what's important and comfortable. If your intuition is sending alarm signals, buy time. Extend your deadline. A prospective employer will usually wait two or three days while you mull over a job decision.

Recognizing Pitfalls
There are certain traps you should avoid when making important decisions. Any one or combination of these hazards can wreck your career, or at least put it in a holding pattern. Be wary of the following pitfalls:

- Taking a job you don't enjoy because you want to be employed.

- Working for someone you don't respect and admire.

- Producing or selling goods or services you don't believe in.

- Failing to follow a course of continuous education.

- Failing to balance loyalty to yourself, your career and your organization.

- Relying on long experience with one company for security.

- Refusing to consider out-of-town openings when you change jobs.

- Accepting a promotion to a job you don't find attractive just for money or prestige.

- Failing to take a cut in salary when it could further your career.

- Getting too much unsaleable experience.

- Sticking to a specialized field without evaluating whether jobs in the area are in demand.

- Resigning in a snit.

- Rushing into a job without evaluating it carefully.

- Taking a job that has poor chemistry.

- Staying in a job or taking a job because of security.

Going for It

If your intellectual and emotional preparation are sound, if you have done whatever you can to manage the risk and protect yourself against disaster, and if the decision still feels right, it's time to get going. No matter how elaborate the preparation, the next stage always demands a leap into the unknown. In addition to situational unknowns, you will have to face the unknowns deep within yourself. All rational planning leads, if only momentarily, to an act of faith. This moment of free-fall may disrupt your sense of orientation. But because it usually brings with it a heady sense of relief, this minute may also feel like the least risky step in the whole process. For example, a study of skydivers showed that most felt less afraid when they were actually about to hurl themselves into space than they did when they were on the ground deciding whether or not to go up for a jump. You will probably discover the same applies to you.

A dream begins to become a reality only at the moment of action. A race doesn't begin until one leaves the starting blocks. From that point on, competence, commitment and determination will decide your future. Decide now that you will succeed and become a Quester. If you want to, choose to, and take the right steps, you will become one. Don't give in to thoughts of failure. Remember, setbacks are just opportunities to learn. They are detours on the road to attaining your goals.

A dream begins to become a reality only at the moment of action.

Confirming Your Acceptance

After you have accepted an offer and established a starting date, confirm this acceptance in writing. Also write to any other interviewers who made offers. Thank them for their consideration and advise them that you have accepted another position. This polite follow-up will help should a desirable position become available in the future. As well, tell everybody who helped you in your job search that you accepted the stated position, and thank them for their assistance.

Resigning from Your Present Job

Of course, before you move to a new position or start a new business, you must resign from your current job. The starting date of your new job should permit sufficient time for an orderly completion or transfer of unfinished tasks. Maintain good relations with your former employer, and try to avoid harming the morale of colleagues. You may need their help in the future.

7. Evaluating Your Decision

The good feelings that result from taking a risk (even if the results don't turn out as you hoped) can be incredible. First, there's the gain of seeing yourself as a survivor, as someone who can accomplish something. Mastery—the sense of accomplishment and achievement that comes from seeing that you can control a difficult situation—is another impor tant gain. When you test yourself by risking, you force yourself to grow by calling on skills, talents and perceptions you have never used before.

The urge to risk reflects the need for achievement. Correctly approached, taking risks can enhance that sense of accomplishment so intimately connected with self-confidence. Many people say that, even when things didn't work out, they were nevertheless pleased with themselves for venturing, asserting themselves, testing their mettle and not stagnating.

Another good feeling comes from learning more about yourself whether you succeed or fail. The lessons you learn from your setbacks are sometimes the most precious. Risking gives you the opportunity to explore your needs, values, coping skills and bottom line.

When you've worked hard at making a decision, take time not just to enjoy it, but to evaluate it, too. Doing so can help you learn to become more effective in making future decisions. Ask yourself the following questions:

• *Do I feel good about making the move?* Are my job needs being met? Am I using my skills and abilities? Is my level of job satisfaction (as measured by *The Job Satisfaction Questionnaire*) any higher?

- *What other gains am I deriving from the move?* What did I lose?

- *What factors contributed to the success of my move?* Or, what contributed to my failure?

- *If I were to do it all over again, what would I do differently?*

- *Who was most helpful in the process?* How can I strengthen that relationship? Who let me down? Does he or she know?

- *What pleasant and unexpected surprises did I encounter in my move?*

- *How do I feel about the degree of success (or failure) I have achieved?* If my efforts are not successful, what can I do to turn this misfortune into an opportunity or advantage? What did I learn from the experience? Would I do the same thing over again?

- *How do I feel about myself as a result of taking the risk?*

Evaluation is a continuous process. Assess your needs, goals and job satisfaction periodically to determine if your developing personality fits your position and lifestyle. When you feel that your job or some other component of your life needs modifying, make the necessary changes to bring it into harmony with your personality. Remember, nothing remains static. To continue to grow and develop, you must constantly modify who you are. Don't wait for a crisis to clear your vision. Don't miss out on the joys of living. Achieve the well-being that comes from living your life to your fullest each and every day.

If, after three, six or 12 months, you find you are not reaching your goals, seek help. Many people have difficulty translating their ideas into action, but with the help of a competent professional, they can accomplish this. Do what you must to complete your task. Accept the possibility you may have made an error. Learn from your setbacks. Next time, you will succeed!

Keep Going

As you grow and develop your potential, you'll find the rewards are enormous. Along with the satisfaction that comes from using your full range of abilities, you'll develop greater independence, self-confidence, maturity, purpose, flexibility and the power to affect change. You will become stronger and wiser, but don't stop there. Most importantly, risks merely open the door to even greater risks. If you take the right chances—those that encourage growth and fulfillment—you will find you will want to take more risks. Each time you gamble, risking becomes a little easier.

There really is no substitute for risk as a way to grow. Knowing you have honestly faced the painful struggle and accepted the tradeoffs and losses involved, yet moved forward in spite of them, is extremely gratifying. To have a satisfying life, you will need to risk again and again until you have created the best possible life for yourself—a life in which you feel comfortable being yourself, without apology or pretense. Create a life in which you can continue to have choices, grow and be authentic.

Life is a challenge, meet it.

Life is an opportunity, take it.

Life is an adventure, dare it!

About the Author

Carole Kanchier, PhD, is uniquely qualified to write and talk about change. With over 25 years of demonstrated success in the career, empowerment, learning, development and business fields, she has researched career/life transitions, writes about change and empowerment, counsels individuals experiencing transitions and conducts varied workshops on issues related to the forgoing.

Author of the award-winning, best seller, *Dare to Change Your Job and Your Life*, Dr. Kanchier is an internationally recognized columnist. Her columns have been syndicated on the CanWest newswire, www.working.com and World Wide Media. In addition, Kanchier's work appears in publications such as *Psychology Today, San Jose and Silicon Valley Business Journal, Malaysia Business, USA Weekend Magazine, New York Post, Brazil Super Interessant Especial Magazine* and *Encyclopedia of Career Decisions and Work Issues.*

Dr. Kanchier has taught at University of California, Berkeley and Santa Cruz, and the University of Alberta, and was a visiting fellow at the Institute of Transpersonal Psychology, Palo Alto. She is an invited speaker at numerous conferences, and is quoted in many publications. Professional and community groups on which Kanchier has served include chair, Career Change Committee, National Career Development Association, and Advisory Board member, College Admission Counseling Program, University of California, Berkeley. Kanchier is regularly featured on local and international broadcasts including WNBC-TV and CNBC, New York; CBC and CTV, Toronto; KPIX, and KQED, San Francisco; and CBC and 1130 News, Vancouver.

A creative visionary, Dr. Kanchier has a reputation for being at the leading edge of many personal, career and employee development strategies.

Dr. Kanchier is available for media interviews, speeches and workshops.

Contact:
Carole Kanchier, PhD
Ph: 1.888.206.0108
Email: Carole@daretochange.com
Website: www.daretochange.com